CHEVROLET TRUCKS 1955–1959

HOW TO BUILD & MODIFY

Dennis W. Parks

S-A DESIGN

CarTech®

CarTech®

CarTech®, Inc.
838 Lake Street South
Forest Lake, MN 55025
Phone: 651-277-1200 or 800-551-4754
Fax: 651-277-1203
www.cartechbooks.com

Edit by Wes Eisenschenk
Layout by Monica Seiberlich

ISBN 978-1-61325-584-1
Item No. SA501

Library of Congress Cataloging-in-Publication Data

Names: Parks, Dennis, 1959- author.
Title: Acumen : Chevrolet trucks 1955-1959 : build and modify / Dennis Parks.
Other titles: Chevrolet trucks 1955-1959
Description: Forest Lake, MN : CarTech, [2020]
Identifiers: LCCN 2021058721 | ISBN 9781613255841 (paperback)
Subjects: LCSH: Chevrolet trucks–Conservation and restoration–Handbooks, manuals, etc. | Chevrolet trucks–Maintenance and repair–Handbooks, manuals, etc.
Classification: LCC TL230.5.C45 P37 2020 | DDC 629.28/73–dc23
LC record available at https://lccn.loc.gov/2021058721

Written, edited, and designed in the U.S.A.
Printed in China
10 9 8 7 6 5 4 3 2 1

CarTech books may be purchased at a discounted rate in bulk for resale, events, corporate gifts, or educational purposes. Special editions may also be created to specification. For details, contact Special Sales at 838 Lake Street S., Forest Lake, MN 55025 or by email at sales@cartechbooks.com.

DISTRIBUTION BY:

Europe
PGUK
63 Hatton Garden
London EC1N 8LE, England
Phone: 020 7061 1980 • Fax: 020 7242 3725
www.pguk.co.uk

Australia
Renniks Publications Ltd.
3/37-39 Green Street
Banksmeadow, NSW 2109, Australia
Phone: 2 9695 7055 • Fax: 2 9695 7355
www.renniks.com

Canada
Login Canada
300 Saulteaux Crescent
Winnipeg, MB, R3J 3T2 Canada
Phone: 800 665 1148 • Fax: 800 665 0103
www.lb.ca

CONTENTS

DEDICATION

To all of those grandpas who took us for rides in their old pickup trucks and then parted with their pride and joy a few years later when we needed something to drive. Also, to Linley and Cabren.

ACKNOWLEDGMENTS

A very sincere thank-you goes out to everyone who helped with this book, as I could not have done it without you. Thanks again (in no specific order) to Keith Moritz at Morfab Customs, Todd Brown, Tim Moon, Sam Kimbrough, and Tom Kuhn.

I also want to thank Roger Ward at Bad Paint Company and John Kimbrough for all the information they have provided over the years and for the proofreading that they have done on my manuscripts.

ABOUT THE AUTHOR

Aside from a few Ford hot rods (a 1929 Ford Model A Tudor sedan and a 1927 Ford Track T roadster), all my vehicles have been Chevy trucks. Beginning with a 1957 GMC, I have owned a 1976 Custom Deluxe, a lowered 1982 Custom Deluxe, a 1990 S-10, a 1951 Advanced Design pickup, a 1991 Silverado, a 2002 Silverado, a 1955 Task Force pickup, a 1968 C10, a lowered 2008 Silverado extended cab, and finally, a 2014 Silverado four-wheel-drive. While I have lost track of the miles I have driven, most of them have been behind the wheel of a GM truck.

I have also spent quite a bit of time writing about and photographing hot rods and vintage trucks. My magazine articles have been published in *Street Rodder*, *Hot Rod*, *Midwest Rod and Machine*, *Truckin'*, *Rodder's Digest*, *Musclecar Classics*, *Street Rod Pickups*, *Street Rod Action*, *Supercar* (Australia), *Classic Trucks*, *Street Rod Pickups*, *Custom Rodder*, *Rod & Custom*, *Super Chevy*, *Custom Classic Trucks*, *American Rodder*, *Hot Rod Trucks*, *High Performance Pontiacs*, *Rodding USA*, and *Hot Rod New Zealand*.

In addition to being a full-time senior technical writer for a pharmaceutical benefits manager, I have written several automotive how-to books: *How to Build a Hot Rod Model A Ford*; *How to Build a Hot Rod*; *How to Paint Your Car*; *How to Restore and Customize Auto Upholstery & Interiors*; *How to Plate, Polish, and Chrome*; *How to Build a Cheap Hot Rod*; *The Complete Guide to Auto Body Repair*; *Hot Rod Body and Chassis Builder's Guide*; *Automotive Wiring: A Practical Guide to Wiring Your Hot Rod or Custom Car*; *How to Restore and Customize Automotive Interiors*; and *Automotive Rust Repair and Prevention*.

INTRODUCTION

Almost everyone loves pickup trucks. I think this is because we all have at least a few fond memories of them from a simpler time. One of my oldest pickup truck memories was when my grandpa would haul my aunts, uncles, and cousins in the back of his 1957 GMC to Sinkin' Creek in the Missouri Ozarks to cool off in the water.

Some 8 or 9 years later, my mom, dad, and I went to visit my grandparents just a couple of weeks prior to my 16th birthday. Grandpa was sitting in his favorite chair, and we were both watching the St. Louis Cardinals play baseball on TV.

Out of the clear blue, he turned to me and said, "I guess you'll be needin' somethin' to drive here pretty soon, won't ya, son?"

"Well, yes, sir," I replied.

"What would you think about my old truck?" he asked.

"Well, sure," I quickly replied.

Quite honestly, I had dreams of a Chevy II, Dad's 1968 Chevrolet Impala, or possibly a Camaro. As many of you will remember, having your own set of wheels meant freedom. Sure, it meant having a job, but that is the case with any vehicle. It did not really matter what it was or how it looked, having your own vehicle was a good thing.

You can imagine my disappointment when Grandpa told me that he would sell me his truck for $300. I had been mowing lawns, but I only had $50 saved up. Next came what was probably one of the best life lessons that I ever learned. Dad, Grandpa, and I drove to the bank in town. They told me to have a seat in the lobby, while they went to talk to the bank president.

After what seemed like forever, the bank president called me into his office. I soon signed for my first loan. To borrow the additional $250, it cost me $262.50, which I had to pay back within six months. I did not have to pay monthly payments; instead, I could pay whatever I wanted, whenever I wanted as long as it was paid in full within six months. Those words pounded in my mind for the rest of the day. Yes, I paid it off before it was due, but I still have the passbook that showed those payments.

I drove that truck throughout my junior year of high school but ended up selling it after about a year. I always told myself, and most anyone who would listen, that I would have one of those Task Force trucks again. Close to 30 years after seeing someone drive my first truck away, I had the opportunity to buy another one: a 1955 Chevy pickup.

Besides simply wanting one of these trucks, I felt that a truck book would make for a great project as well. In 2005, I had written numerous articles for various rod magazines and my fifth automotive book had just been published. As this is written, that was 15 years ago. During those years, other books and hot rod projects took greater priority for various reasons. Finally, those truck dreams that first came about while in high school came true, as well as this book that I have wanted to write for almost as long.

My first goal for this truck is to drive it every chance that I get, meaning that it will get driven to work daily. Winter weather will be the only deviation from that. I plan for it to look good, drive and ride quite well, and haul stuff when necessary. It will have a static drop so that it will have a good stance, along with several modern conveniences, but retain the classic good looks. Like all automotive projects should be, it will be built to please me rather than anyone else.

This book will show you how to do that with your truck if you desire. But do not expect lessons in applying clear over rusty sheet metal or creating fake patina. I much prefer to make the vehicle look good and then wear it out by driving it.

WHAT TO BUILD?

While meandering aimlessly along a back road can be a worthy ambition when your truck is finished (or at least drivable), having a plan is particularly important during the building process. You need to have a destination in mind. Knowing from the beginning how you want the finished truck to look, feel, and drive, as well as how you plan to use it, will make it easier to accomplish your goal.

Good planning will help keep you on track during the build and help eliminate rework. In addition to the extra labor to redo something, rework often creates the need for different parts, which adds to the financial aspect of the build. This does not mean that there can be no deviation somewhere along the line, but to finish the build, there needs to be a target for which to aim.

This 1955 Chevy Stepside has all the makings of a solid daily driver. It has been lowered a bit but not so much that it is not practical to drive. The tires are a common size that could easily be replaced if necessary. Dual exterior mirrors that the driver can see with are very practical.

Determine What You Want

What is the purpose for this truck when it is finished? How will it be used and how often? While these may sound like silly questions, taking the time to answer them completely and honestly will help you develop a plan to build the truck you really want. Is this truck going to be used as a daily driver, a weekend cruiser, or perhaps as a show only vehicle? In reality, it cannot be all three in the same truck.

Daily Driver

If the truck is going to be a daily driver, practicality, reliability, and serviceability are key concepts to keep in mind. Now, that does not mean that it cannot be a very cool truck. You just need to plan accordingly.

Practicality

Practicality for this daily driver vehicle means that it will safely and efficiently get you to and from your destination on a regular basis regardless of weather, time of day, or road conditions. Will it haul you, your passenger, and the necessary cargo? Whether that cargo is merely a lunch box, a school-age son or daughter and his or her tuba, or a room addition's worth of 2x4s and plywood is for you to decide.

Other considerations might be to include or not include creature comforts such as air-conditioning (A/C), a stereo, or heated seats. Convenience items range from a map light to a Bluetooth navigation system, and include cupholders, a cell phone charging jack, and lockable storage.

Of course, practicality will overlap with reliability somewhat. Will shifting gears all the time or an automatic be more practical for the different people who may be driving the truck? How many times do you want to replace the clutch before your newly licensed driver gets the hang of it? But then again, having the ability to pop start a manual shift is practical if the starter and/or battery goes south.

Reliability

Reliability takes into consideration the drivetrain, brakes, suspension, and wheel/tire combinations. Having an 8-71 blower atop a big-block Chevy with racing slicks is not going to fall into the reliable category for a daily driver that the wife uses to drive the kids to school.

Choosing a stock straight six, one that is modified, or a V-8 is up to you. If it is reliable, it is good. Being stranded along the side of the road is not how you want to be seen "enjoying" these old trucks. Naturally, reliability overlaps serviceability too.

Serviceability

Serviceability is where we find out that all those locations or mounting methods chosen for all those components during construction may not have been the best choice when the truck is finished. Everything being easily accessible is a key point to remember during a vehicle's construction. While roadside failures may not be issues to repair, they seldom happen while the truck is parked in the garage where your tools and a floor jack are handy.

If the truck is going to be a daily driver, it is going to need to be serviced. This is going to include oil changes, regular radiator maintenance, tire rotation, and engine tune-ups. Even if it is taken somewhere else for an oil change, you do not want to make the job a challenge. Someone could potentially do more harm than good if they botch the job. Being able to replace an electrical fuse if needed without being a contortionist is also a good thing.

What is used as a fuel tank and where the filler is located are also important. It is safe to say that unless the truck is restored to original, the fuel tank will probably be relocated to beneath the bed, simply because paint fumes inside the cab are awful. Is the filler in the bed floor or somewhere else? Will whatever you may be hauling or a tonneau cover cause interference with that? Does the filler need to be outside the bed?

Will this be a commuter vehicle or a shop truck? Perhaps that question should be rephrased as, "Are you going to use this as a car or as a truck?" If it is going to be used mostly for transportation, as in hauling people, making the interior and the inside of the bed a bit nicer may be a good choice. Go with the upholstery and carpet that is somewhat plusher and finish the bed wood real nice.

If the truck is going to be used as a truck, plan accordingly. It can still be nice, but more durable materials will be needed. Perhaps use a rubber floor mat instead of carpeting and a heavier rubber mat or spray-on bedliner for the cargo area.

Lastly, use components that can be kept clean. Most people don't want

This 1958–1959 GMC long-bed Fleetside may not be pretty, but it sits right and features some custom wheels and tires. Knowing that this photo was taken on the Southwest Missouri Hot Rod Hundred Reliability Run, the truck must get the job done.

to spend the entire weekend polishing the chrome on a vehicle that is going to be driven to work during a rainstorm on Monday morning.

Weekend Cruiser

If the truck is only going to be used on the weekends, most of those daily driver issues still need to be considered. However, your response to them might be somewhat different. It still needs to be drivable, whether that is merely around town or around the country.

If you are not going to be driving the truck every day, a different location for the battery may be chosen. It may make sense to install some remote battery terminals to make it easy to maintain the battery's charge. Installing an electronic fuel injection (EFI) unit instead of a carburetor is also an option.

Driving only on weekends affords you the option to include more of the bling that you may or may not want to have. If you have all week to polish and detail everything before going to the next cruise night, it is okay to dress up the old gal a bit.

I think this truck is very tasteful with the smooth look. Anything (such as emblems) that is not needed has been removed. Stock door handles and exterior mirrors make it practical. Wide whitewall tires on custom wheels give it some personality and accent the slightly lowered stance.

Show Vehicle

When I think of a show vehicle, it's a vehicle that is hauled to shows on a trailer (enclosed or not). The only time it is driven is on or off the trailer and into the event venue.

If the truck is not being driven, it doesn't really matter how well it runs as long as you can easily move it into the venue. There is no need for an A/C unit that takes up space under the dash and requires a couple more hoses in the engine bay. Whatever wheels and tires you want to run are okay, as the tires will dry rot before they wear out.

The driver and passenger in this 1957 Chevy short-bed Fleetside really enjoy this truck, which is evidence that you do not have to drive a flashy truck to enjoy it. You can easily take a truck like this to a cruise night on Friday night, then haul home whatever you need for the weekend do-it-yourself project.

Style

Now that we have discussed how the truck is going to be used, it's time to figure out what style it will be. Regardless of how it will be used or how often it will be driven, determine a style for the build. Some common styles are traditional, nostalgic custom, contemporary, or state-of-the-art show truck.

These styles may overlap some. However, be careful not to end up with a discombobulation of pieces, parts, and modifications that simply do not make sense. When in doubt, keep it simple.

Often, not having a plan from the beginning and a lengthy build time causes the builder to use the latest fad. Fads come and go and are often outdated before they are seen in the latest issue of your favorite magazine. So, choose a style early on and stick with it. Even if that style is not all the rage at the time, build your truck the way you want it and to the best of your ability. Remember, good taste never goes out of style.

Other than a slightly lowered stance and radial tires, this truck looks like it just rolled off the showroom floor. With a tasteful amount of chrome and some painted steel wheels, this truck is timeless. It should provide years of enjoyment for the owner.

A showroom stock 1957 Chevy would look very much like this one, except it would sit a bit higher and the tires would be a bit narrower. This one has been lowered a bit but sits more level than if it had a rubber rake to it.

Traditional

When I think of traditional truck styling, it has no major body modifications and a close-to-stock stance. Anything that can be seen on the truck while driving by it on the highway looks to be stock. If it starts, runs, drives, and stops, it is all good.

The drivetrain, suspension, and brakes are open for just about anything. This opens modifications to virtually any engine and transmission combination. Let's face it, there are many engine choices between the original 235-ci straight six and today's 572-ci crate motors. Likewise, multiple transmission choices are available, including overdrive, whether choosing manual or automatic.

There are also many options for installing disc brakes, a wide variety of wheel choices (aftermarket or OEM), and modern radial tires. Building a traditionally styled truck allows for lots of improvements for both drivability and convenience. For first-time builders, this traditional route is probably the easiest, as there aren't any radical changes being made to the truck, merely subtle changes here and there.

Nostalgic Custom

Combine styling cues from the 1950s and 1960s with available parts from that time frame for a nostalgic custom truck. It would also be acceptable to have a slightly lowered stance, perhaps a chopped top, and headlights and/or taillights frenched into the fenders.

Cragar S/S, chrome reverse wheels, or painted wheels with custom wheel covers would complement tinted primer or large-flake metallic paint. And do not forget to add the tuck-and-roll upholstery.

A small-block or a big-block Chevy engine can certainly be installed if the accessories are period perfect. However, a Buick, Oldsmobile, Pontiac, or Cadillac engine would be a logical choice for a true vintage example of a "bucks up" rodder from the 1950s or 1960s. If a shop truck/push vehicle for a race team is the plan, a vintage Hemi from a Chrysler or DeSoto would make for something a little different.

A potential drawback to building a truck in this style is that research is needed to get it correct, just like with any other true restoration. There is no requirement to build anything back to how it rolled out of the factory, but using vintage parts (or reproductions thereof) is essential if the vehicle will be entered in any events that are judged. Sometimes public opinion is the harshest judge out there. Keep in mind that these vintage parts can be difficult to find and more expensive to purchase.

Contemporary

Contemporary is probably the most forgiving style, as it allows for just about any modification from mild to wild. Minor body changes, such as shaved door handles, one-piece door glass (without a vent window), shaved drip rails,

I included this truck as a nostalgic custom simply because the paint has some flattener in it to make it look like primer that has had toner added, and it is riding on painted steel wheels. However, it is very much a contemporary truck that travels to many events.

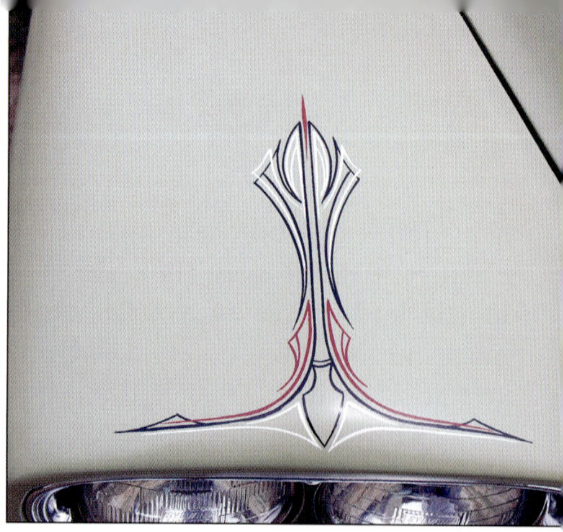

If you are building a nostalgic truck, it really needs to have some pinstriping. The fenders, hood, and tailgate are common locations for pinstripes. Of course, if it can be painted, it can be striped.

Regardless of what you call it, this big-window truck sure sits right. The frenched taillights and rolled pan give it a bit of a nostalgic appearance.

Okay, if this one has you stumped, do not feel bad. It includes a Cameo bed, but the stock bed trim has been removed and replaced with airbrushed trim. I think this gives it a sleeker look, especially with the white paint and polished accessories.

The year 1958 brought on the Fleetside bed option, which gives these trucks an overall sleeker appearance. After bringing it home from the dealer, you could have added the wide whites and peep mirrors and looked very much like this.

There is a lot of nostalgic influence on this lowered 1957 Chevy pickup, including natural-looking patina with some period-perfect pinstriping. Body modifications include a louvered hood and a visor. Five-spoke wheels and narrow whitewalls are other common items from the early 1960s.

shaved emblems, louvers, and relocated fuel tanks, are common. Sectioning or pie-cutting the hood and chopping the top is more advanced, but they have both been done. However, before you get all carried away and start chopping the top on one of these trucks, consider how to chop the wraparound windshield glass.

Front Suspension Options

In addition to body modifications, suspension options are prevalent. Front subframe and Mustang II independent front suspensions (IFS) are the most common. Before anyone realized that a Mustang II front suspension would work on a Task Force truck (among others), subframe swaps were quite common to gain a better ride and upgrade to disc brakes.

Whether the donor car was a Nova, Camaro, or something else, the process is very simple in theory: Cut the front part of the frame off the Chevy truck, cut the front subframe off the donor car, and graft the two back together.

The actual process gets more complicated. Once the front frame is cut off the truck, it is pretty much past the point of no return. A donor vehicle that has a frame the same width as the truck will need to be found. Very few are the exact same width, so a transition in width needs to be accounted for.

It is also essential to determine where to make the frame cuts to maintain the correct wheelbase. It is necessary to fabricate mounting brackets for the radiator and front clip sheet metal. Then, get everything welded back together so that it is square. This was a valiant effort when there was no better alternative.

With the Mustang II–style front crossmember readily available from a wide variety of sources, this makes for a significantly easier swap to gain a better ride and improved brakes. Merely remove the stock front suspension, weld in the Mustang II crossmember between the frame rails, and bolt on the rest of the suspension, and those improvements will be done in a day's time.

To lower the front a bit without an independent front suspension, dropped front I-beam axles are available. When it comes to brakes, the automotive aftermarket has grown exponentially in its offerings. Whether you are using an I-beam axle or independent suspension, disc brake kits (with or without power assist) are available in the stock six-lug or a five-lug bolt pattern. The same braking options are available for the rear, as well.

Rear Suspension Options

For the rear suspension, dual leaf springs, coilover shocks with a four-link, or airbags are all available. If superb handling is desired, a rear suspension from a late-model Corvette could be adapted to the truck. A wide variety of rear axle housings are also available.

All these options allow you to design and build your truck to meet your specific needs for comfort or performance, whether it is merely transportation, a road racer, or something in between. Likewise, wheel and tire options are pretty much limited only by your budget and imagination.

Engine Options

Engine options are practically endless for a contemporary drivetrain. There is a wide variety of displacements and aspiration. Of course, small-block and big-block Chevrolet engines would be the natural selection and would be the easiest to install due largely to easily accessible motor and transmission mounts. Single 4-barrel carburetors are common, and dual 4-barrels or three 2-barrel carburetor setups are also popular without breaking the bank. Superchargers and turbochargers will all fit beneath the hood of these trucks too.

This engine compartment certainly qualifies as clean with the LS3 engine. The black matte finish coordinates nicely with the glossy white sheet metal. Notice how the heater and A/C lines have been routed through the passenger-side inner fender, minimizing clutter beneath the hood.

With the expanse of the GM family of vehicles, several transmissions are available in manual or automatic. Staying with the GM family, there are also the LS and LT series of engines in a variety of displacements and their related transmissions from which to choose. Being from a different generation, these LS components require different mounts, accessories, and external components. However, those are all available from a variety of sources.

Interior Options

Interior options are limited only by your imagination and budget. Bench seats from later-model trucks and SUVs are available from salvage yards and sometimes as new vehicle take-outs from shops that perform upgrades on new vehicle purchases. The latter is often a bolt-in-and-go transplant, while something from a salvage yard may require some upholstery work.

If bucket seats are desired, shop those same places. The seats can also be found in the automotive aftermarket or custom upholstery shops. It simply depends on whether the seats are ready to install or if someone will need to be hired to recover them. Other interior components, such as door panels, carpeting, and floor consoles, fall into that same category.

Paint Considerations

When it comes to exterior paint, simply choosing a color or colors can be a daunting task. Choosing between a single-stage paint and a base coat/clear coat system will have more to do with how the truck will be used and if you plan to paint it yourself.

If you plan on driving the truck daily, consider going with a single-stage paint. It can easily be touched up in the case of rock chips and/or collision damage. Single-stage paint might also be a good choice if you are painting the truck yourself and this is your first paint job.

Base coat/clear coat might be a better choice if it is being applied by an experienced painter. The clear coat provides more UV protection for the color beneath it, and therefore the color is less likely to fade. Although it will cost more in labor fees (your time or someone else's labor rate), a

A bench seat will typically provide more seating capacity than a pair of bucket seats. However, if a center console eliminates the related legroom, you may not have gained anything . . . other than a place to set your hat.

clear coat can be wet sanded, buffed, and polished to a beautiful shine. Of course, regardless of what anyone on the Internet may say, the quality of any paint job is going to depend entirely on the surface finish and preparation.

Another reason to use base coat/clear coat is when a multicolor paint scheme is used, whether that is a simple two-tone combination or wild graphics. At the risk of oversimplifying the process, the first color is sprayed and then cleared. Each additional color is sprayed and cleared, and then the entire vehicle is sprayed with clear to provide one smooth surface.

If you are looking for a retro paint style, the white over just about any color has a very traditional look to it. Removal of any unnecessary emblems and trim help accent the natural body lines. There is nothing wrong with simple.

State-of-the-Art Show Truck

If this style is desired for the truck, a vivid imagination and deep pockets are needed. There is nothing wrong with this choice, but it is not for the faint of heart. Attend a few International Show Car Association (ISCA) shows or the Specialty Equipment Market Association (SEMA) show before beginning your truck project. To run with the big dogs, every detail of the build must be perfect. Forget just making it better than when the truck rolled off the assembly line, it must be flawless to compete in this crowd.

The overall design of the truck must captivate the audience. If they don't look, you're not even in the game. After getting their attention, the design and execution must be top notch to keep them drawn in, asking to see more.

For a wild multicolor paint job like this, base coat/clear coat is the most practical way to go. The base color, black in this case, is applied, color sanded, and then cleared. The clear at this point provides a blank canvas for the flame painter. If he or she makes any mistake, that error could be corrected without damaging the base-color paint below. The multicolor flames are added and then the entire truck is cleared.

After the truck is complete, forget about ever driving it, other than into and out of an enclosed trailer for a show. Then, look forward to judges' comments such as, "The paint should have been two shades brighter," or "I think polished button-head bolts would have looked better than the chromed 12-point bolts in that application."

If this is the style you want to pursue, I wish you the best. Personally, I want to drive my truck as often as I can. A thumbs-up from someone during my commute to work sure makes the workday better to me.

Notable Facts

While this section in no way tells everything about the subtle differences in these trucks, it is information worth knowing. There was a significant change in design midway into the 1955 model year. The 1955 first series was the last of the Advance Design trucks that began in 1947. The 1955 second series was the first of the Task Force trucks that ended in 1959. This book discusses the latter of the two.

A 12-volt electrical system became standard in the Task Force trucks. Power steering and power brakes were new options. From 1955 to 1959, a 235-ci straight six was the standard engine in Chevy trucks. A 265-ci V-8 was optional through 1957 with a 283-ci V-8 available in the 1958 to 1959 models. Being corporate cousins, GMC trucks were standard with a 248-ci straight six in 1955, but that changed to 270 ci in 1956. Optional V-8 engines were available as 288 ci in 1955, 316 ci in 1956, 347 ci in 1957, and 336 ci in 1958–1959.

Dual headlights were introduced as standard equipment in 1958, along with a new hood, grille, and front fenders. The 1955–1957 front clip sheet metal can be installed on a 1958–1959 model as an assembly and vice versa; however, individual components do not interchange. This also applies to Chevrolet versus GMC.

In 1958, A/C was now a factory option, along with the option of a Fleetside bed. On the 1958–1959 Fleetside models, the bed lengths were 78 and 98 inches, respectively. On Stepside models, bed lengths were 78 inches throughout the model run. Long-bed Stepsides were 89 inches on 1955–1957 models and increased to 97 inches on the 1957–1959 models. However, in 1957, Stepsides were available in either 89- or 97-inch bed lengths.

Included in the Task Force models are pickups (Stepside, Fleetside, and Cameo), panel trucks, and the Suburban.

Photo Gallery of Different Styles of Trucks

The following are examples of Chevy and GMC trucks originally manufactured in model years 1955 through 1959. ■

Other than being lowered and having large-diameter custom wheels, this truck is visually stock in appearance. The two-tone paint was a factory option, and the painted mirrors, the bumper, and the grille were stock.

The fit and finish look great on this truck. Other than removal of trim and emblems, no apparent body modifications have been made. Note that the sheet metal behind the chrome grille appears to have been painted black, and therefore invisible. Some enthusiasts are very picky about this, while others are not.

Photo Gallery of Different Styles of Trucks *CONTINUED*

On this truck, the sheet metal behind the grille is painted body color, providing quite a different appearance than if the sheet metal was painted black. While I believe that this matching sheet-metal color is correct from the factory, it is your choice. It is one of those trivial things that is often open for debate.

This 1958–1959 truck has been smoothed to even remove the exterior door handles and relocate the stock fuel tank. The polished grille appears to float within the black grille opening. The body color accented by one other color (black in this case) and chrome is very tasteful.

This satin black 1957 Chevy truck gets driven on a regular basis, so it was built with practicality in mind. With a front suspension via a subframe swap, it has a 500-ci Cadillac engine beneath the hood.

Okay, if you do not understand a vehicle's rake, study this photo. The front end sits considerably lower than the back end of this truck. While this much rake might be a little more than what some people would desire, it does illustrate the concept.

Seeing this truck really brought back memories of my first truck: a 1957 GMC. Yes, there was a lot of bumper and grille on the front of those Jimmys. The bumper guards are separate from the bumper, so they can be used or removed, whichever you prefer. Some love 'em while others hate 'em.

Other than the capped-off bedsides, this is a good look at the rear view of a stock Stepside bed, taillights, and bumper. All quite simple and straightforward, which is one of the reasons so many people really like these trucks. You can also see the deluxe rear glass is considerably larger than the standard cab rear glass.

I do not see anything about this truck that would prevent anyone from driving it daily. The color should be relatively easy to keep clean and the tasteful amount of chrome will not take a long time to maintain. The stock mirrors will make driving in traffic a breeze.

The grilles on the 1958–1959 trucks simply prove that chrome plating was big during that time frame, as that is a lot of sparkle for the front end of a pickup truck back when chrome plating really was chrome plating on metal.

This truck could be called nostalgic due to its satin black paint with pinstriping, or it could be called contemporary. Regardless of what you call it, it looks great and would be welcome in most any garage. The interior looks to be painted orange already, so I suspect the final body color will match that eventually. It is always a good idea to drive a vehicle for a while to make sure everything works before you paint it, if you can.

A stock-height GMC with the voluptuous bumper guards, dual spotlights, and a tonneau cover makes for a tastefully done traditional truck.

Here is a nostalgic custom truck if there ever was one. This truck has been lowered and rolls on wide whitewall tires on chrome reverse wheels. The tailgate has been through the louver press several times, while the taillights have been frenched into the fenders. The tubular nerf bar shouts 1950s hot rod.

Not sure if the finish is paint with flattener added or primer with toner added, but it sure looks nostalgic. The outside rearview mirrors look like stock units that have been shortened a bit. Not having windshield wipers makes one think this does not get driven daily, still, it is cool.

There was a time when every service station, mechanic's garage, or body shop in town had a shop truck that served as a rolling billboard for their services. That does not seem to be the case as often anymore. This very traditional truck looks great, whether the business is real or imaginary.

If you are looking for a project, do not forget panel trucks and Suburbans from this era. This is most likely a newer four-wheel-drive chassis beneath this panel, but there is nothing wrong with that.

This green 1956 Chevy looks to be a very contemporary build with the larger-diameter custom wheels, removed emblems, and monochrome paint. Judging by the headrests, it looks to have some late-model seats inside.

One of these trucks does not have to be fancy to be enjoyable. Looks like this one still has the stock suspension, and that is more than surface rust around the wheel wells. Still, I would bet it gets driven as often as not.

This is a nice nostalgic custom right here. Shiny paint in the stock two-tone configuration as from the factory, some full wheel covers, and a lowered stance all look great.

My 1955 Chevy truck the day after I took delivery of it. I honestly bought it sight unseen (other than photos) off the internet. I will just say, be careful doing that. Still, it was in better condition than anything I could find locally, and it was about half the price.

CHAPTER 2

Plan What You Want

Now that you've determined how the truck will look, it is time to figure out what it will take to get it there. You can think about various aspects of the truck at any time, but in this chapter, we will discuss the chassis, the body, the drivetrain, and then the other systems that are necessary.

If the truck has not yet been purchased, think a lot about the required elements before going forward. Regardless of the truck's intended use and build style, do you have what it takes to build a truck? Do you possess the necessary tools and the required skills to use them? Do you have room to store all the pieces and parts that are disassembled while you are working on it? Will portions of the work need to be done by a professional? If so, how much, and what will it cost? For many of us, we do what we can and pay for the rest as we go to get the truck on the road, but it often takes a long time from start to finish.

Where to Start

Would it be better to purchase a completed truck that is ready to enjoy? That would be a relatively large expense at one time, but that might be a better way to go, especially if there was any hesitation when answering the previous questions. There are always trucks available for sale, but really look the truck over in person and take it for a lengthy test drive before buying it.

How good is the craftsmanship, the fit and finish, the ride, and the performance? When you find that "perfect" truck, ask yourself what it needs to be what you want it to be. Do not hesitate to take a friend with you and listen to your friend's comments on it.

Swapping out a set of wheels and tires is relatively inexpensive and simple. A new paint job or a new interior can be simple, but they can be expensive in a hurry due to the labor involved. Just do not fall head over heels in love with a finished truck that needs to be rebuilt.

Sometime after I bought my project truck, I found this one for sale in my area. As I recall, it was a running, driving truck, but it was listed for about three times what I paid for mine. That would not have been bad, but it had the stock drivetrain and suspension, and it needed some rust repair.

Perhaps buying someone else's partially finished project truck is a better alternative. There will still be work to do or to have done professionally, but it is certainly an option. If someone else has already done all the chassis and bodywork (and done it well), it is close to being a drivable truck, especially if it was purchased for the right price. Installing an engine (salvage yard or crate motor) and transmission is simple if the motor mounts are already installed. There may be lots of little things to

This is what I purchased for about a third of the price. It did not have an engine or transmission in it, but I was planning to do a complete ground-up, frame-off rebuild anyway. So, this one had less stuff for me to get rid of.

do, but most of them are simple and easy.

Project trucks are easy to find because some builders get in over their head due to lack of talent or money. Some professional shops even have project vehicles for sale in various stages of completion. Still, just like when buying a completed truck, check out the craftsmanship of what has been done, determine what still needs to be done, and do not hesitate to negotiate on the price.

Chassis

A purist may insist on using a frame that is original to these trucks. If that is you, do you have an original frame or know where to find one? There are many groups on social media that connect enthusiasts around the world, so do not hesitate to join them, especially the ones that serve as classified ads for parts.

If you have a stock frame, what modifications, if any, do you want to make? To get the desired stance, will you need to use airbags or will dropped spindles suffice? Or, will a set of big and little wheels and tires provide the correct rubber rake? Do any of the frame crossmembers need to be replaced or does the entire frame need to be straightened?

Reproduction versus Stock

If you are not satisfied with the frame you already have, there is a growing list of companies that manufacture reproduction frames and chassis for these Task Force trucks. For the uninitiated, the frame is basically just the two main frame rails, the crossmembers that connect them, the body mounts, and the radiator mounts. To become a chassis, the suspension components are included with the frame. Depending on who and where it is purchased from, the suspension components may be installed or may be packaged separately but included with the price.

If the stock frame is solid and not twisted beyond repair, using it will almost always be less expensive than purchasing a reproduction chassis. However, while expense can be a major factor, time and effort does figure into the overall cost of a build

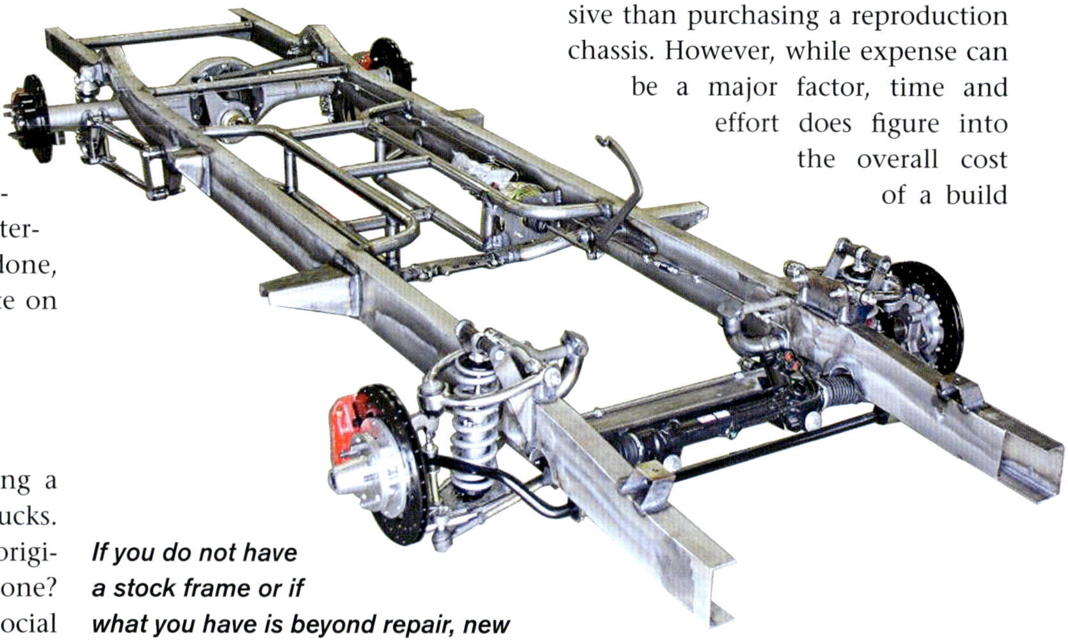

If you do not have a stock frame or if what you have is beyond repair, new frames and/or chassis packages are available from a variety of sources. New frames are straight, square, and usually boxed. This serves as a great foundation for your truck project, whether you start with just a perimeter frame or purchase a chassis complete with brake lines. (Photo Courtesy Pete and Jake's Hot Rod Parts)

and the enjoyment of doing it. The longer that a project drags on, the more likely it is to not be completed.

Starting with a clean, non-rusty chassis can do wonders to get a truck project started off on the right foot, but convenience does come at a price. Typically for an additional fee, the suspension and steering components can be installed, along with brake lines. If you go this full route for a chassis and you take delivery in the morning, you could have wheels and tires and the engine and transmission installed by early afternoon. There is a lot to be said for that.

Whether you are resurrecting an original Task Force truck or building one from new parts, a good cab is a great starting point. Unlike just a few years ago, brand-new reproduction steel cabs are available with the small- or big-window option. They may seem pricey, but the price for the entire cab and doors is comparable to the typical replacement parts alone. (Photo Courtesy Dynacorn Classic Bodies)

Body

Much like chassis, we now have the option of using a brand-new cab and other sheet-metal components for these trucks or using new patch panels to repair the existing trucks. That was not the case when I had my 1957 GMC pickup 40-plus years ago.

Bodywork is a labor-intensive process (therefore expensive) and has a very important impact on the quality of a finished paint job. Doing much work to repair 60-year-old sheet metal can be a waste of time and effort, unless you are very skilled at it.

That said, combining new sheet metal with old can be a nightmare. It is important to remember that even as they left the factory, the body lines and gaps were not consistent and were built to larger tolerances than we are used to today. Yes, they can be made to be perfect, but it will take time. My personal strategy is to work toward consistent gaps, rather than tighter gaps . . . after all, they are just trucks.

The stock hood of my truck and the reproduction front fender have a severe gap about two-thirds of the way back. This will be addressed somewhere along the line, but the solution has not yet been determined. At the leading edge of the hood, the gap is a bit big at about 1/4 inch, but farther back, it is more like 1/2 inch. Not acceptable.

Again, determine how the cab, bed, and other body components fit into the budget as far as money, time, and talent. Of course, that can be said for the entire project.

Engine

Unless some over-the-top chassis and suspension or radical bodywork will be done, the engine is the first place to really personalize a truck. For a contemporary-styled truck, there is a wide variety of GM engines in the small-block or big-block variety that will fit quite nicely under the hood of these trucks. However, remember the W-series 348 and 409 engines if a bit of early 1960s nostalgia works for the truck.

If you are looking for more horsepower, a GM LS motor would be a popular choice, as they have been used to create upward of 1,000 hp. Between salvage yards, a donor car, a rebuilt engine, or a new crate motor, there is bound to be a suitable engine within the budget.

In addition to the engine itself, choosing the various components for aspiration, exhaust, and other accessories will affect the drivability, reli-

The engine bay of these Task Force trucks is big enough to put most any engine that you want beneath the hood. From mild to wild, any engine can be personalized and detailed, or not, as you see fit. Beneath the hood of this aqua beauty is a no-frills, reliable powerplant. There is never anything wrong with plain and simple when it works.

This engine bay is dressed up a bit, but it is still well organized, and everything is easily accessible. Having a minimum of wires and hoses makes for an attractive engine. The polished components compliment the white paint nicely.

Notice how the firewall has been smoothed and has no hoses or wires coming through it. The A/C and heater hoses have been routed outside the inner fender and come into the engine compartment in a very accessible location near the front of the truck.

Connecting the steering column to the steering box and avoiding the exhaust at the same time is often a challenge with some vehicles. However, with a bit of planning, it is not much of a problem on Task Force trucks. Just remember that if more than two U-joints are used, a pillow block (AKA support block) must be used to prevent the steering shafts from looping.

ability, and reactions from others, as well as the budget. Will it have a stock carburetor on the stock inline-6, have a blower on a big-block, or somewhere in between? Whatever is done, make it a clean installation and pay attention to details. Do that, and you will get the greatest comments.

Transmission

With its location in the truck, the transmission is probably the least-seen major component. However, it has a major impact on the drivability of the truck. Does it sound more appealing to shift gears or just put it in gear and go? Will health issues make pressing in the clutch to shift gears a challenge?

Will the truck be doing lots of stop-and-go driving or be mostly on the open highway? Will the truck be pulling a trailer? Providing honest answers to these questions will assist

Overall, this truck is top notch and is very well built. With the glasslike black paint; however, a lot of the details that are there simply get lost.

Even though the paint is satin black (opposed to glossy), it looks great on this daily driver truck. Some well-placed wire ties would go a long way toward detailing the engine compartment.

In a world where 4-barrel carburetors are everywhere, three deuces look great atop this small-block Chevy. Black wire loom does a good job of disguising the multiple colors of the wire inside of it. Electrical wiring needs to be different colors for a reason, but too many colors can be distracting in an engine compartment.

There is a lot going on in this engine compartment: a body-color-painted radiator, lots of wires, and hoses running around a lot of polished and shiny metal. It does not look like any expenses were spared, still . . .

With the brighter body color, an engine with several polished components makes more of a statement than a similar truck with black paint. Overall, this engine is detailed quite nicely, using attractive hose clamps and button-head fasteners.

in choosing a transmission. Generally, the smaller the engine displacement or horsepower, the more gears the transmission should have.

Manual

Beginning with manual transmissions, there are four major common transmission manufacturers: BorgWarner, Muncie, Getrag, and Saginaw. Getrag is a relatively recent addition to this lineup. The table on page 20 provides some basic information about these manual transmissions.

Automatic

OEM automatic transmissions used in GM vehicles are also manufactured by General Motors. They range from 2 speeds in a Powerglide to 10 speeds in a 10L80 or 10L90. The latter two were a mutual effort between Ford and General Motors.

Some common automatic transmissions used by hot rodders include the TH350, TH400, and 700R4. The TH350, typically paired with small-block engines, is known for strength and versatility. Like the TH350, the TH400 is a 3-speed automatic transmission that has gained great popularity in the automotive aftermarket. It was com-

Common Manual Transmissions			
Manufacturer	**Transmission Model Number**	**Gears**	**Basic Description**
BorgWarner (Tremec)	T-10	4-speed	4-speed manual currently made by Richmond Gear
	T-5	5-speed	5-speed manual currently made by Tremec
	T-56	6-speed overdrive	6-speed manual overdrive currently made by Tremec
	TR-6060	6-speed overdrive	6-speed manual overdrive currently made by Tremec
	TR-6070	7-speed overdrive	7-speed manual overdrive currently made by Tremec
Getrag	260	5-speed	5-speed manual made by Getrag
Muncie	M20	4-speed	4-speed wide-ratio manual made by General Motors
	M21	4-speed	4-speed close-ratio manual made by General Motors
	M22	4-speed	4-speed heavy-duty close-ratio manual made by General Motors
Saginaw	M26/27	3-speed and 4-speed	3- and 4-speed light-duty (less than 300 hp) wide-ratio manual made by General Motors

Common GM Automatic Transmissions			
Manufacturer	**Transmission Model Number**	**Years Manufactured**	**Basic Description**
General Motors	3L80HD	1971–1994	Heavy-duty version of TH400
	Super Turbine 400/TH400/3L80	1964–1992	Medium duty
	TH350/TH350C/TH375B/TH250/TH250C	1969–1986	Medium duty
	TH375	1972–1976	Light-duty version of TH400
	TH200/TH200C	1976–1987	Medium duty
	TH200-4R	1981–1990	Medium duty
	TH700R4/4L60	1982–1993	Medium duty
	4L30-E	1991–2001	4-speed light duty
	4L60-E/4L65-E	1992–	4-speed medium duty
	4L80-E/4L85-E	1991–	4-speed heavy duty
	5L40-E/5L50	2000–2007	5-speed medium duty
	6L45/6L50	2007–present	6-speed medium duty
	6L80/6L90	2006–present	6-speed heavy duty
	8L90	2014–present	8-speed heavy duty
	8L45	2016–present	8-speed light duty
Ford–General Motors	10L80	2017–present	10-speed
	10L90	2017–present	10-speed

Decoding the GM automatic transmission model number:

Example: 4L30-E

- 4 is the number of forward gears.
- L simply means that it is a rear-wheel-drive transmission.
- 30 is the GVWR rating (x100).
- E for electronic.

Desiring an overdrive transmission, I chose a 700R4 transmission for the shop truck project. With its low first gear, tall rear tires, and 3.73:1 rear-end gear, it should be fun to drive around town. With the overdrive, it should cruise down the highway just fine.

monly found in two-wheel-drive and four-wheel-drive heavier duty trucks. In 1990, the TH400 was renamed 3L80, meaning it has three speeds, is longitudinally positioned, and is rated for up to 8,000 pounds GVW.

Introduced in 1982 to replace the TH350 is the 700R4 that was targeted to improve fuel economy. This automatic transmission features a 30-percent overdrive. Like all GM transmissions, it was renamed in 1990 as the 4L60 or 4L60E.

In addition to improved fuel economy, it also includes a lower than normal 3.06:1 gear ratio first gear, which provides great acceleration from a standing start. Us old guys gotta have some fun every now and then. Gearing of the 700R4/4L60 is 3.06 for first gear, 1.63 for second, 1.00 for third gear, and 0.70 for fourth gear. The reverse gear in this transmission is 2.9:1.

Rear Axle Housing

Many rear axle housings that fit are available, such as GM's 10- and 12-bolt rear axle housings. It is critical to have your wheels and tires mounted and then placed between the rear fenders to measure and determine the axle width needed to fit between the two wheel and tire assemblies. Then, find one that fits.

However, if you do not yet have the wheels and tires, you can still determine the required axle width. The width between the outer bedside and the inner fender lip on a Stepside (or the outer side of the wheel housing and inner fender lip on a Fleetside) is 12 inches from the factory. The bed width, which is the distance between the bedsides on a Stepside (or between the wheel housings on a Fleetside), is 50 inches.

On most wheel and tire assemblies, the tire bulges out 1 inch to 1½ inches wider than the wheel on both sides of the wheel. If you add a 1/2 inch for clearance, that allows an 8-inch wheel to fit with no problems. You can run a wider wheel, but that will typically require using some mini wheel tubs.

Backspacing

How does that determine the axle width? Wheel manufacturers produce their wheels in different but standard backspacing. Many offer custom backspacing, but we do not want to go there. Before purchasing wheels, check the catalogs to determine the available backspacing. The backspacing is the measurement between the edge of the wheel on the backside and the mounting surface of the wheel that abuts the axle. Common backspacing for 8-inch wheels are 3.500, 3.750, and 4.500 inches. There are others, but these are common.

For this example, we will use an 8-inch wheel with 3.750-inch backspacing. To determine the axle width

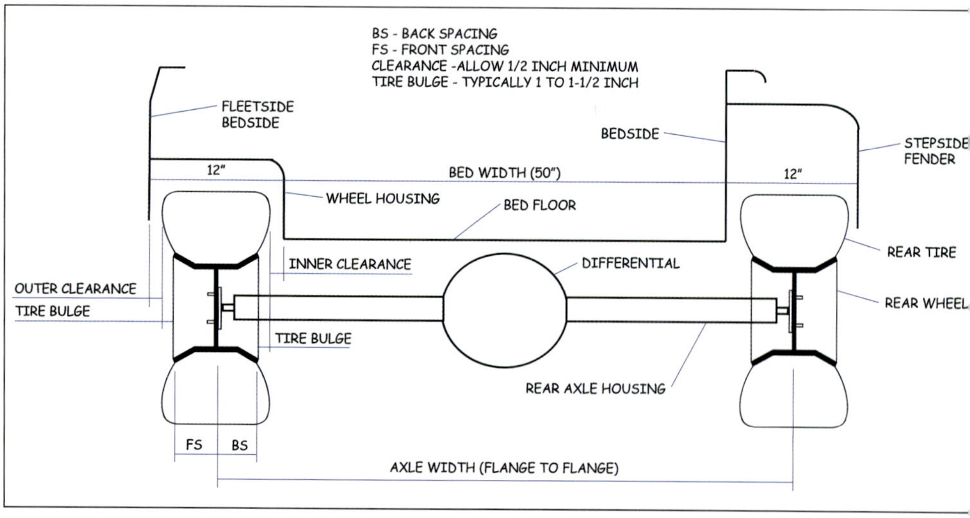

Common questions on social media are "What size tires can I put on the back of my truck?" and "What width rear axle do I need?" One question cannot really be answered correctly without knowing the answer to the other. You simply need to do a little research and some simple math.

While a GM 10- or 12-bolt rear end would be a good rear end for a Chevy or a GMC truck, I chose to go with a Ford 9 inch for the shop truck project. Thanks to the hot rod aftermarket, these are available through a large variety of vendors and in a perfect width for any wheel and tire combination.

(flange to flange), use the following equation:

(backspace + back tire bulge + inner clearance) x 2 + bed width = axle width
(3.75 inch + 1 inch + 0.5 inch) x 2 + 50 inches = 60.5 inches

Remember that increasing the backspacing will move the wheel/tire assembly inward (possibly necessitating wheel tubs). Wheel spacers can be used to move the wheel/tire outward slightly if the axle is a bit too narrow. Decreasing the backspacing will move the wheel/tire assembly outward (possibly causing the wheels to stick out past the fenders).

While purists may despise the use of a Ford 9-inch rear beneath their Task Force or Apache truck, rest assured that there are more Bowtie engines beneath the hoods of Ford hot rods. A great thing about the Ford-style rear axle housing is the dropout third member. This allows for the changing of rear gears quickly and easily if it is ever needed or wanted. While it requires some jigs and fixtures, it is relatively easy to narrow a 9-inch Ford rear end, so they are readily available at whatever width you need.

Open Rear or Limited Slip

Besides finding the correct width axle housing, there are a few other things to take into consideration: the gear ratio and an open rear end or limited-slip differential. The answer to these considerations is based largely on how the truck will be used.

The gear ratio will have the biggest effect on gas mileage, acceleration, and pulling power. If high-speed driving is going to be the norm, a higher gear (lower numerically) would provide the best gas mileage. Conversely, if pulling power is going to be necessary, a lower gear (higher numerically) would provide more torque, everything else being equal. If city traffic and highway commuting will both be common, a gear ratio somewhere in the middle would provide a good compromise.

Determining RPM

One cannot simply look at the rear end gear ratio only and know how it is going to perform. The engine, transmission, and tire diameter are equally as important. The following equation can be used to determine revolutions per minute (RPM), miles per hour (MPH), rear-end gear ratio, and tire diameter if three of the four are known. This equation is based on a 1:1 final drive gear ration when in high gear.

RPM = (MPH x rear-end gear ratio x 336) ÷ tire diameter
MPH = (RPM x tire diameter) ÷ (rear-end gear ratio x 336)

As an example, if the truck has a 4.11:1 gear ratio and is turning 4,500 rpm with a 26-inch rear tire, it would theoretically be running 85 mph. With everything else the same, changing to a tire with a 30-inch diameter would increase the speed to 98 mph. Increasing the tire diameter effectively lowers the gear ratio.

If limited on the tire diameter, performance can be increased by changing rear-end gears. For example, with 30-inch tires and 4.11:1 gears, the engine must turn 2,762 rpm for the truck to run at 60 mph. To run that same speed with 3.0:1 gears, the engine can slow down to 2,016 rpm. Raising the gear ratio (lower number gears) will turn faster MPH and the same engine speed.

If using an overdrive transmission, modify the equation to include the final drive ratio of the overdrive (typically around 0.7) as follows:

RPM = (MPH x rear-end gear ratio x final drive ratio x 336) ÷ tire diameter

With no overdrive, 3.0:1 gears, and 30-inch-diameter tires, the engine would need to turn 2,352 rpm to run at 70 mph. With an overdrive transmission, the engine could slow down to 1,646 rpm to maintain the same MPH.

Choosing an open rear end versus one with a limited-slip differential is typically a personal preference. If the truck will be driven year-round and/or pull a trailer, limited slip will provide better traction in subpar conditions.

Other Components

Even with the major components of chassis, body, and drivetrain determined, there are still plenty of other things to decide. These include the suspension, wheels and tires, the brake system, fuel system, and cooling system, along with a variety of other smaller but not necessarily less-expensive components.

Determine what you want, where to get it, and what the budget for this project is. Items to get the truck drivable and safe need to be determined up front. All trucks are built on a budget; some are just more restrictive than others. There are some components that would be nice, but they may need to wait until later due to their expense. It is always possible to add a set of fancy wheels and tires later. Automotive projects are most enjoyable when you participate at a level that is comfortable for you and your family.

One of the best ways to find out what is available and what everyone else is using is by going to events where trucks similar to yours are in attendance. Even if your truck is not drivable, go as a spectator and talk to truck owners and parts vendors. It is better to ask questions sooner than later. Although there are small events throughout the country, larger events will have more to offer. Check out Goodguys Rod & Custom Association (good-guys.com) and the National Street Rod Association (nsra-usa.com) to find an event near you or across the country.

Suspension

Popular choices for front suspension are the stock parallel leaf springs supporting a dropped axle, an independent front suspension using the Mustang II–style crossmember, or a Corvette independent front suspension. Yes, there are other choices, but these are probably the most popular. Replacement parts are available, and the installation is straightforward.

For the rear suspension, popular choices are the stock parallel leaf springs supporting a more streetable rear axle housing or a parallel four-link setup. Kits for either of these are available from a variety of sources.

Wheels and Tires

Besides supporting the truck and putting the motive power to the ground, the selection of wheels and tires plays an important part in the aesthetics of the vehicle. No matter how slick the paint may or may not be, if the truck does not have the right stance, it is not going to get the good reactions that it should. Sure, it might be a likable truck, and everyone may think it is cool, but if it has that "just right" stance, it will get much more appreciation.

These rally wheels and BFGoodrich radials were bought specifically for the shop truck project, as they were what I wanted at the time. However, the project has taken way longer than planned, and now the tires are past their DOT expiration date, even though they still have full tread. Since the wheels are a multi-bolt pattern, I will use them for rollers on the next project and buy a new set of wheels and tires for the truck when it gets painted.

Determining what is perfect is difficult at best. Having a bit of rubber rake (rear tires that are somewhat larger diameter than the front) will always improve the stance whether the truck sits really low with an airbag suspension, is at stock height, or is somewhere in between.

Front wheel and tire assemblies must be able to not only fit beneath the front fenders but also turn to steer the vehicle. The front wheels must also be sized to adequately fit with disc brakes, if being used. With bigger brakes being exceedingly popular, bigger wheels are necessary.

Rear wheel and tire assemblies simply need to fit beneath the truck and between the fenders or wheel openings. It is always good practice to have at least 1 inch of clearance between the tire and the sheet metal when the vehicle is at rest. During cornering or aggressive driving, the tires might close in on that a bit, but most likely will not rub. An aesthetic thing that many truck owners do is put too small of a tire in the back of their trucks. The Stepside fenders and the wheel tubs on a Fleetside are huge and need to be filled to look pleasing.

Brake System

Unlike back in the late 1970s when I had my 1957 GMC, there are now several sources for disc brakes for both front and rear. Front disc brake conversion kits are designed for the spindles being used. So, while shopping for front disc brakes, purchase a kit for the stock truck spindles, the Mustang II, or whatever other front suspension system is being used.

The Mustang II uses specific rotors to provide a 4.75-inch bolt circle or 4.5-inch bolt circle, which allows the use of GM wheels. Rear disc brake conversion kits are also designed for the specific rear axle housing being used.

Stock Task Force truck spindles never looked as good prior to being outfitted with disc brakes from Wilwood Engineering. The kit features six-piston calipers (available in red or black) that will provide considerably more braking force than the stock drum brakes, hands down. (Photo Courtesy Wilwood Engineering)

Fuel System

One of the first decisions to make for the fuel system is whether to use the stock fuel tank. If the truck still has the original tank, verify that it is not leaking anywhere and is not full of rust. A rusty stock gas tank will ruin all of your hard work.

If you want to continue using the stock location, reproductions of the stock gas tanks are available. However, the stock location of the tank inside the cab behind the seat leaves a lot to be desired in most people's minds.

Unless the truck has been sitting outside in the fresh air with the windows open for a long time, there is probably still at least a hint of gasoline fumes inside the cab. For this reason, most contemporary truck builds remove the stock gas tank and install a new gas tank beneath the truck bed. This eliminates new gas fumes in the cab, locates the new tank between the frame rails (making it a bit safer in case of an accident), and provides a bit more weight to the rear axle.

Many gas tanks that fit between the rear frame rails of these trucks are available. A stock or reproduction tank for an early Ford Mustang seems to be a popular conversion. These tanks have a stock flange on each side that allows for convenient mounting to the truck's frame rails.

A variety of other custom fabricated steel or poly tanks are also available. Some mount to the frame rails with flanges that allow for simple installation by bolting the flange to the frame rails. Others require steel straps to be used to support the gas tank from underneath. Depending on the suspension being used, the stock rear crossmember may need to be relocated to provide enough room front to back.

Filler Neck

After choosing a fuel tank and location, determine where the filler

For anyone wanting to use stock spindles, Wilwood Engineering now makes a disc brake kit specifically for that application. Included in the kit are the rotors, calipers, mounting brackets, brake hoses, pads, bearings, and hardware. Contact a local dealer for more details. (Photo Courtesy Wilwood Engineering)

While it was a convenient location for the stock gas tank when it was built originally, right behind the seat and in the cab is not a good location. The fumes alone are enough reason for most people to relocate the tank. The fact that if the vehicle is in an accident and any damage is done to the tank, it could likely be pouring gasoline on the occupants is another reason to consider relocating the tank.

Regardless of which tank is used (several are available that fit nicely), the typical location is between the rear axle housing and the back of the truck, between the frame rails. The gas filler neck can be routed up through the floor or to the outside of the bed, such as in one of the fenders. To ensure that the tank fills easily, route the filler neck with sweeping curves, rather than sharp bends.

neck should be located. It should be obvious, but to be safe, the filler neck should be routed as straight as possible and must be higher than the top of the tank.

Depending on the tank used, the fill point can be in one of the rear fenders, in the area on the side of the bed in front of the rear fenders, or directly through the bed floor. The filler neck is not required to be perfectly straight, but any sharp turns are going to slow the fill process. The location of the fill point will have some bearing on what type of cap can be used.

Fuel Line

If you are using a carburetor and an engine-driven fuel pump, the fuel line can be a single run of 3/8-inch fuel line and the necessary fittings. Run a piece of flexible fuel hose (rubber or braided stainless) out of the tank to a piece of hard line located at the frame rail. This hard line can then be bent as needed to conform to the contour of the frame rail and run forward to a point near the fuel pump.

Use a flexible fuel hose to connect the hard line to the fuel pump. This flexible hose allows for engine movement due to torque. Fuel line can then be run to a fuel filter and then to the carburetor. Just like brake lines, fuel lines should be secured to the frame rails to avoid movement or rubbing that could cause damage.

Fuel Pump

If running an electronic fuel injection (EFI) system, include a return fuel line back to the tank. Also use an electronic in-tank fuel pump and a carbon dioxide (CO2) sensor in the exhaust. Routing of the fuel line and the return line is like when using a single line.

Cooling System

Having a cooling system that will keep your truck running cool is important. This requires a radiator that allows coolant (antifreeze) to flow through it easily and enough airflow to keep the coolant cool. A heavy thumper engine and/or running an air conditioner will increase the demand on the cooling system. Using an electric fan along with a cooling shroud will increase the radiator's performance. If possible, use a separate transmission cooler for an automatic transmission because the transmission does not need to run as hot as the engine will run.

Everything Else

As the late-night television commercials say, "But wait, there's more." Choosing the seats to be used, the material in which to cover them, and the color can be a challenge. What type of steering wheel, which steering column, and whether the shifter should be on the column or the floor are other common questions. What about a wiring fuse panel and where should it be installed? Which gauges do you want to use, digital or analog? What about floor covering, cupholders, stereo, or other electrical accessories? They all take up physical space and a portion of the budget, so planning is important.

Establish the Overall Parts List

So how do you keep track of all the necessary parts that go into a truck project? Simple, make a list. Creating a spreadsheet of required/desired parts is a common practice for me for most any project, automotive or otherwise. This spreadsheet can start out as a rough, high-level outline of what is required to complete the truck, starting with rolling chassis, drivetrain, brake system, body components, interior components, and labor. Then, begin thinking about the various pieces and parts that are required and add them to the list in the correct category.

Include the component, manufacturer, vendor, part number (if available), and the manufacturer's suggested retail price (MSRP). Doing this will allow you to begin determining a real budget.

As parts are purchased, highlight the items to purchase next to ensure that everything is included. When they are received, highlight them in a different color to indicate that they have arrived. If this prevents you from ordering just one item that you already have, it is worth the effort.

Having this list does not mean that you are required or restricted to purchase only the next item on the list by any means. It simply serves as a list of parts to get from starting to finishing your truck project.

These seats look comfy, are very stylish, and have adjustable backs for occupant comfort. The dash panel has been decluttered significantly, housing only the gauges, headlight switch, HVAC controls, and two A/C vents. This truck also features one-piece power windows and cruise control.

Attention to details is what matters. The dash has been customized to mirror the driver's side onto the passenger's side; however, that is not an uncommon modification. The detail that caught my eye is the inside rearview mirror being moved from above the windshield to the dash. Additionally, a small pedestal was added to the dash to support the mirror, making it look like a factory design.

The PRC radiator is made of aluminum and includes an integral framework that serves as the core support. Included in the package price is the A/C condenser, two electric fans, an overflow tank, and a remote transmission cooler. Note that any radiator material is soft, so exercise extreme caution during handling to prevent damage.

These bucket seats are from a Pontiac Sunfire, but a Chevrolet Cavalier would have similar seats. They are in decent condition, are similar in style to the aftermarket seats I planned to purchase, and were substantially less expensive. They will be reupholstered later in the build. A custom floor console will fill the void between the seats.

1955 Chevy Pickup Project Phase One				
Component	Manufacturer	Vendor	Part Number	MSRP
Rolling Chassis components:				
Stock frame & basic body components	General Motors			$1,400.00
Front Suspension (Superide II)	Heidt's Hot Rod Shop	Morfab Customs	BX-307	$2,955.00
Control Arms (Polished stainless)	Heidt's Hot Rod Shop	Morfab Customs	BS-022	$679.00
Stabilizer Bar (Chrome)	Heidt's Hot Rod Shop	Morfab Customs	BS-054-C	$359.00
Ball Joint Caps (Polished stainless)	Heidt's Hot Rod Shop	Morfab Customs	MP-35	$29.50
Steering (power rack & pinion)	Heidt's Hot Rod Shop	Morfab Customs	MP-038-1	$100.00
Rear 4-bar (polished stainless steel w/coilovers)	Heidt's Hot Rod Shop	Morfab Customs	RB-110-SS	$990.00
Panhard Rod kit (bolt on, polished stainless)	Heidt's Hot Rod Shop	Morfab Customs	RP-103-SS	$195.00
Wheels, 15 x 7 front, Hot Rod Rallye	Wheel Vintiques	Summit Racing	WVI-38-571204	$133.90
Wheels, 16 x 10 rear, Hot Rod Rallye	Wheel Vintiques	Summit Racing	WVI-66-601205	$297.90
Center Caps (Stainless Steel, taxi plains)	Wheel Vintiques	Summit Racing	WVI-1002-S-1	$83.80
Lug nuts		High Ridge NAPA		$50.00
Tires, 225/60R15 front	BFGoodrich T/A Radials	Summit Racing	BFG-03175	
Tires, 345/xxR16 rear	BFGoodrich T/A Radials			
Rear Axle Housing and Axles (Nine inch Ford)	John's Industries	RJay's		
Nine inch Ford third member, 3.70:1 gears, 28 spline, open differential	John's Industries	RJay's	JI370	
Rear coilovers	Heidt's Hot Rod Shop	Morfab Customs		
Motor mounts	Chassis Engineering	Morfab Customs		
Power Brake Pedal, Bracket, & linkage		Morfab Customs		
Brake Master Cylinder (1-1/8" 4 wheel discs ports on 2 sides)		Morfab Customs	MC2911	
Brake Booster (7" diameter dual diaphragm)		Morfab Customs	BB072G	
Front Rotors (Replacement)		NAPA		
Bump Stops, Rear Axle	Energy Suspension	Yogi's	9-9137G	
Transmission mount	Energy Suspension	Yogi's	31-2378	
Rear Disc Brake kit (Dynalite Pro 12" w/e-brake, w/ Black calipers)	Wilwood	Yogi's	140-7582	
Rolling Chassis components sub-total				
Drivetrain components:				
Engine (GM 350/290 Base Crate Motor)	GMPP	Weir Chevrolet	19355658	
Transmission (GM 700R4 automatic transmission)	Gearstar	Yogi's	GPT700-2	
Harmonic Balancer (Neutral balance)	GMPP		12551537	
Flexplate (Internally balanced)			471529	
Starter (168 tooth)		NAPA		
Distributor (HEI)			93440806	
Distributor holdown, billet	Billet Specialties	Morfab Customs	BLT65920	
Alternator (100/50 Amp GM 1-wire)		NAPA		

This is merely a portion of the spreadsheet where I track what items I want to use, their part numbers, vendors, and price (MSRP and what I pay with taxes and shipping). Color coding helps to keep track of when parts are ordered and received.

Notice how the underdash panel for the A/C vents wraps around to blend into the upholstery on the doors. The bucket seats with two-tone upholstery and French seams provide a sporty look to the interior of this Apache.

This center console provides room for lots of things, besides the floor shifter. A navigation system, stereo, HVAC controls, power window controls, cupholders, and a place to put your mobile phone all come in handy while enjoying your truck. It also includes some hidden (and possibly lockable) storage.

At this point, I had a fairly good idea of what I wanted the truck to accomplish, what parts I wanted to use, where to get them, and what it was going to cost. Now it is time to start buying parts and getting some work done.

Chassis

As cliché as it sounds, the chassis of the truck truly is the foundation of a build. For that reason, it needs to be as good as it can be for the truck project to be a success. It needs to be structurally sound, square (horizontally and vertically), and serve directly or indirectly as mounting points for almost everything else.

Whether your truck project has been in the family since it was new or you just drug it home earlier today, carefully evaluate the frame before doing much work on the truck. Without pulling the sheet metal off, some parts are not accessible, but you can usually get an idea of the frame's condition by crawling beneath it with a flashlight. If you can put the vehicle up on a lift, that is even better.

Check for Frame Damage

The first thing to look for is obvious damage, such as tears or cracks in the frame. These frames are now 60-plus years old and were designed to be used as work trucks, so that is what most of them have done. It is not uncommon to find original holes that have now been roughed up around the edges from being used as a secure point to hook a chain or other device of disrespect.

Most of these can probably be prettied up with a welder and a grinder. However, if a crack or tear appears somewhere other than near one of these holes, it may indicate that the truck has been involved in an accident. That does not mean that it cannot be repaired, but it is a warning sign to be on the lookout for other related damage. That damage may or may not have been repaired correctly . . . and that may not be obvious at first.

The stock frame for the project truck prior to picking up the cab from the media blaster. A Heidt's Superide II independent front suspension and rear four-link with coilover suspension has been installed. A 290-hp 350 from GM Performance Parts and a GM 700R4 transmission will provide power to a 9-inch Ford rear end. BFGoodrich T/A Radial tires are mounted on painted rally wheels.

Measure for Squareness

Secondly, verify that the frame does not have a twist in it. If you are starting out with a bare frame, it is quite easy to determine if the frame is square by using three jack stands, a level, and a tape measure. On a level surface, put the rear of the frame on two jack stands that are at the same height and in the same position on the frame rails. Now place the front of the frame on one jack stand located in the middle of the front crossmember.

Measure diagonally from a known location (factory hole) on the top front of the left frame rail to a known location on the top right frame rail near the rear of the frame. Record this measurement and then measure and record the opposite diagonal. These measurements should be identical; however, due to the loose tolerances of these vehicles when they were built, they may be off slightly.

Now repeat this process for the front half and back half of the frame.

After measuring, set a level across the frame rails from side to side. Ideally these would all be level, but it may be that the garage floor or whatever the jack stands are setting on is not level. However, if the front measurements are similar, the rear measurements are similar, and the level is consistent from front to back, the frame is probably okay. If the measurements are more than a 1/4 inch off, the level is inconsistent, or the frame is lifting itself off one of the rear jack stands, it has some twist.

If the body is mounted on the frame, the frame can be taken to an autobody alignment shop to be measured. There, it can be measured very accurately with precision equipment. Regardless of how the measurements are taken, the frame can probably be straightened while in the alignment shop. Shops that do this type of work typically charge an hourly rate, and it may take three to five hours. However, it will be money well spent.

Since the cab, bed, and suspension components mount to the frame, it is critical that the mounting locations align. If the frame is bowed out or concave, the cab and/or bed mounting bolts may not align. Likewise, mounting the suspension to a frame that is out of level and out of square will make a proper wheel alignment almost impossible.

Original Frame

Using an original frame or a reproduction thereof is always the simplest choice when building one of these trucks. Chances are that you already have the original frame if you already have a truck. The cab mounts and bed mount holes are already in the correct location. The radiator mounts are in the correct location to work with the front-clip sheet metal. If they are missing, they can be replaced.

If the original frame is square, straight, and structurally sound, there is really no reason to not use it. However, unless you are doing a purely stock restoration, it will require some updates, most all of which are readily available in an ever-growing aftermarket. Even if you are restoring the truck, having an original frame will make buying and finding parts that fit and work much easier than working with a frame from a different make and model.

Frame Straightening

Necessary repairs, such as collision damage or rust issues, should be addressed as early in the building process as possible. Automotive body shops deal with collision repairs such as frame straightening on a regular basis, so the fact that the truck is 60 years old and not a brand-new vehicle should not become a problem, whether the cab and bed are on it or it is a bare chassis. It is all about laser measurements and hydraulic pushing/pulling capabilities.

In some situations, especially with older, tougher frames, some amount of heat may be required to bring everything into alignment. Any discoloration caused by this can be addressed in the prime and paint process.

To be fully assured that the frame is not too rusty to use, it should be media blasted. This will quickly reveal any rust, whether it is merely surface rust or something more severe. Even if the frame really is in good condition, now you will know that it is indeed solid. Anyone who has been around these old trucks has probably

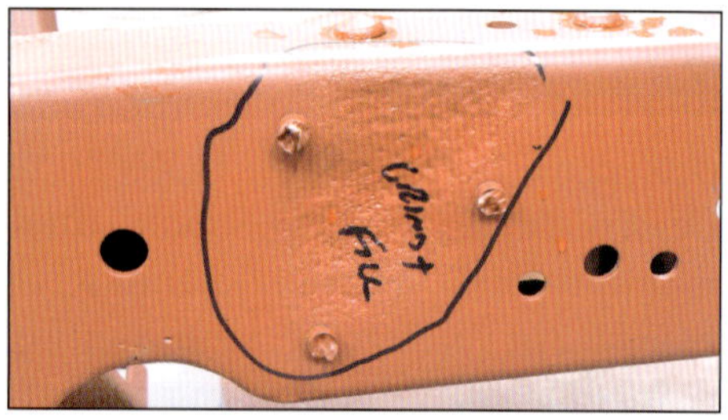

The encircled area is where the original shock bracket was mounted to the frame, hence the remains of the three mounting rivets. Pitting of the frame is most likely from dirt and moisture being trapped between the frame and the shock bracket. There is no rust through, so some body filler will eventually have this looking great.

While installing the Heidt's IFS crossmember, we realized that the front frame horns were tweaked a little to the left. A trip to Jerry's Auto Body got them all straightened out, even though it took a bit of heat, thus the discoloration.

seen more than one that had a shiny new paint job to make it look good to a potential buyer, only to find that the frame was full of freshly painted rust.

It is not uncommon for any vehicle in this age range to have some surface rust or even some minor pitting. The minor pitting can be addressed with some body filler prior to applying the final paint to the frame. If there are rust-through areas in the frame, the situation now requires some thought and a workable plan to resolve it.

Frame Repair

When it comes to frame repair, remember that this frame is the major structural component of the project. While you may or may not be competent with a MIG welder, welding on the vehicle's frame is more serious than welding in a sheet-metal patch panel. A TIG welder is also suitable for welding chassis components. The material is going to be quite a bit thicker and is going to be under more stress than the body's sheet metal. If you are not up to the task of the welding required, hire a competent professional to do the work. Safety is more important than pride.

If a crack or tear appears in the web portion of the frame, it can be reinforced by welding a piece of steel backing material onto the inside of the frame web. It would then make good sense to box that area of the frame as well. Simply boxing the frame or a portion thereof without repairing an existing crack would be a waste of time, as it would not fix the original problem.

Frame Modifications

Modifications to the frame typically consist of boxing the frame to make it stronger and to upgrade the suspension. However, some of them were equipped with V-8 engines directly from the factory, so for a mild small-block engine, boxing is not an absolute requirement.

Being a simple ladder style with multiple crossmembers makes these frames stout to begin with. That said, if the plan is to go with a high-torque engine or do any high-performance driving of any sort, boxing the frame is a good idea.

Boxing the Frame

Boxing an original frame is easy to do, but it requires time and patience to do it correctly. If the stock crossmembers are in place, they will interfere with installing the boxing plates. The boxing plate can be notched around the crossmember or the crossmember can be modified to fit the now slightly narrower span. Unless you already have some commercially available boxing plates, you would need to have some cut out of 10-gauge (1/8-inch) sheet metal.

Since the frame rails are not a consistent profile, a pattern needs to be created. This can be done two different ways: by using poster board or by using heavy craft paper. With the poster board, hold it in place with one hand and then use a permanent marker to draw a line on the poster board along the top and bottom of the frame rail. Cut this out and then trim to fit exactly as it should. A single piece of poster board will not be as long as the entire frame, so continue this process until there are enough pieces to fit together for the complete length.

Perhaps a more convenient method is to use heavy craft paper, or masking paper. This comes in a roll, so it would be easier to make a one-piece pattern. To make it easier to handle, cut a piece off the roll that

Purely a hypothetical situation in this case, but if you wanted to make boxing plates for your stock frame, some areas would no doubt be curved.

Cut out poster board for the area that you want to box. Several pieces of poster board and metal will be needed to do an entire frame. Fold the poster board over the top edge of the frame and tape it in place.

With the top secured, fold the poster board down and then around the bottom edge. Trim the poster board as necessary and press a crease in it at the edge of the frame.

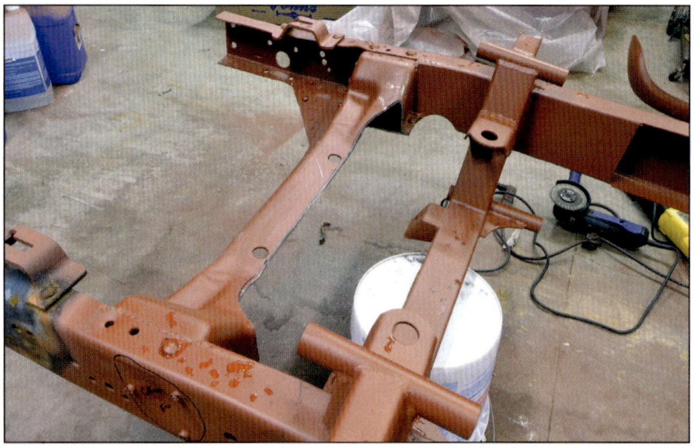

The front frame of the truck is substantially stronger now with the addition of the rectangular steel tube Mustang II front crossmember. The stock front crossmember is simply a piece of stamped steel. In this case, it will be retained; however, it has been trimmed somewhat to facilitate installation/removal of the power rack-and-pinion steering.

The basic stock frame for a 1955–1959 Chevrolet/GMC truck is shown with the addition of a Heidt's MII front crossmember and in primer. The stock suspension and steering have been removed, and the front frame horn damage is corrected.

is long enough to reach from one end of the frame to the other, as well as overlap on the top and bottom.

With the help of an assistant, hold the paper taut against the inside of the frame rails and then tape it in place on each end. Fold the paper along the top edge of the frame rail, putting in a sharp crease as you go. Fold the paper over the frame rail and trim off some of the excess so the paper can be taped to the frame rail. Repeat this process for the lower edge of the frame rail. Cutting at the top and bottom creases in the paper creates a pattern for the boxing plates.

Using this method, the plates would butt to the flanges of the original frame. If you want the boxing plates to fit into the frame rails, trim the pattern accordingly.

With your new pattern in hand, transfer it to the boxing material. A plasma cutter would probably be the best device to use to cut out the metal, but it can be done with a band saw or a cutting torch, if necessary. Clamp the boxing plates into position, check them for the best fit, and verify that they are plumb. It is quite possible that the lower flange of the frame rail is slightly wider than the upper flange.

If the boxing plate is simply welded onto both flanges, it would not be plumb, which could cause problems while building the rest of the truck. Whenever possible, having everything square, plumb, and level is best. If the lower flange is wider, mark or scribe a line where the boxing plate would be plumb. Then, cut or grind off the excess width until the boxing plate can be installed.

Tack weld the boxing plates in several places to ensure that they fit as desired. Then, continue until the boxing plates are completely welded in place.

All commercially available Mustang II suspension kits that I have seen include short boxing plates for use around the new crossmember. This makes the kit easier to install and provides a solid mounting surface to weld to. They also include semicircular boxing plates for the lower side of the frame to allow for the rack-and-pinion steering.

Reproduction Frame

Not having a usable frame is no reason to not build one of these trucks if you want one. Several manufacturers produce reproduction frames for these trucks. Some match the stock profile around the rear axle location very well, while others are merely sections of straight rectangular tubing. While the front and rear crossmembers are typically like the stock configuration, the transmission crossmember can be anything from one simple bar to a collection of round or square tubes that tie both frame rails together, as well as supporting the transmission.

These reproduction frames are typically available in various stages of completion, and therefore different price ranges. At the lower end of the price spectrum is the bare frame, including the frame rails, the crossmembers, and cab/bed mounts, depending on the make and model of the truck. A bit more up the price range, the frame includes front suspension, rear suspension, and a master cylinder mount with brake pedal. Farther up the list are a rear axle housing, brakes, and brake lines.

These packages are often referred to as Stage 1, Stage 2, and Stage 3, but they are not always consistent from one manufacturer to another. Therefore, always verify exactly what is included before doling out that hard-earned pay.

Many of these reproduction frames are available with a Corvette C5/C6 suspension front and rear. Others use the Mustang II independent front suspension and four-link or parallel leaf rear suspension. Worthy of note about all these reproductions frames and suspension components is that while they are reproductions, each manufacturer design and builds them as they see fit. Therefore, some will look more authentic than others, while others may look to be stronger and beefier than others. It will always be a good suggestion to shop around and ask others what they liked and what they did not like about what they have used.

Frame Swaps

A common question about these trucks seen on various social media pages is "What frame should I put my project truck on?" The answers vary, but I will always believe that an original 1955–1959 Chevrolet or GMC truck frame or a reproduction thereof is the best answer. There are still a lot of these trucks out there that can be saved, and the automotive aftermarket has embraced these trucks substantially. Simply put, there is no reason to reinvent the truck wheel or chassis.

Unless you are an engineering guru who simply wants to attempt to assemble a bunch of mis-matched parts just to see if it can be done, there is no good reason to attempt to adapt one of these trucks on a different chassis. That is not to say that it cannot be done, but it is unlikely that the project would be completed. There are always project vehicles like this that never see the light of day.

Suspension

The truck's suspension supports the truck's unsprung weight and keeps the tires in contact with the driving surface. It consists of a group of components that include shock absorbers, springs, and a method of locating the front and/or rear axles to the frame.

On the 1955–1959 Chevrolet and GMC trucks, the stock front and rear suspensions were similar in design, having a set of parallel leaf springs for each axle and a tube shock absorber for each wheel. The axle, front or rear, is clamped to the spring with a pair of U-bolts. Each spring is secured to the truck frame at each end.

At the rear of the front spring and the front of the rear spring, the spring is in a fixed position, unable to move. To allow for suspension travel, the opposite end of the spring is connected to the frame with a shackle, allowing the spring to move up or down as necessary. As the name implies, the shock absorber absorbs, or cushions, the rebound of the axle as it moves up and down while traveling on uneven roads.

By the very nature of this type of suspension, there is a limited amount of axle travel, which is governed by the length of the spring shackle. With the stock front I-beam axle and/or the rear axle not having any significant amount of flex capability, if one end moves upward, the other end is forced to move downward.

For instance, if one tire falls into a pothole, the tire on the opposite end of the axle is going to tend to pull away from the driving surface. In similar fashion, if the tire on one side goes up on a curb, the tire on the opposite end is going to be forced downward. On an irregular driving surface, this causes a rough ride that gets worse at a higher speed.

Independent suspension is an improvement over the stock suspension, be it front or rear. The independent front suspension (IFS) or independent rear suspension (IRS) provides a smoother ride since each wheel can move up or down independently of the opposite wheel.

Front Suspension Assembly

Assembly of the stock front suspension of a Task Force truck is a straightforward task if you pay attention to what you are doing and keep

A look at the stock front suspension prior to any modifications shows the rearmost crossmember (just below the firewall) supported the rear mounts of the engine. The front suspension is simple in design: an I-beam axle, parallel leaf springs, and shocks that have already been removed. At the top of the photo is the steering box. In the front is the right-side radiator mount.

safety in mind. Begin by supporting the front of the frame with jack stands located somewhere forward of the front spring hangers. The rear portion of the frame must be supported also, but this can be by the existing rear suspension or jack stands.

Position the jack stands so that they maintain the frame in a balanced position. Insert a new spring eye bushing into each spring eye. Place the rear end of the front leaf spring into the frame-mounted spring hanger and then insert a pin through the spring hanger and the spring eye bushing. Secure this in place with a lock washer and nut.

Insert the pin of an open shackle through the bushing at the opposite end of the spring and the other pin of the shackle into the spring hanger hole in the side of the frame. Slide the shackle plate over the pins and secure with two lock washers and nuts. Repeat the same process for the opposite side of the truck. Whenever installing new or reinstalling old springs, it is always a good idea to replace the spring eye bushings.

Using a floor jack or other suitable means of support, move the front axle beneath the parallel leaf springs. Lift the axle and secure it to the springs by installing two U-bolts from the top side, around the spring, and through the axle plate on each end. Secure each U-bolt with two lock washers and nuts. Secure the lower end of a tube shock absorber to the mounting pin on the axle and the upper end onto the frame mount.

Spindles can be installed before or after the axle is installed. If the existing kingpins are worn, they should be replaced. Applying some lubricating grease to the kingpins will make them easier to install. When in the proper position, secure the kingpins by inserting the pin through the hole in the end of the axle and passing it through the notch in the kingpin. Secure this pin with a nut on the opposite side of the axle.

Stock Front Suspension Lowering

When using a stock-style front suspension, there are a variety of things that can be done to lower the truck in the front and not spend a bunch of money. New springs that are not as stiff as the stock springs can be installed. The springs can also be installed beneath the front axle to move the wheel centerline slightly higher in relation to the frame.

While the stock axle has a 4.5-inch drop from the factory, it can be dropped some more. However, dropping an axle is a learned craft and not one that should be taken lightly. In other words, do not attempt to do this yourself, as a failure could be catastrophic. The price to have an axle dropped is exponentially less than the damage it would cause or the liability that would be incurred if something went wrong.

Other than the placement of the axle above or below the springs, the assembly of a stock or modified dropped axle suspension is the same.

Except for welding in the crossmember, be it Mustang II, Corvette, or something else, installing an independent front suspension is no more difficult than installing the stock front suspension. The only real difficulty is getting the crossmember in the correct location, and that is not a problem if you can read assembly instructions and a tape measure.

Independent Front Suspension Installation

Unlike the stock-style suspension, installing an IFS will be much easier if the front sheet metal is removed first, or if the vehicle is on a lift rack. This will provide more access for welding the front crossmember in place. In addition, all the original bracketry will need to be removed, including spring hangers, shock mounts, and the steering box. All these pieces can be discarded, as they will not be used with the addition of an IFS.

Instructions for the IFS kit provide exact measurements for locating the front crossmember between the frame rails. Before the crossmember can be welded in place, weld in the front boxing plates. Also, using a front sway bar may require mounting holes to be drilled in the crossmember. This will be much easier to do prior to installing the crossmember.

After the crossmember is welded in place, the rest of the assembly is bolted in. This includes the upper and lower A-arms, the spindles (stock height or dropped), and the steering rack-and-pinion.

Air Suspension

Air suspensions typically have the same hardware as any other suspension system, except that airbags replace the springs. This requires components that are designed for airbags, just as non-air systems require components that are designed for conventional leaf or coil springs. The airbags require an air compressor and/or an air tank along with the related controls.

The appeal of an air suspension system is that it lets the driver adjust the ride height of the vehicle at the touch of a button. It is easy to adjust the height to one that is convenient for driving and then lower it substantially, or "lay frame," while parked. Some people simply do not understand the appeal of that. However, there is a practical application for using an air system, especially on the rear axle.

Much like air shocks back in the 1970s, an airbag system will allow the driver to add more air when hauling a load to avoid bottoming out on the suspension. When the load is removed, some air can be removed for a more aesthetic stance. This is one way to be able to have a cool truck and still be able to use it as a work truck when needed.

For most any front suspension swap or upgrade, at least any that requires welding, having the front sheet metal clip out of the way will make that task easier. Of course, if you are starting with a bare frame, you are already there. On the project truck, the portions of the front fender that were there were solid, but they were not pretty. For that reason, it was decided to replace the front fenders.

Knowing that the front sheet metal will need to be reinstalled eventually, it makes good sense to take as many photos of it as possible to aid when it is time for reassembly. It is surprising how soon a person can forget how this all goes together.

For installation of the Heidt's Superide II IFS, the truck was taken to Morfab Customs. Keith Moritz has installed many of these kits. Excluding taking the front sheet metal off the truck, the suspension swap can typically be done in a weekend. The final welding might take a bit longer, but everything can be removed, replaced, and tack welded in that time frame.

After being thoroughly impressed with a Heidt's IFS and Keith Moritz's installation thereof in a previous 1951 Chevy truck, the decision to go with the Heidt's Superide II IFS was easy to make. Moritz's Morfab Customs did the work this time too.

Stock Front Suspension Removal

1 *Just for the record, on this truck, the top of the front frame rail was at 19 inches before any modifications. That did not include the engine and transmission weight, as they were out of the truck before I bought it. As this is written (MII installed and no drivetrain), the same measurement is 14 inches. With the engine and transmission installed, the dimension is 12 inches, for a net lowering of 7 inches.*

2 *If you plan to use the existing front sheet metal, keep it bolted together and remove it as a unit. To do so, remove just one bolt from the top rear of the fender, one bolt from the lower rear fender, a bolt securing the inner fender to the cab, and a couple of bolts from the radiator (if installed) from each side.*

3 *Without the front sheet metal, it is much easier to see what needs to be removed to install the new front suspension. The stock front member will be retained during the installation but will be trimmed somewhat. The parallel leaf springs and axle could be swap meet items, but they may not be worth the effort.*

4 *Remove the rivets. These old trucks were assembled with hot rivets, so they are usually removed with heat as well. If you are interested in salvaging any of the stock suspension, drill out the rivets. In this case, the old stuff went to the recycler, so a torch took care of most of the rivets.*

5 *Remove the steering box. The curved flat bar in front of the steering box is part of the parking brake mechanism. This could potentially be used without needing to be removed. To clean up everything, I removed it and replaced it with new components. The rivets holding it in place were removed with a hot wrench.*

6 *Remove the linkage that connects the parking brake handle in the cab and the actual mechanism. Since all these parts are going to the scrap bin, it was simply cut in two.*

7 *Remove the nut in the lower end of the steering column that secures the drag link to the steering box. Theoretically, after removing this nut, the linkage to the drag link could be slid off the splines and the steering box removed from the frame rail.*

8 *However, after 60-plus years of dust, dirt, mud, and the resultant rust, the linkage between the steering box and the drag link did not want to come off the splined shaft. Apply some heated persuasion and then use a nut puller to pull the arm off.*

9 *After torching off the rivets that secure the steering box mount to the frame rail, push the splined shaft inward through the frame rail to remove the steering box. Yes, it will take a bit of persuasion from a hammer to get it loose.*

10 Use a steering wheel puller to remove the stock steering wheel.

11 The lower portion of the stock steering column is secured by a plate that is held to the toeboard with three screws. Remove these screws and the plate to remove the steering column.

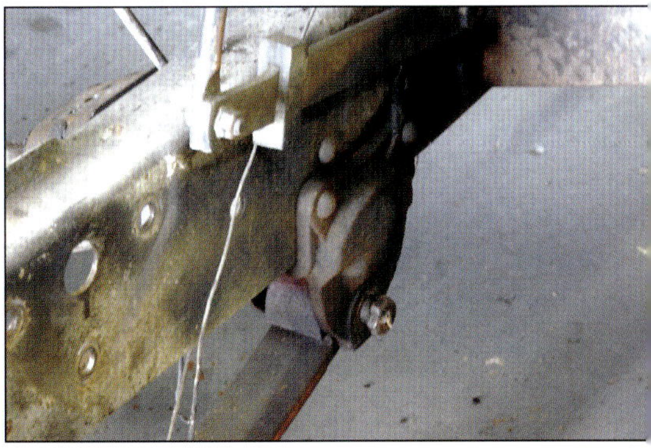

12 Unbolt the two-piece clutch pedal arm from the frame and discard it. Even if using a manual shift transmission, a new pedal assembly will be used.

13 Support the front axle with a floor jack and then remove the rivets that secure the spring shackles to the frame. Do not forget to disconnect the front brake lines. The front axle can then be removed.

14 With the stock suspension out of the way, take a few minutes to check the frame thoroughly for any damage or troublesome areas that may not have been seen before. Now is also a good time to remove any extraneous wires, cables, or anything else that will not be used in the project.

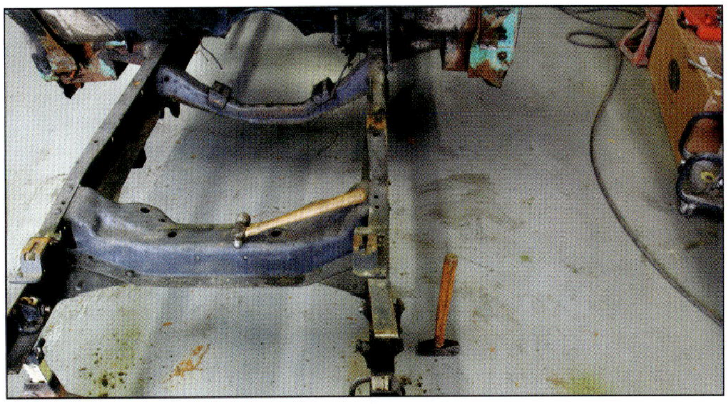

15 After the frame check, it became abundantly clear that the left front frame horn was slightly misaligned. Since the damaged area was not within the area that the MII crossmember would be installed, it was dealt with at an auto body shop later.

16 In the area of the stock steering box, the upper flange of the frame rail is turned up a bit. This would not be a big deal, but the boxing plate for the IFS extends into the area a bit. To rectify this, heat up the frame flange a bit, and then hammer it flat.

Independent Front Suspension Installation

1 *Examine the frame. Here, the frame boxing plate extends into the lipped section of the frame rail. Also apparent in this photo is the fact that the lower flange of the frame rail flares out some and will require trimming prior to installing the boxing plate.*

2 *Apply heat, hammer flat, and repeat until the necessary part of the lip is flattened. The entire lip section does not need to be flattened, but that is an option. In that case, a hammer with a serrated head should be used to shrink the metal a bit, as it will probably be too long to simply hammer flat.*

3 *After heating and hammering, it may be necessary to do a bit of grinding to smooth out the upper flange of the frame rail. That will be done later during preparation for paint.*

4 *Remove the stock axle snubbers, as they will not hit anything on the new front suspension. Be sure to remove them before installing the boxing plate, or the mounting studs will not be accessible.*

5 *Move all the stock front suspension out of the way and clean up the frame rails a bit. Now, the actual installation of the Heidt's Superide II IFS can begin.*

6 *To obtain a high-quality weld, lightly grind the surface areas of the frame rail that the boxing plate will be welded to.*

7 *Use a level to determine the correct location to install the boxing plate so that it is plumb (parallel with the web portion of the frame rail).*

8 *With the boxing plate in position, scribe or mark a line on the lower frame flange that indicates where the frame rail needs to be trimmed.*

9 *Merely as a double-check, set the MII crossmember in place to verify that the fame rail does require trimming before trimming it.*

10 *Read the directions thoroughly and measure twice. With the Heidt's Superide II IFS, the front crossmember location is based on stock holes in the frame. Before welding the crossmember in place, be sure to drill the holes for the stabilizer bar if necessary. Some crossmembers have them while others do not.*

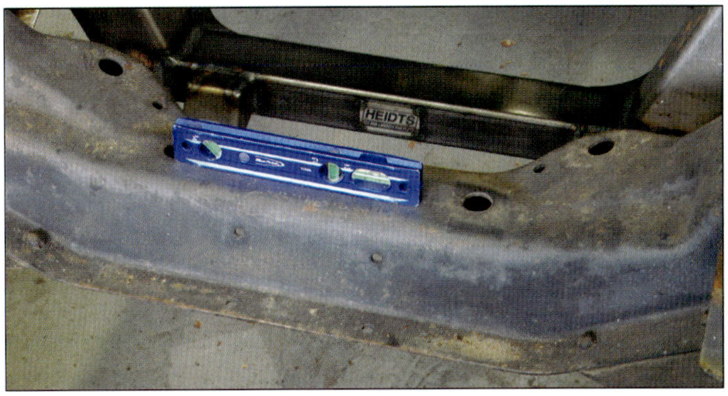

11 *To ensure accurate work when doing chassis work, level the frame before welding anything in place. If it is level before you start, you do not need to compensate while you are welding.*

12 *After cleaning up the lower flange of the frame rail with a grinder, mock up the boxing plate one last time. Mark or scribe a line along the lower edge of the boxing plate. The extra width of the flange will need to be removed.*

13 *Depending on what is available, cut off the excess width from the frame rail flange. A plasma arc cutter will work best, but a pneumatic saw will also work.*

14 *Regardless of what is used to cut off the excess frame rail width, it will probably still require a bit of cleanup work with a grinder.*

15 *While it may seem like a lot of work, take the time to verify that the boxing plate is going to fit correctly, as desired, and plumb. Some may say that no one will ever notice, and they are correct. However, anything that is not square, plumb, or level has great potential to cause many headaches in the future.*

16 *The fit is getting much better after a little bit more trimming and grinding. A truck project is a sizeable investment in both time and money, so take the effort to make it the best you can.*

17 *When the boxing plates fit as good as can be on both sides, muster all the clamps that you have. Clamp the boxing plates in place, and then clamp the crossmember in place as well. Check everything for proper measurements and fit prior to striking an arc.*

18 *Begin by tack welding the boxing plates in place. Skip around from one location to another, and then from one side to another to avoid concentrating too much heat in any one location. You do not want to start bending any portion of the frame at this point.*

19 *Leave the stock front crossmember. While it is nothing to look at, it does provide some additional support in the forward part of the chassis.*

20 *Weld the front crossmember in place. It is now ready to have the other suspension components installed. This certainly looks much cleaner than the stock configuration, doesn't it?*

21 *We are not sure if the prototype chassis included the stock front crossmember or not, but when installing the rack-and-pinion, it was obvious that the stock crossmember required some trimming. A plasma arc cutter will make short work of this, but a pneumatic saw will work too.*

22 *Do not cut out more of the stock front crossmember than necessary. The bulged-out area was first trimmed away to clear the actual rack-and-pinion components.*

23 *Not only is it necessary to trim away enough for the rack-and-pinion steering components to set in place but there also needs to be enough room to install and/or remove the mounting bolts that secure the steering to the new crossmember.*

24 *It is also necessary to have the rack-and-pinion installed in the correct position because the lower portion of the frame rails need to have enough clearance to allow for connection to the tie-rod ends.*

25 *Grind away any surface rust. Then, use the curved boxing plate as a template to mark, or scribe, where the frame rails need to be trimmed.*

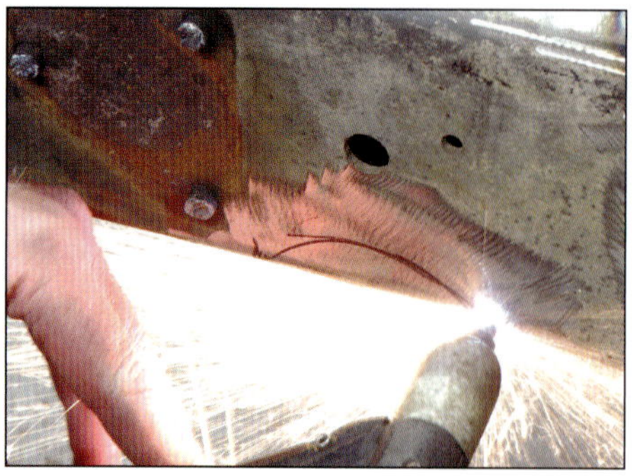

26 *Use a plasma arc cutter or pneumatic saw to cut out along the curved line. It will need to be cut out of the stock frame rail and the boxing plate that was recently installed.*

27 *Use a grinder to smooth the edges of the metal, providing a good fit for the boxing plate.*

28 *Clamp the provided curved boxing plate in place, verifying that the curved boxing plate is centered in the opening. Then weld the curved boxing plate into place.*

29 *Other than bolting on the front suspension components, the installation of the front suspension is now completed. Read that as no more hot wrenching or welding is needed.*

30 *Insert the bushings into the lower A-arms if not installed already. Then install the lower A-arms to the front crossmember and secure by inserting the long bolt from the front side. Place the nut on the back side and tighten. It may be necessary to grind a bit off the end of the tube in the crossmember that the A-arm fits around. It should not be loose, but a slight amount may need to be ground off.*

31 *Install the bushings into the upper A-arms if not installed already. Install the upper A-arms and secure using the same method as the lowers. Note that a rubber mallet may be necessary to push the bolts through the A-arms.*

32 *The new bushings will be stiff, so wiggle the A-arms up and down a little bit before installing the coilovers and spindle.*

33 *Install the coilover by first securing the top end to the upper A-arm with the bolt and nut provided. Slide the upper mounting hole of the spindle over the upper ball joint and secure with a castle nut. Slide the lower mounting hole of the spindle over the lower ball joint and secure with a castle nut. Then, secure the lower end of the coilover to the lower A-arm with a bolt and nut. If necessary, use a floor jack to push up on the bottom end of the coilover to align everything.*

34 *With the coilover and spindle in place, tighten all the mounting hardware. Be sure to install cotter pins in the ball joints.*

35 *Set the rack-and-pinion steering in place and secure with the mounting hardware provided. Thread the jam nuts and tie-rod ends onto the ends of the tie-rod. Straighten both front wheels to the straight-ahead position, then adjust the tie-rod ends inward or outward enough so that they can be connected to the spindle. Secure with a castle nut and a cotter pin. Then, tighten the jam nuts to secure the tie-rod ends.*

36 *Grease and then install the wheel bearings into the rotor, and then mount the wheel/tire assembly. Still a long way to go at this point, but the front suspension is installed, so the truck sits better already.*

Rear Suspension Assembly

For all intents and purposes, installing the stock-style rear suspension is done in similar fashion as the front. The only difference is instead of a dropped front axle, the rear axle housing will be installed. Chances are good that if you are reading this book, you will not be installing the stock rear-axle housing because it is geared way too low for today's driving. To lower the back end of the truck, the leaf springs can be moved to beneath the axle tubes.

A coilover rear suspension will provide a smoother ride and better performance. This setup will require a method to locate and secure the rear axle in place. This is commonly done with a pair of four-link radius rods or a three-link system. In either of these cases, a Panhard bar is required to prevent the rear axle housing from moving laterally in relation to the frame.

Four-Link Rear Suspension

With a four-link (AKA parallel four-link) system, two radius rods with adjustable rod ends mount to the frame forward of the rear axle and to the rear axle near each end of the axle. This locates the axle front to back within the frame.

With the suspension at rest, the radius rods should be roughly parallel with the driving surface. A Panhard bar mounts to the inside of one frame rail on one end and to the rear axle housing on the other end. This locates the rear axle housing side to side. The coilover shocks then cushion the up and down movement.

Three-Link Rear Suspension

A relatively new type of suspension is a three-link, also known as a Y-link. This is like a four-link but has only one radius rod on each side. However, a slightly shorter radius rod mounts to the top of the differential in the back and to a crossmember in the front. All three rods are parallel to each other and roughly parallel to the driving surface. A Panhard bar mounts to the inside of one frame rail on one end and to the rear axle housing on the other end. This locates the rear axle housing side to side, just as with the four-link.

Whether it is a four-link or a three-link system, the pinion angle should not be set until the engine, transmission, and bed are installed. This will help avoid putting the rear suspension in a bind. The location of the Panhard bar can then be established and the coilover shocks installed.

After the pinion angle is set, the rear axle brackets can be positioned and final welded to the rear axle housing. The adjustable rod ends on the radius rods allow for fine-tuning of the setup. When set up properly, a four-link or a three-link system will keep the rear axle centered in relation to the frame and keep the pinion angle constant.

A slight disadvantage of a three-link system is that the center bar attaches to the top of the differential. On a stock-height truck, this would not really be a problem, but if that were the case, you most likely would not go to the trouble to install this type of suspension. However, if you want a low truck, raising the floor might be necessary.

Set the Pinion Angle

If the engine and transmission are already installed, the pinion of the rear axle housing has to be at a specific angle to match the output shaft of the transmission. For example, if the transmission output shaft is pointing down 3 degrees (from level), the rear axle pinion would need to be pointing up 3 degrees

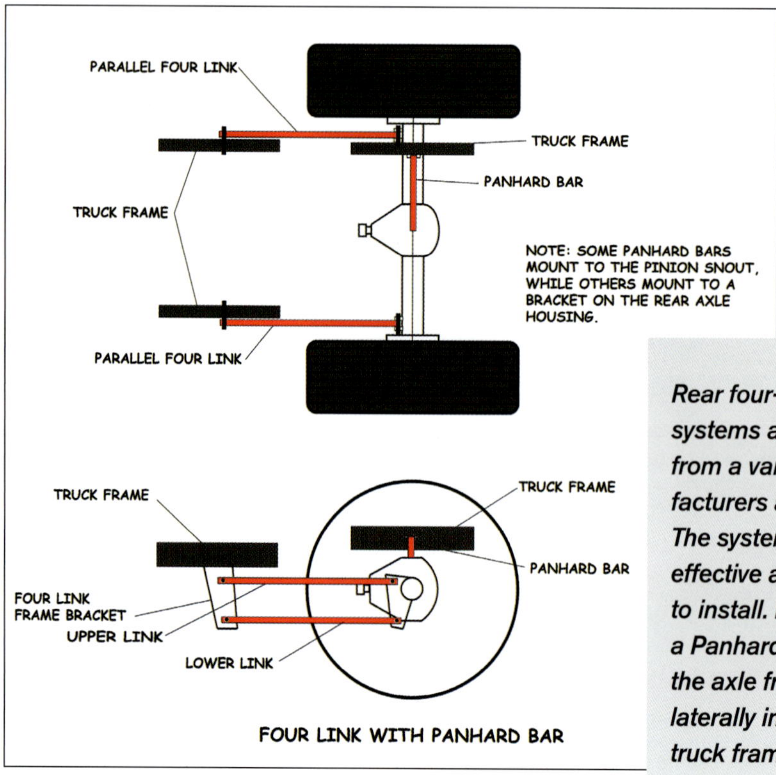

Rear four-link suspension systems are available from a variety of manufacturers and vendors. The system is simple yet effective and quite easy to install. It does require a Panhard bar to prevent the axle from moving laterally in relation to the truck frame.

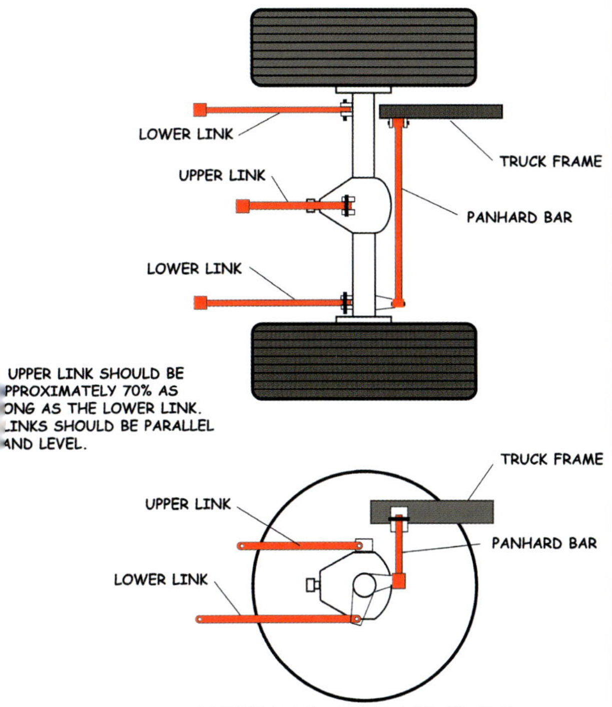

THREE LINK AND PANHARD BAR

A rear three-link suspension system is not as common as the four-link, as most are custom designed and fabricated. The upper link and the lower link are parallel but not in the same plane. While the rear ends of the links mount to the axle housing, the forward ends of the links mount to the truck frame. Just as with the four-link, a Panhard bar is required for the same reason.

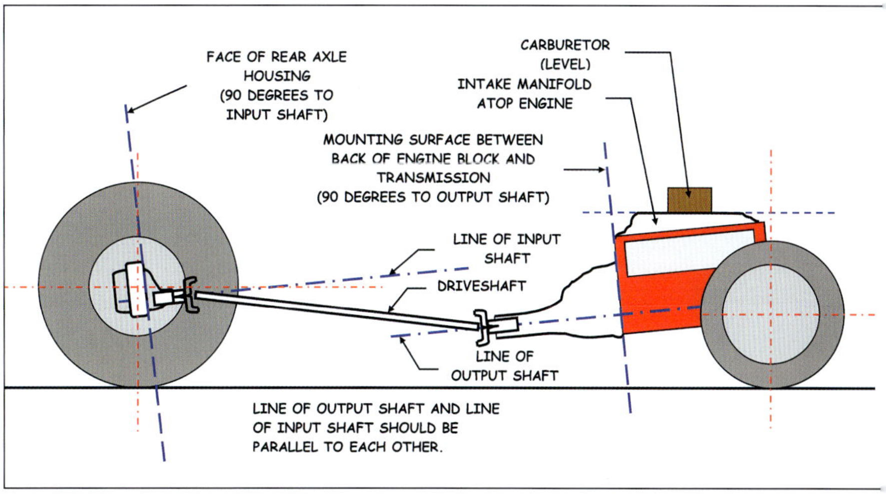

Getting the pinion angle correct is important in minimizing drivetrain vibration and component failure. For a street-driven vehicle, the line of the input shaft into the rear differential and the line of the output shaft from the engine/transmission must be equal and opposite. They are typically between 2 and 5 degrees from level.

When the suspension is fully loaded, the pinion angle must be rechecked and then set to the correct value. In this case, the pinion angle was set correctly (based on experience) and was still set at a correct value. Grind the primer off the axle housing and brackets to allow for good weld penetration.

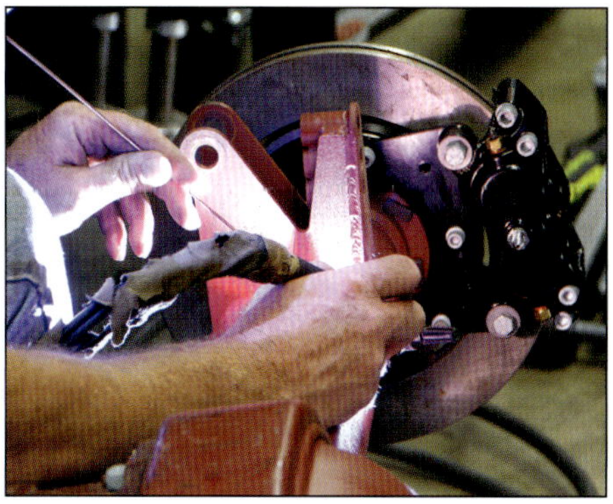

TIG weld the rear four-link brackets in place. If a lift rack is available, the rear axle may not need to be removed from the truck. In this case, it was removed, allowing it to be rotated to allow for good positioning. If the axles are not installed, a fixture bar should be inserted to help prevent any warpage in the axle housing.

(again from level), making the output shaft and pinion parallel. Note that 2 to 5 degrees from level is common for street-driven vehicles. Keep in mind that some trucks have larger tires in the back than in the front. This "rubber rake" (difference in front and rear tire diameters) also comes into play when setting the pinion angle.

When the engine and transmission have not yet been installed, it is necessary to reverse engineer the setting of the pinion angle. This is one of those situations where experience and common sense are both important. It is not that difficult, but you must be thinking about what you are doing to get it correct.

For proper fuel delivery and ultimate performance, the carburetor should be sitting level while the vehicle is sitting on a level surface. Of course, the engine keeps running while driving uphill or downhill, but when you are setting the motor mounts and/or the rear axle pinion angle, set the carburetor at level.

Use an angle finder to determine the relationship between the mounting surface of the intake manifold (where the carburetor mounts) and the output shaft of the transmission if the transmission is mounted to the engine. These will be roughly parallel but may differ by a few (less than 5) degrees.

If the transmission is not mounted to the engine, you can determine the relationship of the

After the pinion angle is set and the four bar axle brackets are final welded to the rear axle housing, the Panhard rod can be installed. Depending on the kit used, the Panhard rod may be bolted to the frame or bolted to a weld-on bracket. The opposite end may mount to the pinion snout or to the housing itself. A Panhard rod must be used anytime that coilovers (or a transverse spring) are used to minimize lateral movement of the body in relation to the chassis.

intake manifold and the surface of the rear of the engine where the transmission bolts to the engine. These measurements will be roughly 90 degrees different, so make sure to add or subtract properly to determine what the output shaft angle is in relation to the intake manifold. Making a simple sketch may make it easier to double-check the accuracy when taking these measurements and recording them. The output shaft from the engine/transmission should be parallel to the pinion shaft (input) to the rear axle housing.

Based on this information, temporarily set the pinion angle and tack weld the suspension in place for the construction phase. When the suspension is fully loaded, the pinion angle must be rechecked and set to the correct value, and then the axle brackets welded solid.

Stock Rear Suspension Removal

To make the installation easier, remove the bed from the truck prior to replacing the rear suspension. Simply remove the four or six bolts that secure the bed to the frame. Typically, four average guys can lift the bed off without too much trouble. Just be sure to have a plan as to where to put the bed before you lift it off the chassis. In this case, I had already sold the original bed at a swap meet to help pay for the new suspension. With this project being planned to be a keeper, I am replacing most all the marginal sheet metal.

Stock Rear Suspension Removal

1 *Begin the rear suspension swap by supporting the rear frame of the truck with a pair of jack stands. Then, support the existing rear axle housing with a floor jack and remove the rear wheel/tire assemblies.*

2 *To salvage the stock rear suspension, remove the leaf springs from the frame in the same manner as removing them from the front. However, in this case, the stock suspension was heading to the scrap metal yard. Therefore, a torch was used to cut the U-bolts that secure the rear axle housing to the springs.*

3 *Remove the frame mounts that secure the rear spring hangers to the truck frame. Use a torch to heat the stock rivets and then knock them out. Be sure that the rear axle housing is adequately supported prior to removing the springs from the frame.*

4 *If installing a four-link rear suspension, the stock front spring hangers need to be removed from the frame to make way for the new four-link frame brackets.*

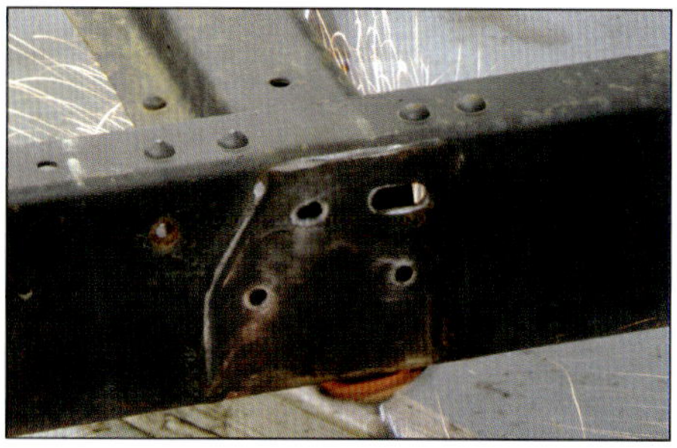

5 *In addition to removing the stock rivets from the side of the frame, any that are located on the bottom of the frame where the new four-link frame brackets mount will need to be removed. The heads can be ground off and the rivets then punched out.*

Rear Four-Link/Coilover Installation

Just as on the 1951 Chevy truck, this project is receiving a Heidt's four-link with coilover suspension and a 9-inch Ford rear axle housing. It gives a great ride but still allows the truck to haul almost any cargo desired.

Rear Four-link/Coilover Suspension Installation

1 *With the stock rear suspension and axle housing out of the way, the rear suspension swap is extremely easy. The brackets that secure the front ends of the parallel four-link mount to the stock holes of the now-removed front spring hanger mount.*

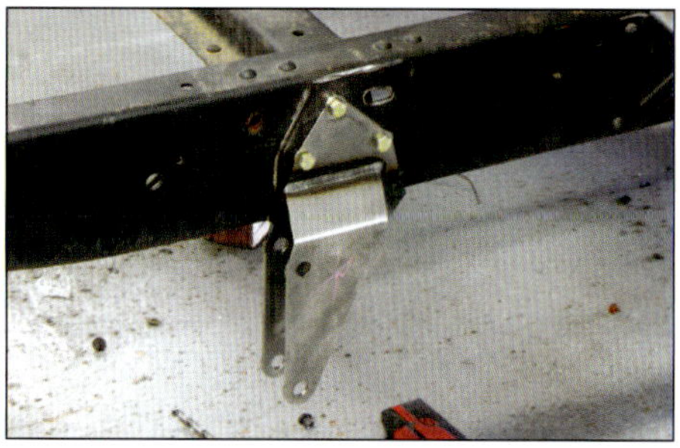

2 *While different kits will be similar, the frame brackets may be different. Be sure to install the frame brackets on the correct sides of the truck. On this kit, the holes for the four-link are located closer to the rear of the mount, so this is the passenger's side (right side).*

3 *Install the new coilover crossmember by securing it to the frame using the designated stock holes in the frame. Be sure to mount the crossmember with the longer shock mount tubes toward the front.*

4 *The parallel four-link is made up of four bars with a fixed mount on one end and an adjustable heim joint on the opposite end. For the four-link to work properly, the individual links (bars) must be the same length. The easy way to verify that they are the same length is to place a long bolt through the end of all four bars, adjusting as necessary.*

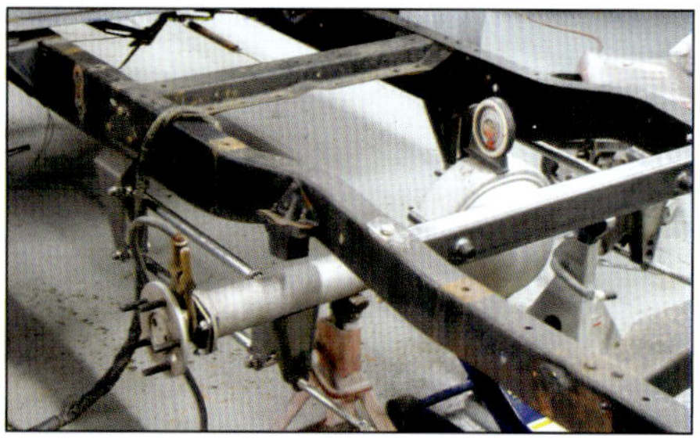

5 *Install the four-links into the frame brackets with the adjustable heim joints on the axle end, and secure them with the bolts provided. Move the rear axle housing into place front to back and laterally and support with floor jacks. Adjust the length of the four-links as necessary to reach the axle brackets. Secure the four-links to the axle brackets and secure with the bolts provided.*

6 *Using an angle finder mounted to the rear axle housing, rotate the axle housing to the approximate pinion angle. Verify that the axle housing is located squarely in the frame and is centered side to side, then tack weld the axle brackets to the axle housing.*

7 *Note that the final welding of the rear axle brackets will be done after the engine and transmission are installed to verify the correct pinion angle. Coilovers and the Panhard bar will be installed at that time.*

8 *Although the final ride height is not yet set due to no bed, no front sheet metal, or drivetrain weight, the stance is considerably better than with the stock suspension.*

Brakes

Brakes are safety items that should be the best available. They don't necessarily need to be the most expensive, just the best. With more power under the hood of our trucks these days and the "unrefined" driving habits of others, having good brakes is a necessity now more than ever.

At one time, I owned a 1968 Chevy C10 that had a 383 stroker motor under the hood. While the previous owner had done a good job of making the truck go fast, he had left the stock drum brakes on all four corners. During one of my first drives in the truck, I quickly (and in a bit of panic) realized that installing disc brakes was to be the next improvement. No one wants to learn auto bodywork out of necessity.

Front Brake Installation

While the Task Force trucks were originally equipped with drum brakes on both axles, disc brakes are a vast improvement. With the bulk of the weight (and therefore the stopping power) in the front, I cannot imagine why anyone would consider installing drum brakes on the front. The automotive aftermarket has provided us with a wide variety of disc brake kits. They are affordable and easy to install.

With the frame supported on jack stands, remove the front wheel/tire assembly if they are already installed on the truck. Use the two bolts provided with the disc brake kit to secure the brake caliper mounting bracket to the back side of the spindle. Grease the inner and outer wheel bearings, then install them and the bearing retainer seal into the disc brake rotor. Slide the rotor onto the spindle. Note that applying a bit of silicone or other lubricant onto the spindle can help the rotor slide on.

Align the key in the retaining washer with the key slot in the spindle and slide the retaining washer into place. Secure the retaining washer onto the spindle with the spindle nut. Tighten the spindle nut sufficiently to fully seat the bearings, then back it off one-half turn. Spin the rotor to verify that it turns; it should. Then, install a cotter pin to prevent the nut from backing off.

Front disc brakes are included with the Heidt's Superide II IFS kit, as with most other IFS kits on the market. These are 11-inch rotors with four-piston Wilwood calipers. With the superior stopping efficiency and the ease of service, I cannot imagine why anyone would run drum brakes on the front of any vehicle these days.

Next, install the brake caliper. Place it over the rotor and into place so that it can be secured to its mounting bracket with two bolts. Tighten the bolts securely.

Brake Pads

Something to know about disc brake pads is that some must be installed into the caliper prior to the caliper being placed over the rotor. These usually include two long slider bolts on which the ears of the brake pads slide. Other brake pads can be installed (or replaced) while the caliper is in place. These are usually secured by two cotter pins.

If you are going to be running brake lines next, it is best to leave the wheel/tire assembly off. But if that is a project for another time, the wheel/tire assembly can be reinstalled at this time. If the wheel/tire assembly is reinstalled at this time, be sure to tighten the lug bolts. No one should need to remember to tighten the lug nuts if they choose to move the vehicle later for whatever reason.

Rear Brake Installation

With disc brakes up front, some may choose to settle for drum brakes in the rear, due largely to drum brakes being less expensive. However, what price can be put on safety? With the project truck being assembled as part of this book destined for daily use, it is getting disc brakes in the back too.

Although rear disc brakes are more expensive than drum brakes, they are worth the extra money. Installation of disc brakes is simple and less confusing than drums. These units from Wilwood include an integral parking brake. Be sure to disconnect the brake lines anytime the rear axle housing is dropped.

Individual steps may vary slightly from one kit to another, but they are basically the same. Mount the brake caliper bracket to the axle housing and secure with the bolts provided in the kit. Depending on the application, you may or may not need to pull the rear axles.

Install the brake rotor onto the end of the axle and secure. Then, install the caliper over the rotor and secure it to the caliper bracket. Be sure to install the brake pads whenever they need to be installed, depending on the application.

Master Cylinder and Brake Booster Installation

There are several kits available for relocating the master cylinder beneath the floor. They typically include the brake pedal, mounting bracket, power brake booster, and master cylinder. Moving all of this cleans up the firewall tremendously. The mounting bracket bolts to the frame, so installation is very straightforward.

The only real challenge to doing this is filling the master cylinder with brake fluid. If desired, an access hole can be cut into the floorboard of the truck cab. However, most folks do not want to take a chance of spilling brake fluid on their carpeting, and for good reason. To avoid this, mount a remote fill reservoir under the hood at a more accessible location. This will require a cover on the master cylinder that will accept brake lines from the reservoir.

Part of the talent of building any custom vehicle is knowing how to make everything work, especially service or maintenance items. This Wilwood remote-fill brake fluid reservoir can be mounted most anywhere that will make it easily accessible. It is much more attractive under the hood than a huge master cylinder hanging on the firewall.

Residual Check Valves

Another important thing to remember is that if the master cylinder is mounted lower than the actual brakes (such as below the floor), a residual check valve needs to be installed approximately a foot from the master cylinder in each line. For disc brakes, this should be a 2-pound valve, which is usually blue in color. For drum brakes, this should be a 10-pound valve, which is usually red in color. The residual check valve prevents brake fluid from running downhill, away from the brakes.

Brake Line Routing, Bending, and Installation

When it comes to routing and bending brake lines, it will be easier if the cab and bed are off the frame and out of the way. It does not always work out that way, but if you can plan to run them while these obstructions are out of the way, you can save yourself some trouble.

Before bending the brake line, determine approximately where the couplings will be located. This will assist you in knowing how many pieces of brake line to buy and in what lengths. My personal thought is that while I can flare brake lines correctly, I am still more confident in a factory flare. However, I do know that flares will be required in some cases.

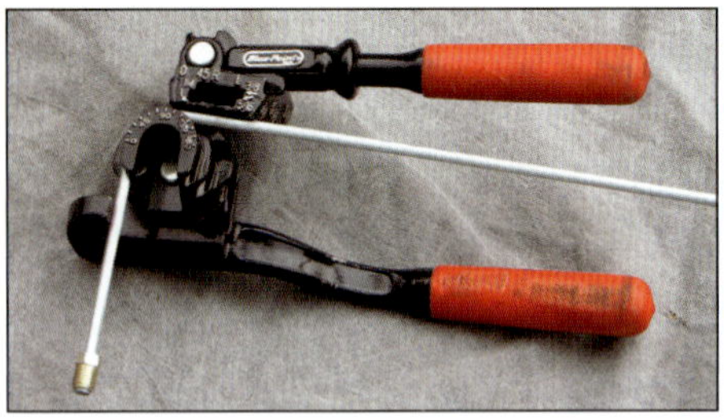

My tubing bender is the only Snap-on tool that I own, but it was worth the investment for brake lines and fuel lines. Like most tubing benders, it can bend the three different sizes that are commonly found in automotive use. However, the difference is to make much tighter bends. For 3/16 tubing, the centerline radius is less than 1 inch. Smooth tight bends tend to make for a more attractive brake line installation.

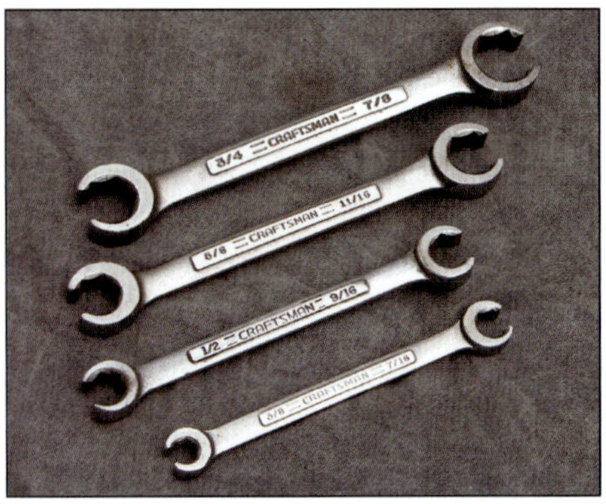

When working with brake or fuel line fittings, a box-end wrench will not work. A standard open-end wrench will work. However, stubborn fittings that are made from a soft material are easy to round off. Flare-nut wrenches make contact on four sides of a hex nut to provide better contact.

With the master cylinder being located beneath the floor, it calls for residual check valves. Begin with a 12-inch-long piece of 3/16-inch brake line from the master cylinder and route it toward the frame rail, bending as required. Install an appropriate (2-pound or 10-pound) residual check valve.

Remember that regardless of the master cylinder's positioning in the truck, the brake line to the front wheels should come from the larger of the two cylinders. If they are the same size, it should come from the one closest to the pushrod. You could continue with the next length of brake line; however, whether you are running to the front or rear brakes, there is going to be a section of straight line of some distance.

Beneath the floor is the new master cylinder, power booster, and brake pedal arm. A 2-pound check valve in each line prevents brake fluid from backing away from the braking components. When the master cylinder is higher than the brakes, gravity does this. The master cylinder cap is designed with two inlets (one for each cylinder) to be filled through a remote reservoir.

To minimize the number of connections, which potentially translate to leaks, run the brakes from the wheel/tire assembly toward the master cylinder. This allows some room for compensation if the brake line is a bit longer than it needs to be and for you to retain the factory flare.

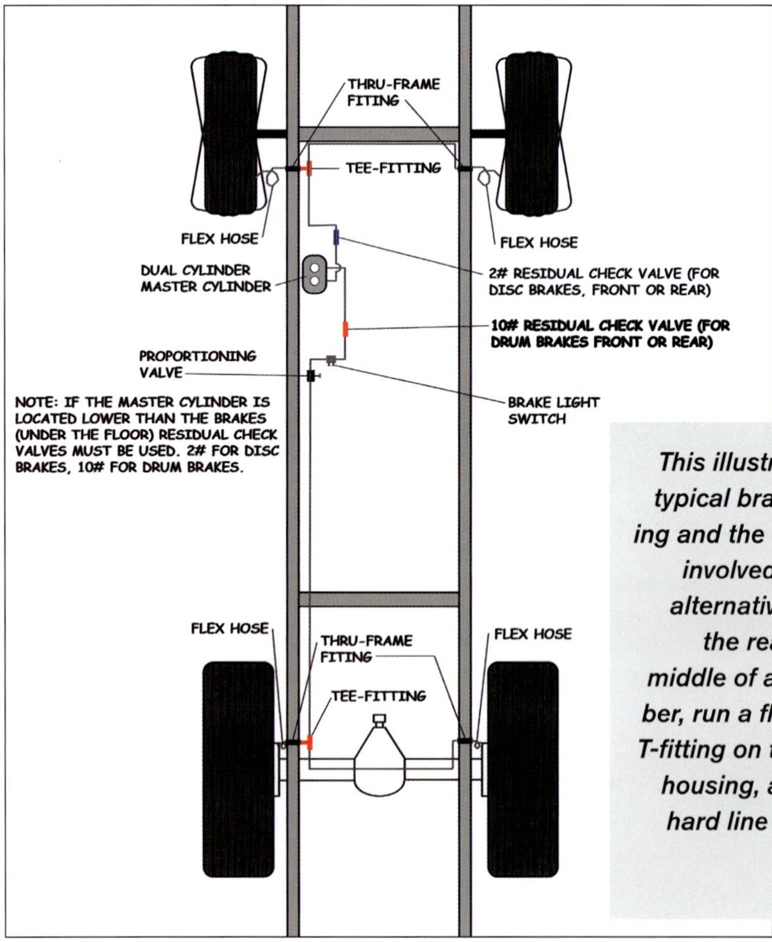

This illustration shows typical brake line routing and the components involved. A common alternative is to route the rear line to the middle of a crossmember, run a flex hose to a T-fitting on the rear axle housing, and then run hard line to each rear brake.

At all four brake line locations, 3/16-inch hard line runs from the master cylinder along the inside of the frame rail to a bulkhead fitting. The bulkhead fitting passes through the frame rail and then connects to a braided stainless-steel hose that connects to the brake caliper.

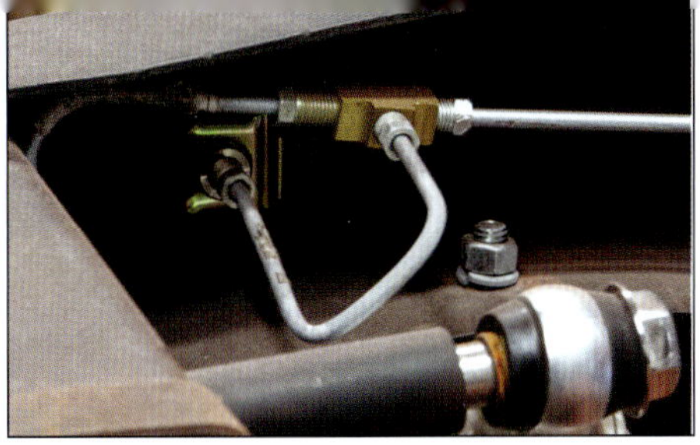

This is the brake line connection at the left rear wheel. The line running to the right runs forward directly to the master cylinder. The short line coming from the brake line T connects to a bulkhead fitting to pass through the frame rail. It connects to a braided stainless-steel hose that runs to the disc brake caliper. The line exiting to the left continues along the rear cross-member to the right rear frame rail.

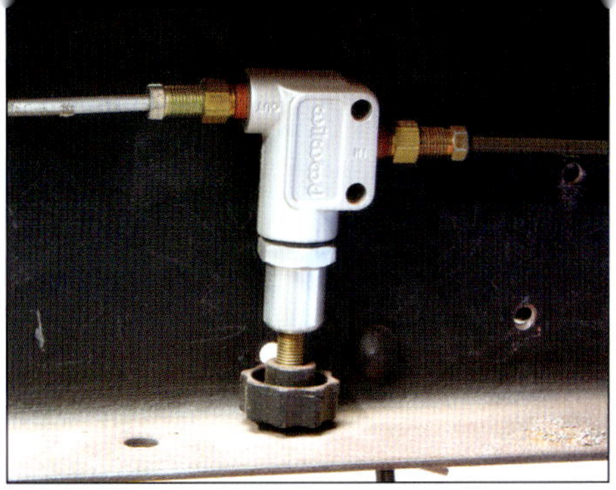

This adjustable proportioning valve is located inside the left frame rail between the master cylinder and the rear brakes. Since most hot rods have larger rear tires than in the front, the adjustable valve allows for fine-tuning of the brakes. As a proportioning valve, there are specific inlet and outlet connections.

Front Brake Lines

For the front brakes, connect a flexible brake hose to the caliper and determine where to mount it to the frame. This can be a through-frame fitting if the location is in a boxed area of the frame, through a bulkhead fitting if in an unboxed portion of the frame, or in a tab welded to the frame. Be sure to mount the frame fitting in a location that will allow for both turning and suspension travel of the wheel/tire assembly.

Hoses are available in different lengths, but they cannot drag on the ground. Using the appropriate fittings, connect a length of brake line to the right front brake line hose and route it toward the left front brake line hose. This commonly routes the brake line along the backside of the front chassis crossmember.

Locate a T-fitting so that both front brake lines can be routed to it. Then, route and bend the brake line to connect to the front residual check valve. Secure the brake line to the frame and/or crossmembers as required with the brake line clamps of your choice. While the brake hoses need to flex to allow for suspension travel, the hard lines should be secure so that they do not move. However, keep in mind when bending lines to allow for using a flare nut wrench for easy assembly/disassembly.

Rear Brake Lines

For the rear brakes, use that same basic procedure. Whether using disc or drum brakes on the rear, there is a choice of running a flexible hose to each rear brake with hard line between them or running one shorter hose from the frame crossmember to a T-fitting located on the rear axle housing.

Some builders prefer to run the hard line across the rear crossmember and frame with a flex hose at each wheel. The single-hose installation requires running the hard line across the rear axle housing. Regardless of how the brake lines run from one side to the other, there needs to be a T-fitting somewhere to run both sides to one line that runs forward to the master cylinder.

Wheels and Tires

If running custom aluminum or chrome wheels, the tires can simply be mounted and balanced and then bolted onto the truck. However, there are several versions of steel wheels that are popular for these trucks. To avoid falling victim to rust, they need to be painted or powder coated. Unless you are already set up to do your own powder coating or you are planning to start that as a business, you can probably find a professional shop to do that.

On the other hand, priming and painting is easy, and it requires only a spray gun and an air compressor. If you have these, after a trip to the local automotive paint store to purchase primer and paint, you are all but done. If the wheels are used, it may be wise to have them media blasted to remove any old paint and ensure that the wheel is still structurally sound.

If the wheels are new, wash them with soapy water, rinse, and then dry. Be sure to use an air gun to blow water out of any crevices. Then, clean with wax and grease remover by spraying it on and wiping it off with a clean paper towel.

Mix up the two parts of an epoxy primer, then apply per the instructions for the specific epoxy primer being used. After the epoxy primer has dried, use a Scotch-Brite pad to smooth out any runs or sags, and to prep for the paint. Clean the wheels again with wax and grease remover, since they have been handled again. Mix the single-stage color and hardener and then apply the paint in accordance with that product's information sheet. Let air dry or force dry if an oven is available.

Tire-mounting equipment is rough on freshly painted wheels, so it is probably best to let the paint cure for at least a week before having tires mounted. If possible, have the wheel/tire assembly balanced on a machine that can simulate a road force to the mounted assembly. This will optimize the balance, therefore providing a smoother ride and even tire wear.

Painting the Wheels

1 *Wash the steel wheels with soapy water, rinse, and then dry. Use an air hose to get all the water out of the crevices. Then clean the wheels with wax and grease remover to remove any oil or anything else that might prevent good adhesion of the epoxy primer.*

2 *Spray the wheels with epoxy primer, such as PPG's DPLF in the color of your choice. After allowing the primer to dry, use a Scotch-Brite pad to remove any imperfections, such as runs or drips. Blow away any dust and then clean again with wax and grease remover.*

3 *Hang the wheels so that they can be accessed from both sides. Wear the appropriate personal protection for the paint product being used, and then apply the paint of choice in accordance with the manufacturer's instructions.*

Let the newly painted wheels cure for as long as practical before mounting and balancing the tires. These wheels are now Omaha Orange, which was a stock color for these trucks when they rolled down the assembly line. That will be the body color when this truck gets painted, as well.

The shop truck was finally looking like a truck again. In a moment of extreme optimism in having the truck on the road soon, I bought a used Fleetside bed from a 1958–1959 truck just to make the truck a bit more practical to drive. Sadly, getting the truck on the road did not happen that summer. But it did make me realize that even though this truck had been a Stepside from the factory, a new Fleetside bed would be in its future.

The front sheet metal still needs some tweaking to fit as I would like, but the original hood is back on it. However, the front fender extensions and inner fenders may call for some expert assistance to fit correctly, as there are several panels that share common bolts and bolt holes.

CHAPTER 4

Body

There is no doubt about it, bodywork is labor intensive when it is done correctly. Whether you are doing the bodywork yourself or are paying to have it done, it is going to cost you in one way or another. And just to clarify, the bodywork that we are talking about at this point is repairing collision damage, replacing rusty panels, and making them all fit together to look like a truck.

The many hours of applying filler, block sanding, applying filler primer, and sanding yet again prior to even beginning to think about applying paint will be discussed in chapter 8. Of course, this paint-prep bodywork is expensive too.

With bodywork potentially taking such a bite out of your truck-building budget, it makes great sense to start with the best body available. However, if you are an accomplished tin bender and can make repairs to a less-appealing cab yourself quite

The passenger-side door did not fit very well. Both front fenders were loose in front of the door since the lower fender bracket had rusted off the truck, which is a common occurrence on these trucks. A quick solution to getting this truck on the road would have been to throw in a junkyard drivetrain and go. However, I plan to keep this truck forever, so it became a frame-off rebuild.

While there was no indication of why, someone trimmed a section out of the front of the Stepside step on both sides and drilled several 1/4-inch holes in the rear fenders. Also, the door did not fit correctly at the bottom. These things can all be addressed, but that needs to be figured into the budget one way or another.

Except for the remaining hole from a sloppy stereo installation, the dash was in surprisingly good condition. Just as with most truck projects, the seat had been a mouse hotel at one time and there was a hint of gasoline fumes. Like the bed, the seat and the doors were sold at a swap meet to help finance the project.

The cab steps and doorsills were iffy at best, making replacement the logical option.

The angled toeboards seemed solid, but the flat floorboards were rough and had soaked up lots of moisture. Replacement panels are readily available, so you can bet these were going to be replaced.

Having a new cab, such as this one from Dynacorn, would have certainly gotten my truck on the road sooner. The doors are already hung, no floorboard panels to replace, and no rust to repair. With reproduction chassis also available from various sources, building these trucks can be a lot more enjoyable. (Photo Courtesy Dynacorn Classic Bodies)

The fit of the door was simply not acceptable. After closer inspection, it was obvious that this corner of the cab had been hit hard at some time and the repair was less than stellar. In looking at a plan view, the back panel should be straight. This one did not have a curve; it had a bend in it. Seeing that originally was quite disheartening, but installing a replacement cab back panel made it all good.

While the bed's sheet metal was straight and not in the worst condition, it was rusty where moisture and dirt had been trapped between the bed wood and the bedsides. It also had lots of random holes drilled in various places. Of course, those could be welded shut, but the bed was sold instead.

easily, you can potentially save yourself some money. The more you can convince the seller that those repairs will be labor intensive to repair, the more likely you may be to save a few bucks on the purchase price.

What this all boils down to is making an accurate assessment as to which body parts can be used "as is," which can be repaired, and which should be replaced. Unlike years ago, there are now a lot more sheet-metal pieces and parts available for these trucks. Some pieces may require more effort to fit them correctly or as desired, but these reproduction pieces are still typically better than starting with a flat piece of sheet metal and a hammer.

With the availability of a brand-new complete cab, this can be an important decision toward completion of your truck project. While the price tag of a new cab may seem like a steep price to pay, by the time you purchase a few oversized sheet-metal pieces and have them shipped to your location, that new cab might not be all that much more expensive. And if you are paying the going shop rate to have those panels installed, the new cab looks better all the time.

It is not my desire to influence anyone into or out of purchasing a new cab, but it is an option to consider prior to doing any bodywork on your existing cab.

Prior to having this Fleetside tailgate media blasted, it was obvious that it was already shot. Still, it would be a good panel on which to practice welding patch panels because you would not have to worry about making it any worse.

After having the tailgate media blasted, we got an undistorted view of its true condition. Someone with some decent fabrication and welding skills could resurrect this tailgate, but it would take a while.

Repairs

A multitude of factors contribute to the unfortunate condition of many of these trucks that are available. First, they are now more than 60 years old. For humans, that is not as old as it used to be. Like they say, "It isn't the age, it's the mileage, and the roads were not all paved." That could not apply to anything more than it does to old pickup trucks, with *trucks* being the operative word.

They were built to work, and often never saw a garage at the end of that workday. They have hauled animals and all sorts of other payloads. They have had their doors slammed unmercifully for no real reason. They have driven on dirt roads, gravel roads, and highways. Since they were not the family sedan, accidental damage was often never repaired, and a thorough car wash was a rarity. They have been what many of us learned to drive in. Simply put, they have had a rough life.

Prior to making any modifications to your truck's sheet-metal components, it makes sense to first repair any damage caused by collision and/or rust or fix anything that does not work properly. This includes doors or a hood that do not open and shut properly. It simply makes no sense to attempt to modify panels that are not properly aligned or that are attached to rusty panels that may require replacement due to rust issues. That is unless the modification can be done at the same time as making the repair.

For the reasons already mentioned, it is unlikely to find one of these trucks (that has not been restored) to be in pristine condition. However, a cheap coat of paint can hide a multitude of sins. So, prior to doing any bodywork on the cab, bed, or any other sheet metal, it is well worth taking the time to investigate it as thoroughly as possible.

In many cases, this calls for having the paint removed by media blasting or a chemical stripping process. Getting down below the paint and primer is often the only way to know with any amount of certainty what condition the underlying sheet metal is in. This may seem like an unnecessary expense and in a rare instance, it might be. However, if it uncovers improperly repaired damage or unresolved rust issues, it is much better to find that in the beginning of the project than at the end.

Rust Removal

Chemical stripping and media blasting are two common forms of rust removal. Either of these will remove paint, primer, wax, and rust from the sheet metal. Chemical stripping can be completed commercially by using a dipping process, or it can be done at home in your shop through a manual process. Likewise, media blasting can be done commercially or by anyone who has the correct equipment, but the process is the same regardless of where it is done.

For either process, the pieces and parts should be disassembled as completely as possible. If areas of thick body filler are known to exist in a panel, the filler should be removed prior to chemical stripping or media blasting to yield the best results. A simple method of doing this is with a 36-grit disc on an orbital sander. If thick body filler is not removed before the panel is chemically stripped, the filler will begin to peel but will not come off completely. The body filler will prevent the stripper from stripping the surface beneath the filler, making the entire process a waste of time.

Chemical Stripping

Chemical dipping is relatively economical, depending on the size of the project. For large pieces, such as complete cabs, or numerous smaller pieces, having them dipped commercially is the practical way to go. Large pieces are placed on a rack and dipped individually, while small parts get placed in baskets and then dipped.

Parts being dipped go in a hot tank of a caustic solution for between four and eight hours to remove wax, grease, and paint. The parts are then rinsed with plain water for three to four hours to remove the caustic solution. De-rusting is done by placing those parts into a second vat that is full of de-rusting solution and connecting an electrical charge.

Opposite of what is used in the chrome plating or powder coating processes, the electrical current is reversed to pull the rust away from the metal that is being stripped. This de-rusting process may take up to about 40 hours and then the parts are rinsed with plain water again to neutralize any remaining de-rusting solution.

Parts that are chemically stripped should be primed with epoxy primer as soon as practical to prevent the formation of surface rust. A benefit or drawback of chemical dipping is that the stripping solution will get to all surfaces of the parts that are immersed. This will remove all rust but may leave areas of good metal with no protection if you cannot access them to apply epoxy primer and paint or undercoating.

If you simply need to strip one or two pieces, such as a pair of swap-meet fenders for instance, you can do this yourself. Purchase 1 to 2 gallons of Aircraft Stripper from a local auto parts store, along with some cheap paintbrushes and disposable pans. Do not spend a lot of money on the brushes and pans because you will need to dispose of them when you are finished.

You will also need some rubber gloves and a filtered mask. Make sure that you cover as much of your skin as you can because paint stripper will burn bare skin. Be sure to follow all the safety precautions on the product label.

One thing that the instructions for paint stripper do not tell you is to use 36- or 50-grit sandpaper to scuff the painted surface prior to applying paint stripper. Scuffing allows the paint stripper a better opportunity to penetrate the paint, thereby using less stripper and saving time in the actual stripping process.

Place the vehicle or parts on a concrete surface that can be hosed down with water after the stripping process. Check with the source of paint stripper for recommendations on disposal of the used stripper that will be rinsed from the parts being stripped. After scuffing the painted surface, spread the paint stripper on with a paintbrush. Be patient and wait for the stripper to work its way through the multiple layers of paint and primer.

As the paint bubbles up, use a scraper or a razor blade to peel the softened paint from the surface. For stubborn spots, apply additional paint stripper. After all the paint is removed from the panel, neutralize the stripper by rinsing with lots of water. Then, proceed with bodywork or applications of body filler or primer.

Media Blasting

For a long time, river sand was used extensively for media blasting, hence the now-outdated term of sand blasting. However, sand can quickly put heavy scratches into light sheet metal and will produce significant heat, causing shee-metal panels to warp.

In lieu of sand blasting, a great way to remove paint, peeling chrome, and rust is by blasting with a more appropriate media, such as silica sand, aluminum oxide, plastic media, or walnut shells. However, you cannot simply start blasting away at your parts.

Remember these three important things when media blasting: 1) Mask the area that should not be blasted. 2) Use the appropriate blasting media. 3) Remove all the blasting media when the job is complete. You must also wear proper safety apparel, including eye and respiratory protection.

No matter what type of media is being used, media blasting will leave a slightly textured surface. Therefore, machined surfaces, bearing surfaces,

Paint Stripping

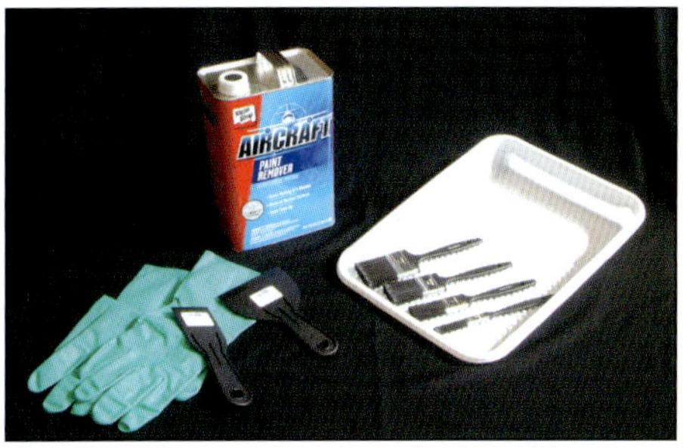

1 *When dealing with paint stripper, think cheap and disposable, as cleanup is a futile effort. A disposable paint roller liner works well to hold the paint stripper. Cheap brushes in various sizes work well to spread the stripper and push it into nooks and crannies. Flexible paint scrapers work well to scrape the paint off as it bubbles up. Be sure to wear rubber gloves and eye protection.*

2 *Prior to applying any paint stripper, use a Scotch-Brite pad or some 200- or 400-grit wet or dry sandpaper to scuff the surface. This will allow the paint stripper to better penetrate the paint and primer, resulting in better paint removal.*

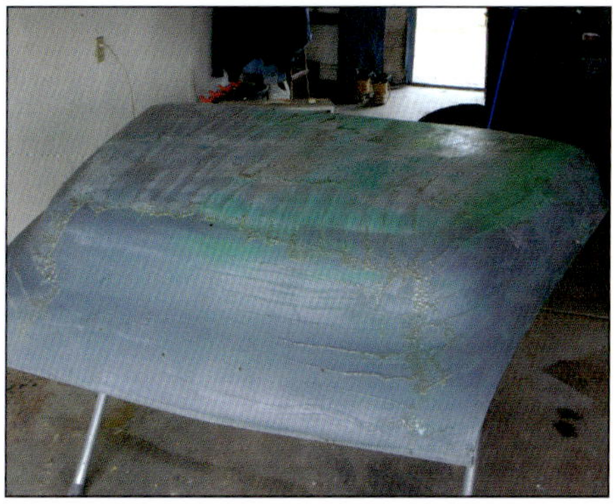

3 *Liberally brush the paint stripper on the surface to be stripped and then give it time to work. Depending on how well the paint has been applied, it may take a while for it to start working. If the painted surface is merely a rattle-can job on bare metal, it will work quickly. If it is baked-on enamel, it will take a while.*

4 *After a short time, it becomes obvious that the gray primer had not been applied very well due to poor surface prep. The original turquoise factory paint lasted longer, so more paint stripper was applied and allowed to sit longer.*

5 *It makes sense that the paint comes off the large, flat area of the hood faster than the front and sides. The flatter areas have been more prone to sunlight heat and snow accumulation. It also stands to reason that the painter probably applied more paint to the closer areas than to those that required a farther reach.*

6 *Paint stripper must be neutralized after use to stop the continued action. This is usually done by rinsing with ample amounts of water, but you should read the product labels carefully to verify what should be used.*

Fresh from the media blaster, the cab is as bare as can be, albeit with a slightly textured finish. The light spots are where body filler has been used as part of a poorly completed collision repair. While it may look okay in the photo, the cab requires a lot of work to be brought up to the desired quality.

The Fleetside truck bed that I bought still had the well-worn and faded original paint on it when I purchased it. To get an accurate look at the actual condition, I had it media blasted at a cost of about $400. It looks better than some truck beds out there, but since I plan to keep this truck forever and new reproduction beds are available, I will buy one of those eventually.

threaded areas, or any other areas that would be negatively affected should be masked from media blasting. Exterior threads such as those on the back of trim pieces can be easily protected from blasting by covering them with a length of appropriately sized rubber hose or tubing. Other areas should be masked with heavy cardboard and masking tape, accompanied by prudent use of lower blasting pressure and a careful aim.

After having it media blasted, the truck bed was sprayed with two coats of PPG's DPLF Epoxy Primer. This will prevent the formation of new rust and will serve as an excellent substrate for additional primers and eventually paint. A good body man could remove the dents from the bedside.

Media used for blasting should be compatible with the material upon which it is being used. If the blasting media is harder than the surface being prepped, you will do more harm than good by hurling hard objects at it. A large volume of softer material passing by the surface is a more appropriate way of freeing the surface of unwanted paint or rust.

Blasting Material

Various materials other than sand are available for use in media blasting. No one material is the best for all stripping or cleanup operations, so be sure to match the media with the task. For removing paint and rust from steel, aluminum oxide is a good choice. A little more expensive is plastic media, which is best for stripping paint from metal, as it does not get as hot and cause warping. Although it is not the best media for any one cleanup project, glass bead blasting does a good job on most any surface. For cleaning soft metals such as aluminum, die-cast, or brass, aluminum shot is best, although it is more expensive.

When choosing a blasting media, you must remember that any scratches or abrasions that you put into the metal while cleaning it will also need to be taken out. An aggressive media will no doubt remove paint and other finishes faster, but if the media is harder than the material that is being blasted, you will get to a point where you are creating more work for yourself.

In addition to the flaking rust, paint, or whatever was on the part prior to blasting, also remove all the blasting media when the blasting is finished. Much of the media used for blasting is recycled and used again, so even if the parts were not oily or greasy, previously blasted parts may have been. Any oil that is present on the parts will cause adhesion problems, so it is imperative that all parts be cleaned thoroughly after being media blasted. Just as parts that are chemically stripped, media blasted parts should be primed with epoxy primer as soon as practical to prevent the formation of surface rust.

A drawback to media blasting is that the media can be difficult to remove from confined areas. It is fine for use on a simple two-sided surface such as a fender. However, on a door shell or a pickup truck cab, some of the media will collect between panels and will be difficult to remove.

Soda Blasting

A relatively new process that is like media blasting is soda blasting. In this case, the media being blasted is sodium bicarbonate (commonly known as baking soda). While this process has been shown to provide good results for removing paint during auto restoration projects, the sodium bicarbonate does not do an effective job in removing rust.

Collision Damage

Perhaps the worst type of collision damage is that which you cannot readily see. An experienced bodyworker will be able to "read" a dent, determine the sequence of the damage, and then undo the damage in the reverse order. However, if a dent has quickly been filled with some body filler and then painted over, it is impossible to read the dent and repair it properly.

The gash in the step area is not really collision damage, still it needs to be repaired or replaced. In this case, it will be replaced as part of the greater floor sill/step replacement.

While a major dent in the sheet metal may be distracting and require attention, having a true assessment of the damage will make it easier to determine if that panel can be repaired or should be replaced. Learn to work smarter, not harder.

Rust Repair

Perhaps the most important step in rust repair is determining and admitting that you have a rust problem. The worst part of the rust may appear as an area of complete rust through, whether small or large. However, the real question is: "How far out does the secondary rust occur?

Use an ice pick or a similar pointed steel probe to gently poke around in the area surrounding what appears to be the worst instance of the rust. If the ice pick goes into the sheet metal with slight effort, there is a rust issue. If the ice pick does not go through the sheet metal, the rust through may be localized, but continue to probe in an outward spiral to determine the extent. After determining the extent of the rust, use some chalk or a permanent marker to outline the area.

Patch Panels

If the rust is limited to an area that can be recreated from a piece of sheet metal or if a commercially available patch panel exists for that area, the best course of action is to cut out the rusty sheet metal and weld in new. With so many patch panels now commercially available for the Task Force trucks and the economical availability of MIG welders, it is no wonder that so many people are rebuilding these trucks.

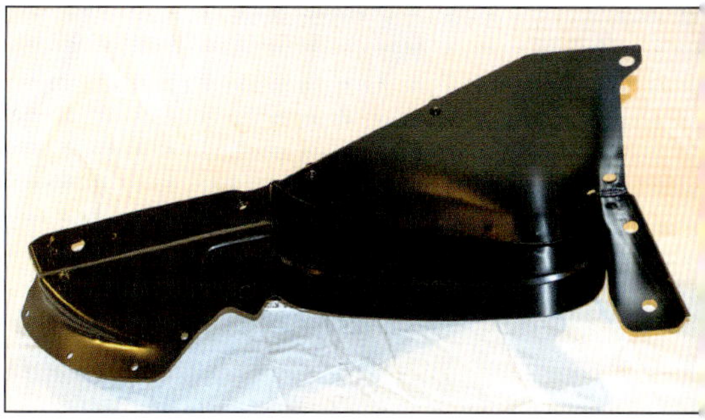

Door patches and various other patch panels can be fabricated by skilled craftsmen from flat pieces of sheet metal. However, a complicated piece like this inner fender extension would require a lot of fabrication time by even the finest craftsmen. This piece and the mate for the other side were purchased through Dynacorn.

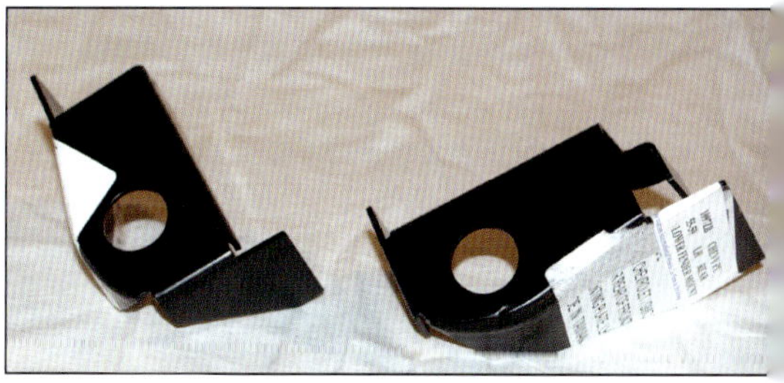

These are replacement lower fender brackets that weld to the lower front portion of the cab and serve as a mounting location for the rear portion of the front fenders. These pieces had rusted off my truck and are missing or damaged on many of these trucks, allowing the rear portion of the front fender to flail around.

Check out the catalogs or websites of the companies that offer sheet metal patch panels to determine what is available. For the most part, these trucks all rust in the same areas, so patch panels are typically made for those areas.

Some patch panels are more

After fitting the front fender into place, the lower fender bracket can be clamped in place. Scuff the mounting location with a grinder to allow for a good weld. To verify proper location, insert the appropriately sized bolt through a fender washer and the hole in the bracket, then thread it into the threaded bung on the back side of the fender. Then clamp the bracket in place.

appropriate if the rust was caught early, while others are bigger for much later in the process when the rust has spread out. Other than a larger panel being more expensive, it is typically better to buy a bigger patch and not need all of it than try to fit a couple of smaller panels together. Also, realize that rust in some areas will call for a complete subpanel assembly to be replaced.

After receiving the new patch panel, verify that it indeed extends to or past the rusty area. Ideally, you simply lay the patch panel atop the old panel and trace around it. Then, using a plasma arc cutter, reciprocating saw, or cutoff wheel, cut out the rust. Clamp the patch panel in place to the good sheet metal, and then weld it in place.

Panel Fitment

Realistically, the main reason to purchase patch panels is so we do not

With the fender still in place, secure the bracket in place with some bead welds from a MIG welder.

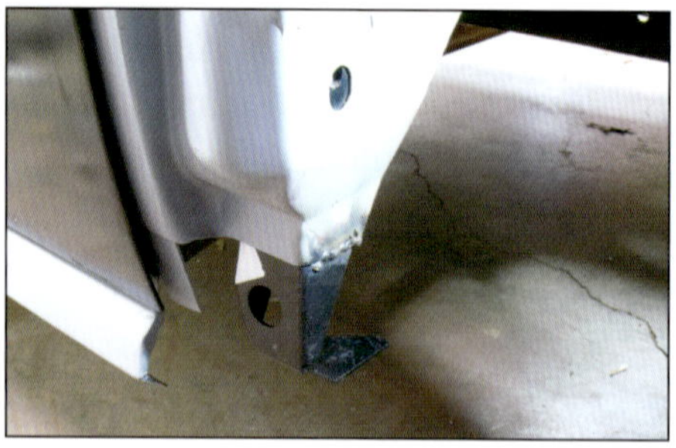

Removing the fender provides a better look at the passenger-side lower fender bracket. Prior to final bodywork, the welding of the bracket will be finished.

have to recreate the intricate body lines. If there is just one of these on a patch panel, it can probably be made to fit well. However, if there are two body lines, it is not uncommon for the area between the two to be too short or too long.

To obtain a perfect fit, it may be necessary to cut the patch panel in two, align the body lines appropriately, and then add or remove metal from the area in between. While this may be an aggravation, it is still probably easier than reproducing the factory body lines yourself.

When replacing a significant portion of the cab floor, it is essential to prevent the cab from moving or flexing prior to cutting out any of the existing floor. Therefore, it makes particularly good sense to have the cab bolted to the frame and braced

Anyone who has done any metal fabrication and/or welding probably already knows about sheet-metal clamps. If you do not have any, get some. The thin tab with the wingnut on top slides down between the two pieces of sheet metal. On the opposite end (below the sheet metal), a piece of square metal slides through the tab to serve as a clamp when the wingnut is tightened. This holds the sheet metal the correct distance apart for butt welding.

adequately to prevent any flexing.

If the doors are in place and they latch properly, they may be adequate support. However, if the doors are not in place, temporary bracing can be done by tack welding some electrical conduit diagonally across the door openings. Just be sure to leave a large enough opening for whomever will be welding in the new panels.

Floor Panels

Replacement floor panels are available, or you can make your own. Which you choose is largely dictated by your access to the necessary tools and the depth of your wallet. The floor panels are flat, so they are not difficult to make, but they should have some bead rolling done to make them stronger and less likely to "oil can." Replacement panels will have the factory pattern rolled into them, but you can be creative if you choose to be.

With the doors off and part of the floor to be cut out, adding some cross bracing to the cab seemed like a good idea. To do that, a few pieces of 1/2-inch electrical conduit was welded diagonally across multiple locations in the cab. This will not serve as protection in a crash but is merely to keep the cab from collapsing on itself.

When installing any patch panels, skip around from one location to another to minimize creating excessive heat in any one location.

I was not going to tell my Uncle Ed, but I will tell you . . . whenever you are welding, be sure to use the proper safety equipment, such as welding gloves at the very minimum.

If you make your own floor panels, use some Kraft paper or thin cardboard to make a pattern. The better the pattern fits, the better the replacement panels will fit. When you are satisfied with the pattern, transfer it to 18-gauge sheet metal. Then, set the replacement panels (store bought or handmade) in place and scribe or mark a line around the perimeter. This line will be where the old portion of the floor is cut.

The original floor can be cut out with a variety of tools: a plasma arc cutter, a pneumatic saw, or a cut-off wheel attached to a die grinder. Prep the area where welding will occur by removing any paint and/or primer. Then, set the replacement floor panels in place and secure with sheet-metal clamps.

Place several short welds around the perimeter of the panel being installed. Continue adding short welds around the perimeter, avoiding concentrating heat in any one place that could lead to warpage. As more welding is completed, the sheet-metal clamps can be removed and the welding finished.

Hot rods and vintage trucks have at least one thing in common: whenever you drag one out of a barn, it has at least a hundred holes in the firewall. At least it seems that way. There are a couple of ways to fill the holes or cover them up.

Weld Holes Shut

To retain the factory profile, you need to weld the extra holes shut. For any holes that are 1/4 inch in diameter or smaller, anyone with some experience can fill the holes easily. For larger holes, cut out a small patch panel from steel sheet metal and weld it in place. This practice can also be used for most any holes in the sheet metal.

A potential issue when welding up a bunch of holes is keeping the panel flat. Still, this is the better method of eliminating unwanted holes in sheet metal. Just be aware that a skim coat of body filler might be necessary after the welding is finished.

If you prefer a smooth firewall, cut out flat aluminum or sheet metal to create a patch panel. This can then be welded in place or glued in place using panel bond adhesive. Remove the hood hinges, the stock battery mount, and anything else that may be mounted on the firewall. Using some

Kraft paper or poster board, make a pattern for the driver's side and the passenger's side of the firewall. Transfer the pattern to the replacement metal and then cut it out. A throatless shear works well for this.

With the metal pieces cut out, check them for correct fit and modify as necessary. Locate and drill the holes necessary for the hood hinges and anything else that you are going to mount to the firewall. Having these holes drilled ahead of time will allow the mounting bolts to accurately locate the panels as well as provide a method to clamp the panels in place while the adhesive cures.

Use a grinder to scuff any paint and/or primer off the factory ribs of the firewall. This is where the panel bond adhesive will be applied. If the panel bond adhesive used is a contact-type adhesive, it will need to be applied to both surfaces, so mark the area on the backside of the panels where the adhesive must be applied.

Using the correct adhesive applicator, apply it to the firewall and the backside of the panel. Set the first panel in place and secure it with the two hood hinge bolts. Then, use some magnetic welding clamps to securely hold the panel in place while the adhesive cures. Check the directions for the adhesive for the proper cure time. Then, repeat the process for the remaining panel.

The cab of my shop truck project needed major surgery. The floor and toeboard, steps, doors, rear cab panel, and various other hidden panels all needed to be replaced. Fortunately, those replacement panels were all merely a phone call and a credit card away.

Many truck builders are curious as to which company makes the best replacement panels. While I have no way to verify the validity, the consensus is that the same company stamps all the panels that are then wholesaled to various vendors. Additionally, we must remember that the tolerances of sheet-metal fit were much looser 60 years ago than now. What this all leads to is that any part or group of parts (regardless of vendor) may fit accurately on one truck but poorly on another. How accurately everything fits together largely depends on how much effort is put into it.

Knowing that the repairs on my truck were substantially beyond my skill level, I took the truck and the replacement panels to my great friend, Roger Ward. He and Todd Brown worked together to completely restore the truck's abused cab.

Patch Panel Installation

1 *These are some of the original pieces of the cab that were cut out. The cab corners, cab back panel, doorsills, and various other pieces were all cut out of the truck and replaced with new. (Photo Courtesy Todd Brown)*

2 *Look closely above the notch in the cab back panel to see where a portion of the cab was replaced, as indicated by the vertical weld. Between the cost of labor and the replacement panels, buying a new cab would have cost less money. (Photo Courtesy Todd Brown)*

3 *After removing all the bad sheet metal, Roger and Todd began resurrecting the cab. The doorsill plate/step was used to establish the distance between the front and the rear of the door opening and was spot welded into place. The doors will be modified to fit the new opening. (Photo Courtesy Todd Brown)*

4 These trucks look a lot different without the back cab panel. At the top of the photo are the remaining scars from the previous body repair. Roger is contemplating the next course of action now that the doorsills/steps are in place. (Photo Courtesy Todd Brown)

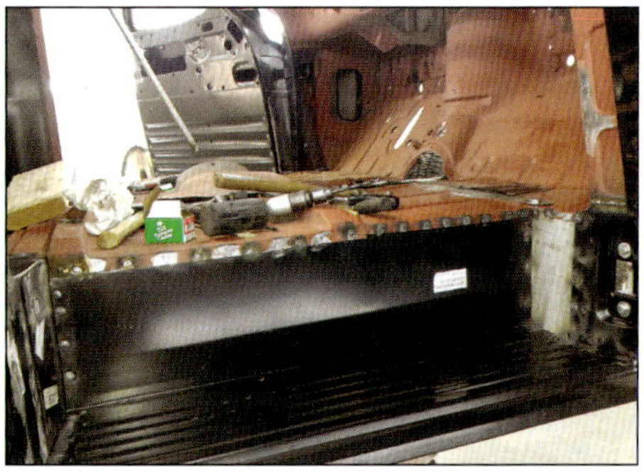

5 With the doors hung, the doorsills/steps installation is completed by spot welding the floor across the top of the vertical portion. A piece of flat sheet metal was used to fill the previous opening at the front of the step. (Photo Courtesy Todd Brown)

6 At this point, the cab is certain to be substantially stronger than it was. The transmission access panel area still requires some work. The stock mounting flange will require some repair prior to using the stock access panel or possibly a new transmission hump that may be added after the transmission is in place. (Photo Courtesy Todd Brown)

7 The replacement back panels are designed to extend all the way to just below the drip rail. However, welding in that area would require some intricate finish work. Learn to work smarter, not harder. Roger and Todd made the splice between new and old across the middle of the window, providing more room for blending. (Photo Courtesy Todd Brown)

9 Even though the sheet metal is not yet perfect in this photo, it is much better than when the truck was first taken to Roger and Todd. Any of the panels that are reddish brown primer are the original sheet metal, while the new panels are the black EDP. (Photo Courtesy Todd Brown)

8 Even though the replacement back panel and the replacement door were manufactured by the same company, the body lines are slightly off from one to the other, and the gap is not quite right. Even though the parts are brand new, they will require alteration to fit perfectly. (Photo Courtesy Todd Brown)

10 This side appears to align a little better as far as the body lines, but the gap between the door and the back panel requires more work. Everything is a tradeoff. The new pieces may not fit like the originals, but they are solid. It is sometimes easier to alter new panels to fit, rather than adjust and repair the original pieces. (Photo Courtesy Todd Brown)

11 *In addition to doors and fenders, several other panels (seen and unseen) required replacement as well. The bad thing about this is that you may not realize that some panels need to be replaced until you are already into the process. Depending on the availability of the parts, this can cause delays in completion of the project, as well as affect the budget. (Photo Courtesy Todd Brown)*

12 *To install the extension to this piece, the epoxy primer had to come off the outside as well as rust from the inside. A sanding disc on a small grinder made quick work of that. All surfaces to be welded must be clean and free of rust, primer, and paint. (Photo Courtesy Todd Brown)*

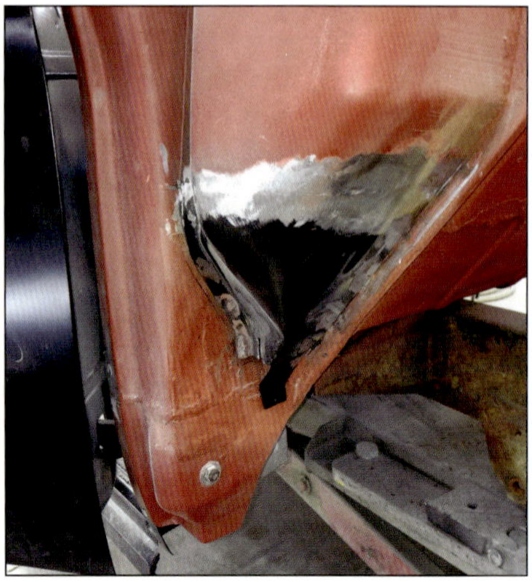

13 *After welding the new panel in place, grind the weld smooth. Apply a coat or two of epoxy primer to prevent the bare metal from rusting. Depending on where the panel is located, it may need a skim coat of filler. (Photo Courtesy Todd Brown)*

14 *The little silver cubes are sheet-metal clamps used to secure two pieces of sheet metal together when butt welding them. The clamps hold the metal in alignment, as well as the proper distance apart to weld properly. To remove the clamps, access the back side of the metal being welded is needed. (Photo Courtesy Todd Brown)*

15 *With a MIG welder and a short amount of time, the driver-side floor panel was installed. Perhaps one of the most versatile skills when building hot rods or trucks is the ability to weld. (Photo Courtesy Todd Brown)*

16 *Since the passenger-side door was a bit too long, the seam along the back side was cut off and the inner and outer door welded back together. There are things about building trucks and hot rods that will make some guys cringe. Paying good money for new parts and then modifying them to obtain a perfect fit is just one of them. (Photo Courtesy Todd Brown)*

17 *The process for trimming the door is to grind away or cut the weld that secures the inside of the door to the outside of the door. Tack weld it back together to check for the correct length. When the correct length is obtained, then weld it back together. Check multiple times that the length remains correct. (Photo Courtesy Todd Brown)*

18 *When the welding is completed, grind the welds smooth. Prime with an epoxy primer to prevent any rust from accumulating. Then finish bodywork whenever the rest of the truck is ready for that stage. (Photo Courtesy Todd Brown)*

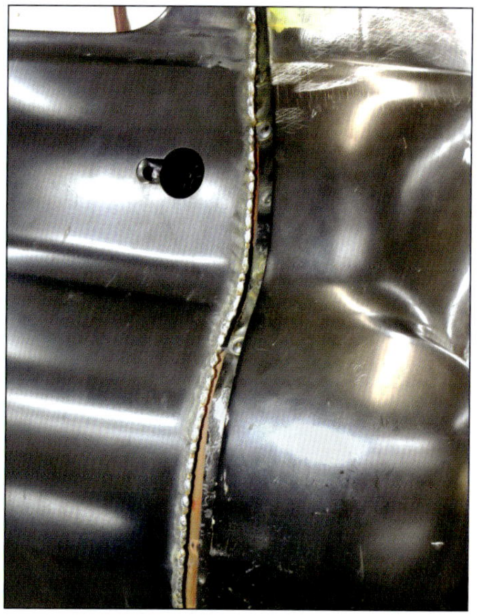

19 *On the driver's door, a weld bead was added to lengthen the door to match the opening. Remember, the reproduction parts are most likely never going to fit perfectly because these trucks did not fit together perfectly when they came out of the factory. Still, with some thought of what needs to be done and the skill to do that work, you can make them fit together nicely. But you may have to cut it up in the process. (Photo Courtesy Todd Brown)*

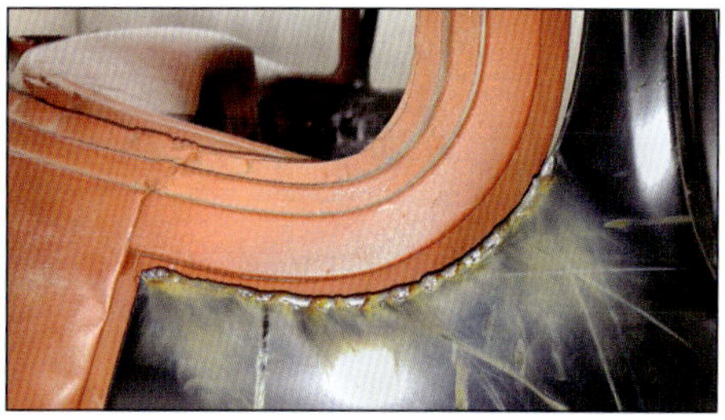

20 *Not only do the doors require extra work to get the length correct, they can use some work around the dogleg of the windshield frame as well. Obtaining the correct fit is all a matter of cutting where necessary, welding back together, and then grinding smooth. It is a lot of work, but it is worth it when it all fits like it should. (Photo Courtesy Todd Brown)*

21 *Even though the door fits much better now, compared to this photo, it becomes imperative to constantly open and close the doors through their full range of motion so that none of the gaps are too tight. (Photo Courtesy Todd Brown)*

22 *While resurrecting the cab, it was determined that the left rear corner of the cab had been damaged severely enough in the past that part of a cab from another truck had been welded in place on the left side. That work had not been done with the precision that we are accustomed to these days. This led to a bit of nip and tuck to the original cab to get everything to fit properly. (Photo Courtesy Todd Brown)*

23 *After grinding all the welds smooth, the cab is looking much better. It may not be perfect, but I plan on driving this truck most every day, so it will be good enough for that. It is difficult to critique bodywork when running down the highway. (Photo Courtesy Todd Brown)*

26 *A new piece of sheet metal was welded into the area where a stereo had previously been installed. This is where two HVAC vents will be installed. The stock ashtray will be retained but might be modified to house some sort of electrical gadget. (Photo Courtesy Todd Brown)*

24 *Both doors fit nicely into their respective openings. Epoxy primer will protect the bare sheet metal until final bodywork is completed, and it will also serve as a great substrate for applying additional coats of primer. (Photo Courtesy Todd Brown)*

27 *A little bit of filler was required to conceal the spot welds that attach the inner step to the floor panel. The cardboard taped to the step serves two purposes: 1) to prevent any globs of fresh body filler from falling onto the step and 2) to provide some cushion for the body man's knees while sanding. (Photo Courtesy Todd Brown)*

28 *With the new back panel in place, it is impossible to determine where the splice is located and hard to imagine that the panel has even been replaced. With both small-window and big-window panels available, it is no longer impossible to convert to one or the other if you cannot find the type of cab you really wanted. (Photo Courtesy Todd Brown)*

25 *A little bit of filler was required in the area where the new back panel was installed. However, making the splice in approximately the middle of the area on each side of the rear window made it easier to blend in the bodywork. Welding the complete panel in place and working it into the drip rail area could have been difficult at best. (Photo Courtesy Todd Brown)*

29 *Some replacement panels, epoxy primer, and some hard work have the truck cab looking almost as good as new. A good next step will be to get all the sheet metal in the same color of primer. Then let the block sanding begin.*

Modifications

Body modifications to these trucks are limited only by imagination and fabrication skills, whether that is yours or someone else's. Some modifications are good, while others are less than appealing. Sometimes the overall idea is good, but the execution simply is not up to par. Other times, the fabrication skills are superior, but the design is atrocious.

This is not meant to distract anyone from being creative. Look to see what others are doing, and then refine and improve upon their ideas. It is probably better to push the envelope than to feed it into the shredder.

There are several body modifications that can be made that will not detract from the classic character of your truck yet will be minor improvements. Some of these could be considered convenience and safety related, while others are purely cosmetic.

Smooth the Firewall

The firewall on most any old pickup truck seems to be filled with holes in one way or another. Some are factory, while others certainly are not. The traditional way of filling these would be to weld all the extra holes shut with a welder.

If they are about 1/4 inch in diameter or smaller, they can be filled with weld. Larger than that and a small round plug usually needs to be welded in place. However, depending on how many holes there are to fill, a lot of time can be spent cutting out plugs, welding them in place, and then doing the required bodywork to get the firewall smooth and flat.

A more contemporary method is to use panel bond adhesive to glue a piece of sheet metal or aluminum sheet over the area. Panel bond adhesive is what most OEM automotive factories use to attach panels together. Being an epoxy, this product is typically applied with a special caulking gun–type apparatus that accurately mixes the two parts during the application.

Before cutting any metal or aluminum, you must first make a pattern. The final pattern will be made from poster board, but for the original, I used some Kraft paper. Cut out a piece of Kraft paper, wrapping paper, or even newspaper slightly larger than the area to be covered. Use some welding magnets to hold the paper in place while pressing it into the edges of the area. Then, trace around the edges with a permanent marker.

Lay the Kraft paper onto a piece of poster board and then trace around the edges of the Kraft paper with a marker. When you are satisfied with the outline of the pattern, cut it out with a pair of scissors. Check the pattern with the vehicle. If it needs to be trimmed, you can easily do that. If it is too short somewhere, you can easily add to the poster board by taping some more on and cutting it to the proper shape.

When the pattern is the desired shape and size, tape it in place or hold it in place with magnets. Mark the hood hinge mounting holes and the stock battery mounting bracket on the back of the pattern from the inside.

Now transfer the pattern onto your piece of sheet metal or aluminum sheet. Cut it out and drill any necessary holes. Just to be on the safe side, bolt the sheet stock in place, to be sure that it fits as it should. This will also allow you to enlarge any holes if necessary. In the case of the hood hinges and battery mounting bracket, they will be covered, so there is some wiggle room on the holes.

Scuff the mounting surface of both the firewall and the sheet stock. Apply the panel bond adhesive to both surfaces per the manufacturer's directions, and then press the cover panel in place. Secure it in place with bolts where applicable and with welding magnets in other areas. After the panel bond adhesive has fully cured, use a bit of plastic body filler to blend in the edges with the surrounding sheet metal. Sand, prime, and paint to match the rest of the truck.

Firewall Plug Holes Elimination

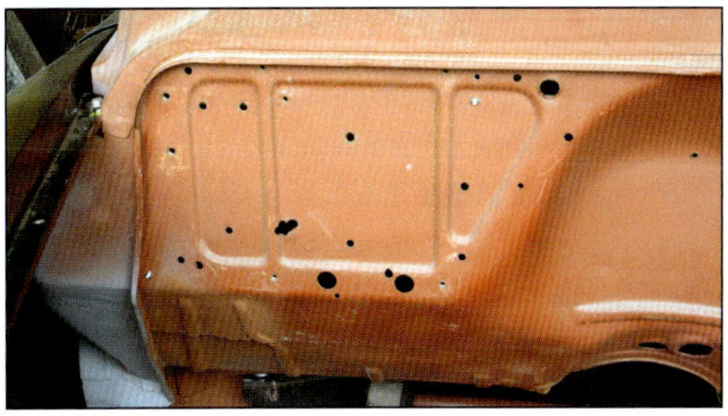

1 *I count 23 holes in the passenger's side of the firewall, with only 6 of them being required at this point (2 hood hinges and 4 battery mounting brackets). Some additional holes will be required to connect the HVAC system, but I am sure that none of the existing ones will be the right size or in the correct location for that.*

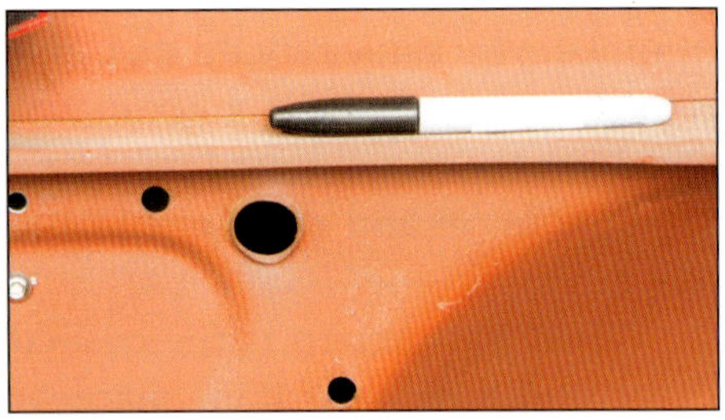

2 *The raised area of the firewall will be the mounting surface for the cover panel. One of the larger holes has a protruding lip around it, so it must be flattened for correct fit.*

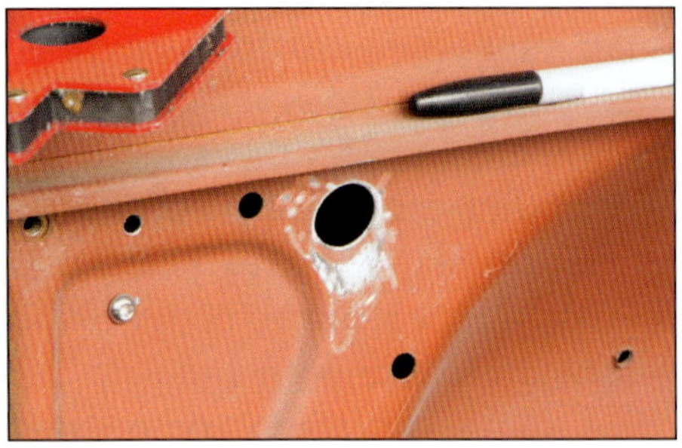

3 *A few minutes with a grinding stone in a pneumatic drill and the lip is now removed, providing a flat mounting surface.*

4 *Holding the Kraft paper in place with welding magnets, press the paper into place along the hard edges, and then mark the crease with a marker.*

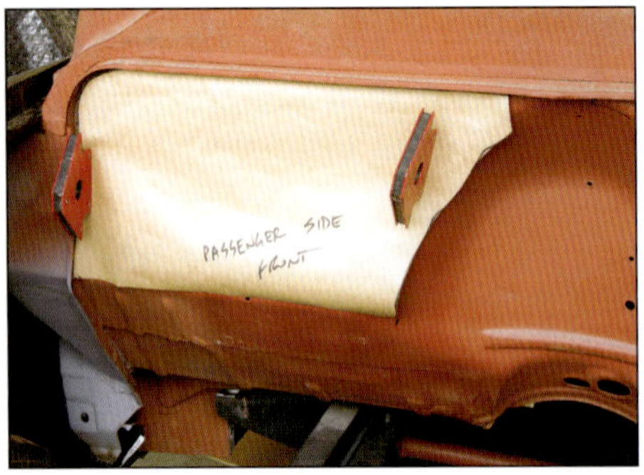

5 *The softer edges may be a little more difficult to determine, but if feathering it in with some plastic body filler anyway, it does not need to be precise at this time. The metal should not be too long at this soft edge, as it will be difficult to trim after it is glued in place.*

6 *Transfer the paper pattern to a piece of poster board. While this may not be entirely necessary, the paper and poster board are both easier to modify, as well as being less expensive than sheet metal.*

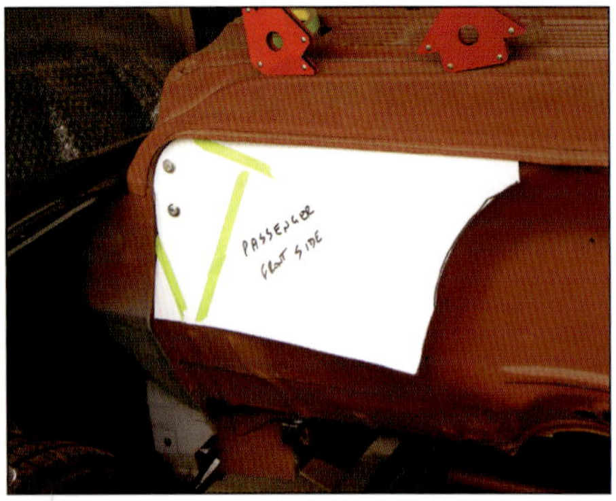

7 *The green masking tape shows where another piece of poster board was added to get the round corner fitting correctly. Additionally, the poster board can be bolted in place to allow for a more accurate pattern.*

8 *The poster board pattern is looking good at this point. It fits in place, and the mounting holes are properly located and are the correct size. Remove the poster board, scuff the mounting surfaces, and then clean with wax and grease remover to obtain a good bond.*

9 *Advances in automotive OEM manufacturing processes have led to advances in the automotive aftermarket as well. Welding the firewall cover plates in place would have been the traditional method, but that would have taken longer and would most likely require a bit of grinding work after the fact. An easier and less time-consuming method is to use panel bond adhesive. It may or may not be better, but it is a viable alternative, with the product and application gun available at the local auto parts store.*

10 *Press the cover panel in place, align any bolt holes, and use them to clamp the cover panel in place. Use welding magnets along the soft edge of the stock distributor recess. After it cures and the small holes in the recessed area are filled, the entire firewall will receive a skim coat of body filler prior to paint to blend in the edges.*

Between the necessary repair of the existing floor and the installation of the larger 700R4 transmission, this area requires some work. For a restoration, a shrinker/stretcher could be used to recreate the missing portion of the floor and the stock transmission access panel used. Most likely, a new panel will be fabricated to cover the area.

Transmission Access Panel

Depending on what transmission is used, it may be necessary to modify the floorboards and/or the transmission access panel. While the access panel in my truck was in reasonable condition, other than having a big hump in it, the area beneath it was partially rusted out. Not really knowing for sure how much room the 700R4 automatic transmission would require, this part of the floor was left "as is" until the engine and transmission were installed.

The plan will probably be to square up the opening, then weld in a new piece of floor that is modified sufficiently to clear the transmission. An alternative would be to use panel bond adhesive to glue the new panel in place. Either of these would eliminate the possibility of access to the transmission through the floor.

If access is still required or desired, the new panel can be secured with several button-head screws. With any of these plans, it will require a relatively small opening with a grommet for wiring to pass through. This will include wires to the neutral safety switch that is mounted to the transmission.

Power Windows

Installing power windows is purely a convenience, but it is just that. While some prefer the stock styling and implementation of the vent window, others believe that one-piece door glass cleans up the look of the truck's profile.

Most of the power window kits for these trucks seem to be used in conjunction with one-piece door glass. Presumably, power window kits are available for trucks that use the stock vent window. A small detail that should be addressed when installing one-piece door glass is to fill the slight depression in the door's window opening that allows for the vent window's division bar. This can be done by welding a slight bead into the area and then grinding and smoothing it to match the surrounding profile.

There is a small strip of metal that connects the outer door with the inner door just below the windowsill. When installing one-piece glass, this support must be cut out. Although it is not as noticeable in this photo as in person, the truck doors have a slight notch in them to allow for the vertical support of the stock vent window. If you eliminate the vent window, an extra detail would be to fill this notch.

Door Latches

While the stock door latches are better than those of the prior body style, there is room for improvement. Installing rotary door latches provides an improvement in occupant safety, not only in preventing the door from possibly flying open while driving but also in staying latched during a collision. True, no one expects to have a vehicle accident while driving their pride and joy truck, but it does happen on occasion.

Smooth the Bumpers

A custom trick that does not take a ton of talent but helps with the appearance of most any vehicle is to smooth the bumpers. What this means is to weld the bumper mounting bolts in place and then grind off the heads. This is not a radical modification by any means, and most people would likely never even notice it simply because they will not see something that is not there. Yet, virtually every passenger car made these days uses bumpers that have no visible bolts, so it must improve the looks a bit.

While smoothing the bumpers is an easy task, getting the gaps consistent between the doors and the cab and doors and the fenders is an entirely different story. To do this, you must develop an eye to be able to look at the overall flow of the body lines, prior to making any adjustments.

At each body panel, ask yourself if one panel is high, if the other panel is low, and which one can be adjusted as necessary. Understand that body fit tolerances simply were not as tight 60 years ago as they are now. Combine sloppy tolerances with a collection of multiple pieces and they simply are not going to fit together as well as some of us would like.

Every truck is going to be different, so there is no real answer other than to learn how to use shims and to not be afraid to trim metal here and there. It may be necessary to cut some panels and weld them back together, making them longer or shorter in the process to get the gaps perfect.

Truck Reassembly

By the time you get around to assembling the cab and other sheet metal, you should probably sit back and relax for a few moments with your favorite beverage and congratulate yourself for getting this far. While it may not sound like an accomplishment to some, there are others who have given up by now. However, you are far from finished, so drink up and get back to work.

Cab

A common question on social media about these trucks is, "What is the best way to pick up the cab to remove from or reinstall on the frame?" Obviously, there are some exceptions, but four average guys in good health can usually lift the cab with doors installed without issue. However, that does not include seating, stereo equipment, and air-conditioning. Having an extra person or two to watch for anything that might be in the way or to give directions is a good idea.

I do not always have a group of friends at the ready whenever I feel the need to move a cab and/or truck bed. But there are alternatives. Some guys have rigged up support, such as a timber passing through both door windows, and picked the cab up that way. That may work, but it seems questionable at best, and the possibility for damage is higher than some would like. A potentially less-risky method is to use multiple straps passing beneath the floor and coming together above the cab and then lifting from one central point with a hoist.

Doors

Removing or installing the doors pretty much requires two people: one to hold the door in place while the other removes or tightens the bolts to the door hinges. It can be done by one person with a floor jack, but even maneuvering the floor jack and tightening bolts at the same time can be tricky by yourself. There is horizontal and vertical adjustment of the doors about the hinge.

The goal will be to center the door in the opening as much as possible. Ideally, the gap will be the same all the way around and the body lines of the doors will blend right in with the body lines of the cab. Getting these body lines correct between the cab and the doors is a must if you want to get the body lines of the fenders to line up as well. Do not expect door latches or weatherstripping to correct door alignment.

To install the doors, secure the door hinges to the cab with two bolts. There is no adjustment in this part of the hinge. With both hinges secured, push both hinges to the open position and slide the door onto both hinges. Install three bolts in the lower hinge and three bolts in the upper hinge, but do not fully tighten them.

Close the door to see how well it fits in the door opening. With the bolts a bit loose, slightly adjust the door as necessary as you close it. When it appears to be centered in the door opening, tighten the three lower bolts. Recheck for fit. When the door fits the best, tighten all six bolts.

The stock door hinges mount to the cab in the same manner with two bolts that thread into cage nuts. The lower hinge (shown) mounts to the door with three bolts, which allows for in/out and up/down adjustment. The upper hinge mounts to the door with three bolts, which allows for the same adjustment.

Exterior Mirrors

Since exterior mirrors on the passenger's door were an option on these trucks from the factory, many of those doors (original and reproduction) do not have threaded holes for mounting the mirror. It is simple to figure out how to install a nut on each bolt from the inside. However, "Where does the mirror belong?" is a common question on social media.

One way to do it is quite simple, and simple is often good enough. Simply tape a piece of Kraft paper or similar over the area on the driver's door where the mirror attaches. Mark the edges of the door and the center of the three mounting holes. Transfer that to the opposite door, using the back side of the pattern. Before drilling any holes, hold the mirror arm for the passenger's side in place for a visual check.

Transferring Mirror Locations to Passenger's Side

1 *The mirror arm mounting holes are threaded from the factory on stock and many reproduction driver-side doors. However, that is often not the case for passenger-side doors. Still, the mirror location can easily be transferred to the passenger's side.*

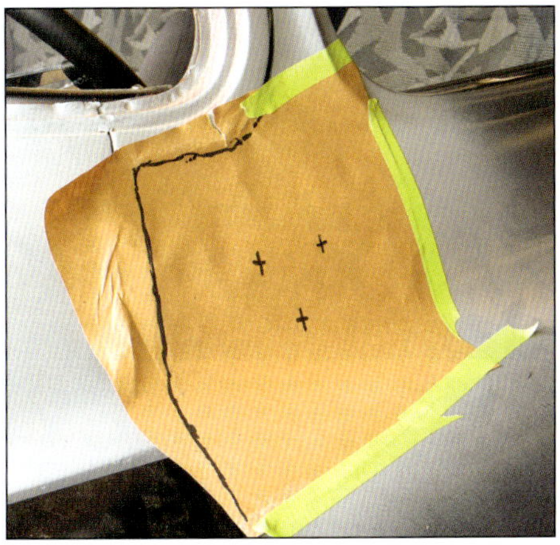

2 *Tape a piece of Kraft paper or similar onto the area of the door where the existing holes are. Outline the edge of the door and the existing holes with a permanent marker. Poke a tiny hole in the paper at the hole locations.*

3 *Remove the piece of paper and locate it on the opposite door so that the back side of the paper is showing. Align the paper with the edge of the door as indicated by your marks. Using a permanent marker, put a mark on the door at the three locations.*

4 *After marking the locations of the new holes and drilling pilot holes, use a step drill bit to drill them to the correct diameter. There is another piece of sheet metal within the door, so it must be drilled as well, but using a standard drill bit.*

5 *Violá, the passenger-side mirror is installed. This is personal preference, but I like to have things visually balanced on a vehicle, therefore the passenger-side mirror. Plus, if you drive in a lot of traffic, as I do, it will be good to have.*

Power Windows

Due partially to becoming accustomed to power windows in my late-model truck, I want them in my '55, which when drivable will become my daily driver. Additionally, I like the look of the one-piece door glass, so it all sounds good. I just wish there had been a template for the one-piece glass included with the kit. I will make a template out of thin plywood, but that will require some time and effort that I didn't really want to spend, especially knowing that I most likely will not get it right the first time.

Window Motor

Upon receiving the power window kit, read the instructions carefully. Verify that the clamping mechanism that secures the window glass is located so that the glass will be above it.

The directions provide locations for drilling five holes on the inner door panel for use in mounting the window riser mechanism. Drill these five holes, remove the bolts from the five mounting locations, and then insert the window riser mechanism into the door. For my kit, it is easier to insert the upper end of the track first and then rotate the assembly while it is already inside the door.

Secure the window riser mechanism in place by inserting the bolts through the new holes in the inner door panel and into their mounting points. Although there is no glass in place at this time, a battery charger can temporarily power the electric window motor up and down.

Power Window Installation

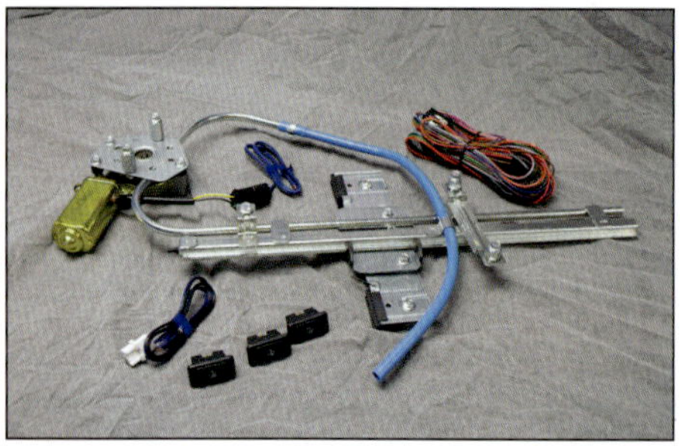

1 *This is merely one of the two window riser assemblies, along with wiring and switches. With this kit, no template for the one-piece glass was included. Some time with a piece of 1/4-inch plywood will cure that. It is flat glass, so most any automotive glass shop can cut that.*

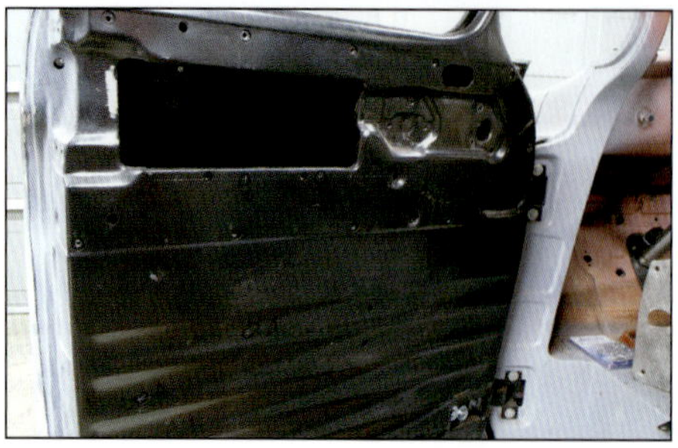

2 *A diagram enclosed with the instructions maps out the five necessary mounting holes that need to be drilled on the inside of the doors. Different kits require different size holes or holes in different locations, so read the instructions with the kit that you use, unless of course, you roll your own.*

3 *After drilling the holes, install the power window mechanism inside the door and secure it in place with the hardware provided. The five new bolt heads stand out easier than the empty holes on a black door. I do not know if this applies to all power window kits, but I found it easier to insert the window riser mechanism upside down and then rotate it within the door.*

4 *Electrical switches that come with the power window kit come with cover plates. When mounting the switches in a central location, just two switches are required to operate both windows. However, if the switches are mounted in the door panels, two switches will be required on the driver's side and one on the passenger's side.*

5 *Using a scrap piece of 1/4-inch plywood and the garnish molding from one of the doors, I was able to make a pattern for the one-piece glass. The inner and outer lines were drawn by simply tracing around the garnish molding. The edge of the glass will fall somewhere between the two. Be sure to allow for the thickness of the glass run channel.*

6 *Flexible rubber hoses were provided with the power window kit to serve as conduit between the door and the cab pillar; however, there were no instructions on where or how to install it. For the time being, I drilled holes in both surfaces in a location where they are accessible from the back. The holes are slightly undersized and the hose pinched and inserted.*

7 *The inner door panel that was included as part of the door latch kit had a drilled hole for use with the stock window riser. Of course, the manual riser handle is not required with power windows, so that hole was incorporated as a location for the power window electrical switch. It simply had to be trimmed a bit for the switches to clear.*

Window Switches and Wires

After choosing a suitable location for the power window switches, the wiring can begin. Note that if the switches are going to be mounted in the door, three switches will be required. Two switches on the driver's side and one on the passenger's side to open the passenger-side window. If the switches are going to be installed in a central location, only two switches are required. Regardless of the switch location, some wires will need to be routed from the cab into the door. This will require some type of conduit to protect the wires when the door is open.

From an electrical power source that is powered when the key is in the ON position, run a power wire to the positive terminal on each switch. Run a power wire from each motor to the positive terminal on the primary switch for that motor. Run a negative wire from each motor to the negative terminal on the primary switch for that motor. Run a ground wire from both driver-side switches to a suitable ground.

From the positive side of the third switch, run a wire to a negative terminal on the passenger-side switch. From the negative side of the third switch, run a wire to the remaining negative terminal on the passenger-side switch.

After the wiring is completed, connect to a power source, and check for proper operation. When all appears to work correctly, insert the glass, and test again.

Rotary Door Latches

Having relied on the stock door latches on my former 1951 Chevy truck and on my former 1929 Ford Model A Tudor and having both of them fail in one form or another, I chose to use rotary latches on the shop truck project. Trique Manufacturing offers its Altman latch that is designed specifically for these trucks, so that was a no brainer. Although the kit seems a bit pricey, the product and related hardware are of high quality, and the instructions make for simple installation.

If not done already, remove the existing door latch mechanisms and interior door panel. Although it may not be necessary, remove the existing door glass to ensure that it is not damaged while cutting part of the door to make room for the latch. Of course, if you damage the glass while removing or reinstalling it, you have defeated the purpose. Your call . . .

Rotary Door Latch Installation

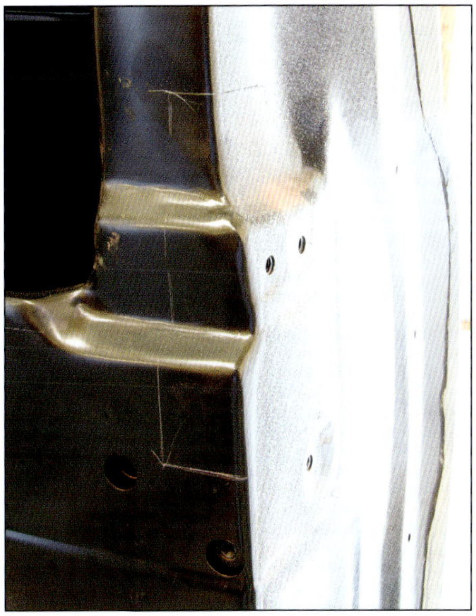

1 *Instructions included with the kit provide measurements and locations for determining the area to be cut out of the inner rear portion of the door. Locate the points according to the instructions, and then scribe a line between the points.*

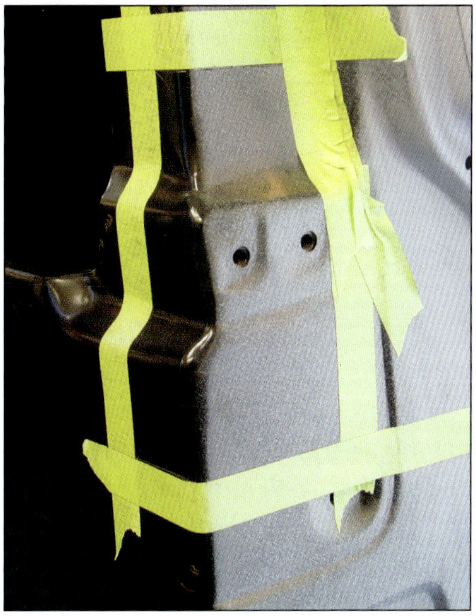

2 *This enclosed area will be cut out. The masking tape is applied to the outside of the line, purely to more clearly show the area that needs to be removed . . . for you (the reader) and me while cutting it out.*

3 *Since the cuts need to be straight and the window channel is just inside this area, the cutting should be done with a cut-off wheel, rather than any type of saw. After cutting out the sheet metal, deburr the edges.*

4 *The interior door panel also needs to be modified for the door latch to fit. Included in the kit is a paper template that needs to be cut out.*

7 *Cut out this area and then deburr any rough edges.*

10 *Secure the two panels together with the hardware provided in the kit.*

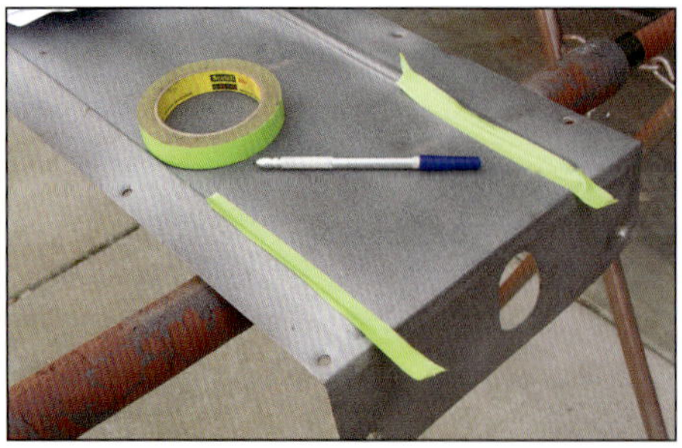

5 *The instructions indicate to measure down 3/8 inch from the upper bead and up 3/8 inch from the lower bead in the stock door panel. The tape has been applied to better illustrate this.*

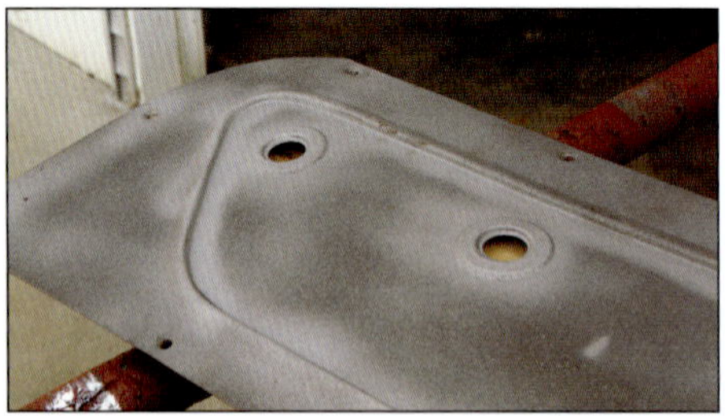

8 *For the new inner door panel to fit correctly, hammer flat the rings around the stock door handle and window riser handle.*

11 *The stock or replacement door latch relay can now be secured to the rotary latch mechanism with one bolt and lock nut. Then, reinstall and secure the door latch relay to the inside of the door with three screws.*

13 *While it can be done without help, having assistance from one other person will make securing the rotary latch to the door panel significantly easier. Secure the latch in place with three bolts and then secure the door panel assembly to the inside of the door.*

6 *Center the template between the two beads and align the fold in the template over the edge of the inner door panel. Mark a line around the template.*

9 *Now position the inner door panel onto the stock interior door panel so that the holes in each panel are lined up. Clamp the panels together and then use the new inner door panel as a template to drill the new mounting holes in the stock door panel.*

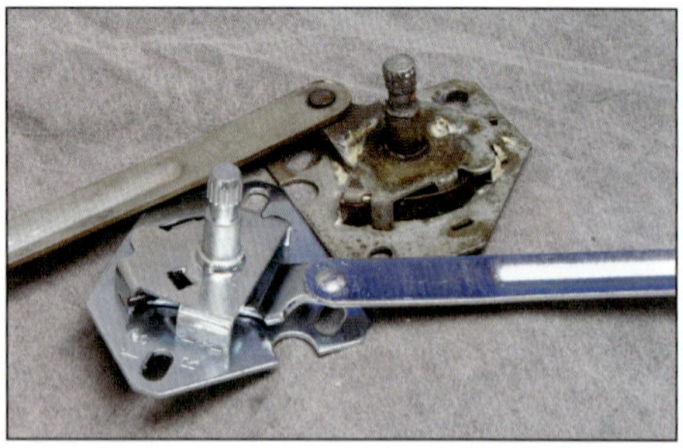

12 *While making this upgrade, take the time to check out the condition of the splines of the door latch relay. If they are bad, now would be a great time to replace them. While the original in this photo is not bad, the other original that is currently in the truck is about shot. It will be replaced.*

14 *This kit would be even better if it included the correct bolts to secure the striker plate to the doorsill. None were included, and the stock bolts have been long gone. If they must be replaced, the correct-size bolts are 12-24 x 3/4. Fun fact: two bolts are missing from this installation as two incorrect-size bolts still need to be drilled out.*

15 *The rotary latch is significantly better in design than the technology of the late 1950s. Safety is a good thing and is no place to skimp.*

Third Brake Light

While third brake lights were not required when these trucks were new and are not required now, having a third brake light is a good idea. I do not want anyone running into my late-model vehicle, but I really do not want anyone running into something in which I have invested significantly more time than money. Fortunately, these third brake lights do not have to be ugly, and some are even quite stylish.

One option is to scour the salvage yards for something that will work or can be adapted to work on your specific vehicle. However, in many mass-production vehicles, the third brake light is merely a surface-mount light that leaves a lot to be desired in the appearance department. A second option is an aftermarket pedestal-mount brake light that can easily be mounted above or below the rear window, usually with just two screws.

A more involved option that looks very slick is a flush-mount light. This requires access from inside the cab, but it does not look obnoxious from the outside and shows quite readily when the brakes are applied. There are two logical places to install this type of light: above the rear window above the rain gutter or below the rear window, which allows a little more latitude as far as at what height to mount the brake light.

Since mounting this light above the rear window will interfere with the dome light placement, it will be mounted below the window in the project truck. This will be more in the line of sight for most drivers and more accessible for installation.

For the third brake light from Hagan Street Rod Necessities, the first step is to determine the desired location. Determine the centerline of the cab and scribe a vertical line or mark with masking tape. Just remember which side of the tape is center if you use this method. The kit includes a steel faceplate with an opening that matches the lens that you purchase.

Determine and mark the vertical centerline of this faceplate in similar fashion. Align the two centerlines and then slide the faceplate up and down until the best location is found. Temporarily clamp the faceplate in place (making sure that it is level) and then scribe a line inside the opening where the light will protrude. Then, remove the faceplate and set it aside.

Several sizes and shapes of lights are available. For this installation, a 6-inch by 1/2-inch slot will be installed below the window in the double wall area of the cab. Use the appropriate-size drill bit to make the opening with the correct radius at the corners. Then, using a cut-off wheel or a pneumatic saw, cut the straight portions of the light's shape.

To install the light housing, a portion of the inner wall of the cab will need to be cut out. This is a simple rectangular cut. From inside the truck, test fit the lens to ensure that it fully protrudes through the opening in the cab. While the opening should be as exact as possible, the lens must fit flush and fully protrude through the opening. The lens will eventually be sanded flush later, along with any necessary body filler if the opening is not exact.

When the lens and the housing both fit properly from inside the cab, mark the appropriate locations for the T-bolt studs to be attached to the inner side of the outer wall. These studs will fit through the slotted mounting holes in the housing. The T-bolt studs can be secured in place by welding them or using panel bond adhesive.

To mount the LED light inside the housing, first slide the heat-shrink tubing over the wire all the way to the LED strip, and then heat the tubing in place. Feed the wire through the hole in the housing. Remove the protective paper strip from the adhesive strip, then position the LED in the center of the housing and press into place. Apply a bead of RTV clear sealant around the base of the LED strip to protect it from moisture.

After the weld has cooled or the panel bond has cured, sandwich the lens between the cab and the housing by sliding the housing over the T-bolt studs. Secure each with a washer and nut.

Use 80-grit paper on a grinder or a dual-action sander (DA) to remove the bulk of the protruding lens. If any filler is needed for imperfections in the cutout, apply it. Then, sand the lens, filler, and the surrounding body with finer grit sandpaper all the way down to 600 grit.

When the lens is flush with the surrounding bodywork, remove the housing and the lens. To eliminate any white light from showing through, apply a coat of black spray paint to the outside of the lens. Reinstall the lens and housing as before, and now polish and buff the lens to remove the black paint from the portion of the lens that protrudes through the sheet metal. Complete the installation by connecting the red power wire to the brake light circuit and the black wire to an adequate ground.

Third Brake Light Installation

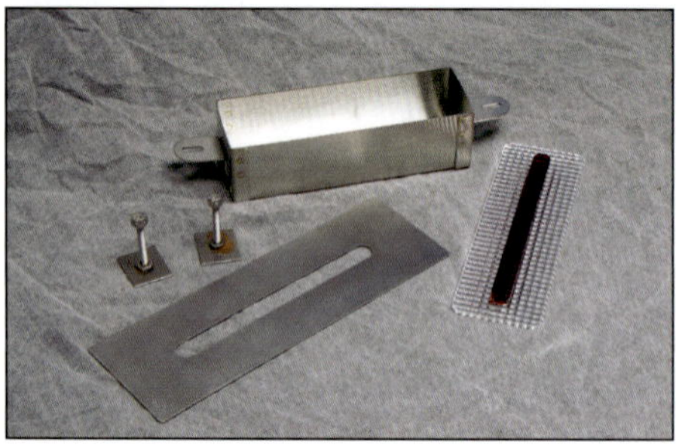

1 *Included with the Hagan LED third brake light is the stainless-steel housing, lens, steel faceplate, two T-bolt studs, and an LED strip (not shown). The cool thing about these lights (they are also available as taillights) is that they are very bright since they are LED and the lens surface can be sanded down flush with the surface.*

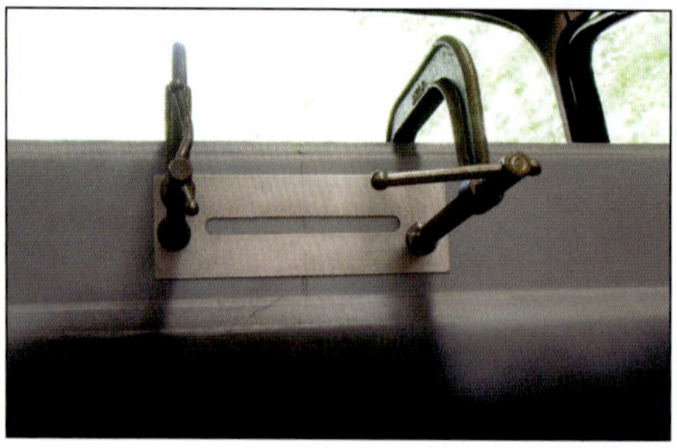

2 *Determine the desired location of the third brake light. In this case, it will be located below the rear window rather than above to not interfere with the dome light in the interior. Then clamp the steel faceplate into place on the outside of the panel to use as a template. Use a scribe to trace around the inside of the opening.*

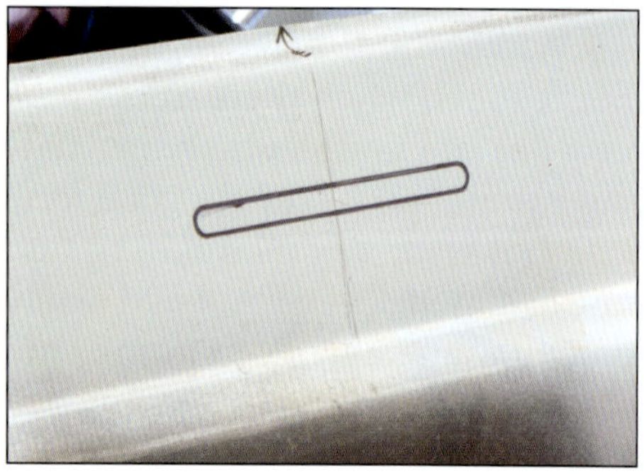

3 *This heavy line shows the area to be cut out. After being cut to the correct size and shape, the lens will be mounted from the inside and ultimately sanded flush for a very cool installation.*

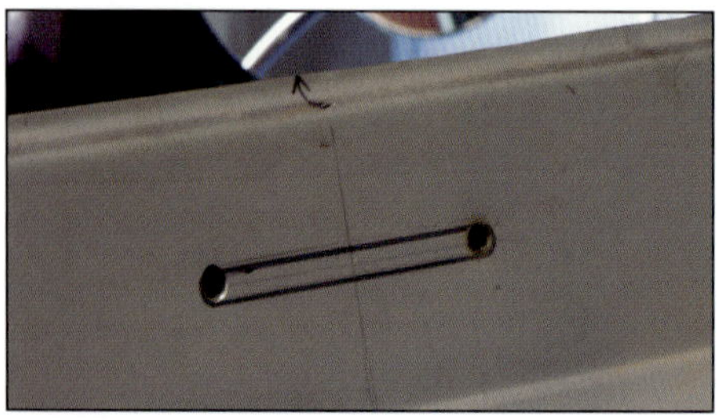

4 *With this being a 1/2-inch-wide lens (different sizes are available) with rounded ends, a 1/2-inch step drill bit was used to cut the ends. While the fit should be as close as possible, part of the beauty of this kit is that a bit of body filler can be used if the opening is not perfect.*

5 *It still requires some trim work for the lens to be able to protrude through the opening. After making the initial cut, a file can be used to enlarge the opening as required.*

6 *The area inside the box must be cut out inside the cab to allow for the housing. In this application, the housing will protrude into the cab area a bit, as the housing is thicker than the double wall area of the cab.*

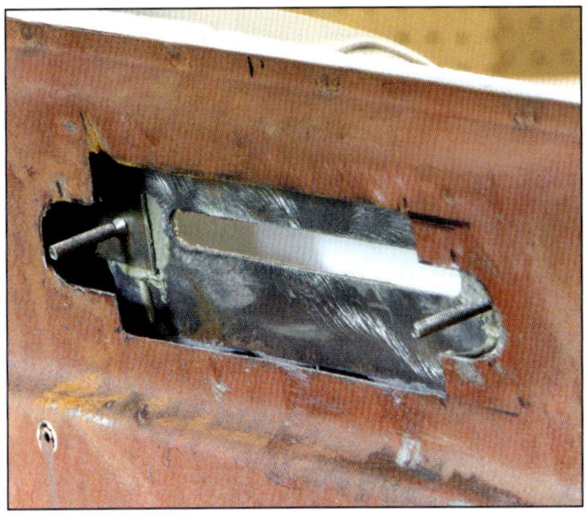

7 *The two T-bolt studs are to be secured to the inside of the outer panel and serve as a mounting source for the housing. The T-bolt studs can be welded in place; however, I chose to use panel bond adhesive.*

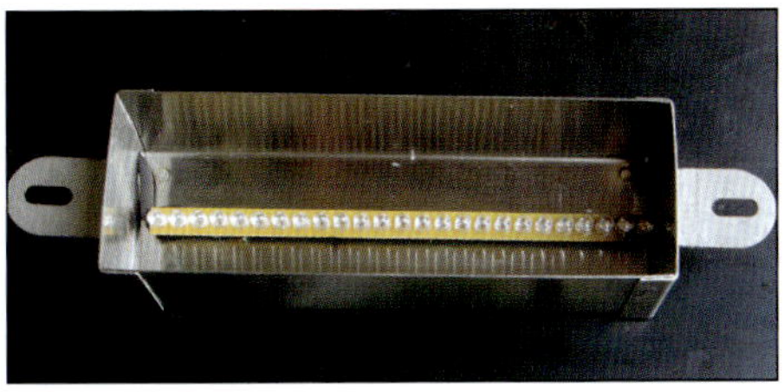

8 *After sliding heat-shrink tubing over the wiring and shrinking the tubing, route the wires through one of the holes in the housing. Remove the paper strip from the base of the LED strip and position it in the housing. Apply a bit of clear RTV sealant around the openings in the housing to prevent moisture from entering the housing.*

9 *Insert the lens and then secure it in place by installing the housing over the studs with a washer and lock nut.*

10 *With the lens protruding through the sheet metal, begin sanding it with 80-grit sandpaper until it is flush with the surrounding surface. Then apply a bit of body filler around the third brake light to fill any imperfections in the cut out sheet metal.*

11 *As the sanding continues, the third brake light will become level with the surrounding surface. Continue sanding throughout the body surface preparation. Just as finer sandpaper smooths the surrounding surface, it will remove the primer, paint, and scratches from the third brake light.*

12 *Using a battery charger to provide power, the third brake light is very bright, even in the garage with fluorescent lights on. So, it should be visible in the daylight and definitely at night, all good things on a truck that gets driven.*

Front Sheet Metal

Perhaps the most puzzling piece of putting one of these trucks together is assembling the front sheet metal. Ask several people how they assembled theirs, and you will get several different answers. There are two fenders, two inner fenders, two fender extensions, an upper grille bar, a lower grille bar, and two inner fender-to-cab braces. Those all eventually bolt to the radiator, the grille, and the cab directly or indirectly as well. While some would think that it makes sense to begin with the grille and work your way out, others say to begin with attaching the fenders to the cab and work forward.

One thing is for sure, successfully assemble everything at least once before any of it is painted. Also, tighten the fasteners enough that the assembly does not fall apart while working with it but not so tight that things cannot be moved around a bit. Yes, having an extra set of hands available would be a good practice.

Do not be surprised if some pieces need to be trimmed here and there, even if they are brand new. Shims

With the engine and transmission in place, it was time to install the front sheet metal. While the front sheet metal will ultimately attach to the radiator core support, I did realize later that it might be better to wait until after the sheet metal is installed to install the radiator. That may or may not apply to a stock-style core support.

Front End Installation

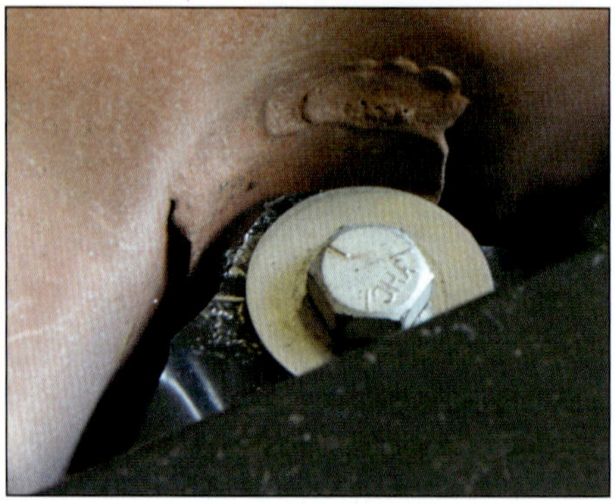

1 *The tab of the replacement fender has been trimmed a bit already since it was hitting on the rounded portion of the cowl.*

2 *To clean up the tab a bit, secure a fender washer to the extreme limit of the slotted mounting hole with a bolt and a nut. Any portion of the tab that protrudes beneath the fender washer is merely excess that will serve as a deterrent to proper fit.*

3 *The fender washer serves as a visual guide in addition to serving as a stop for the grinding stone. Trimming off this slight excess will allow the fender to be pulled in closer to the truck. It is merely a small step in obtaining consistent gaps.*

4 *When working with painted sheet metal, this will certainly require additional sets of hands to assemble. For now, a large sheet of bubble wrap served the purpose. Begin by securing the fender extension to the inner fender with bolts in the two positions shown.*

5 *Then secure the inner fender to the front fender with the three bolts shown along the upper edge of the two pieces. The potential pain point is now installing a bolt at the upper front of the inner fender into the front fender and the fender extension. When these three pieces are secured together, they all become more manageable.*

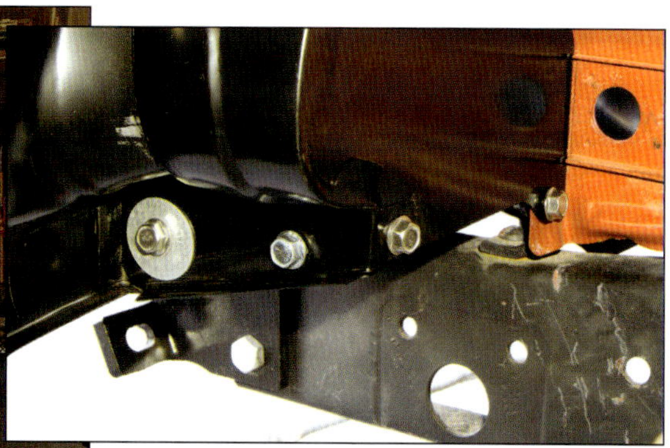

7 *Looking inward through the driver-side fender we see the front fender, fender extension, and primed inner fender (left to right). All four of the bolts shown thread into the backside of the lower grille bar.*

6 *Four bolts secure the lower grille bar to each front fender assembly. A key to installing all parts is to leave them somewhat loose during assembly. When all pieces are secured to each other, they can all be squared up and tightened.*

8 *The grille is secured to the lower grille bar with four sheet-metal screws. They are located within the narrow stands in the lower grille bar that align with the four vertical bars in the grille.*

9 *The upper grille bar will ultimately be secured with a bolt that will come through the front fender and the fender extension. A second bolt will go through the upper grille bar and the inner fender and into a welded nut on the back side of the fender extension. Sheet-metal screws will be installed through the three small holes in the lip of the front fender and into the fender extension.*

10 *After installing the upper grille bar, install the hood latch into the hood latch panel. Then secure the hood latch panel to the upper grille bar with four bolts. The next step will be to install the radiator and core support. Everything is still loose at this point, but it is looking better.*

may also be required to get everything as you want it. Another helpful tip is that from the factory, most of these sheet-metal pieces were bolted together with pointed screws, rather than square-tipped button-head bolts. The point is that the pointed screw will be significantly easier to start when panels are not aligned exactly. Take your time and do not lose your patience. It can be done.

There are several pieces of sheet metal to connect, more holes than you can imagine, and none of them are labeled with "insert tab A here." And in many cases, we are assembling a collection of original parts with reproduction parts, all of which were constructed with somewhat loose tolerances. There seem to be multiple paths toward installing the front sheet metal.

During previous mockup attempts, I realized that the tabs for bolting the upper rear portion of the fender to the cowl near the hood hinge were larger than they need to be. This prevented this portion of the fender from moving inward as far as I would have liked, creating a large gap between the fender and hood. A grinding stone in a pneumatic rotary tool trimmed the tab down quite easily.

The next step is to connect the inner fender, fender extension, and front fender together. The fender extension fits behind the inner and front fenders with the grille opening of the front fender in front of the fender extension. Then, secure the inner fender and the fender extension together with a couple of 3/8-inch bolts.

The fender extension has nuts welded on the backside, so merely install the bolts enough to hold the pieces together. Now secure these two pieces to the front fender by installing bolts through the top edge of the inner fender into the front fender. The front fender has nuts welded to the backside also. Install the bolts enough to hold the piece together but still move a little bit.

After securing the front fender, inner fender, and fender extension together for each side, set them in place and secure them to the truck at the cowl. Shims may need to be installed below the fender tab at this location to obtain the correct body line from the door to the fender. Eventually, the lower rear of the front fender must be secured to the cab as well.

The lower grille bar connects both front fenders. Two bolts pass through the front fender, a portion of the fender extension, and into the lower grille bar on each end. Two additional bolts pass through the fender extension and into the back side of the lower portion of the front fender with one of those passing through the inner fender panel, as well.

Since I was replacing the original grille with a chrome grille, now seemed like the time to install it. The grille (painted or chrome) can be removed/installed with the upper grille bar in place. The grille itself is secured to the lower grille bar with four sheet-metal screws from underneath. Having small fingers will probably be an asset when doing this part.

The upper grille bar connects the upper portions of the front fenders side to side. One bolt passes through the front fender, the fender extension, and into the upper grille bar. Another bolt goes through the inner fender and threads into a nut that is welded to the backside of the fender extension.

Radiator and Core Support

The radiator core support sits atop a mount located on the top of each frame rail and is secured with one bolt in each. The stock-style radiator is then secured to the core support with six bolts. Some aftermarket radiators incorporate the core support as an integral portion of the radiator assembly. In either case, the core support serves to connect the sheet metal (fenders, inner fenders, etc.) from one side to the other.

Bed

After assembling the front sheet metal, the bed (be it Stepside or Fleetside) will be much easier. After all, it is essentially a square box with fewer intertwined pieces. Like the front sheet metal, the bed should probably all be assembled at least one time prior to paint, just to develop a logical sequence of events.

It makes sense to install the front bed panel to each of the bedsides, then install the rear cross sill to tie all four sides together. Then, install the tailgate trunnions and the tailgate. The cross sills should then be installed. At this point, assembly will be easier if the four sides can be set on sawhorses or some other method that allows access from below.

The next step is to install the wooden bed floor and the related bed strips. On a Fleetside bed, the wheel housings need to be installed prior to the bed wood. On a Stepside bed, the rear fenders and steps can now be installed. Again, having an extra set of hands will make the assembly process significantly easier.

Most Stepside fenders and commercially available bedsides already have the mounting holes in them, so alignment is not a major issue. However, the fenders do get heavy, and they are difficult to reach around, so it is a two-person job. While one person holds the fender, another can install two or three bolts and nuts so that the fender does not fall off. Having one person in the bed installing the bolts and another on the outside threading on the nuts usually works well. Just remember to install all the fender mounting bolts loosely before tightening any of them completely.

On a Fleetside, the wheel housings are much more manageable. If not using a rear bumper, whether a Stepside or a Fleetside, a rolled rear pan provides a finishing touch to the back end of the truck bed. Most optional rolled rear pans can be

The radiator core support ties the front fenders together with two bolts on either end that pass through the two holes shown between the hood latch panel and the radiator. In this photo, the radiator is leaning back too far. Note that a piece of plywood, cardboard, or foam core should be placed over the surface of the radiator to protect it during assembly.

Even without the hood in place, the truck is looking better, but it still needs a few tweaks here and there. The driver-side firewall cover needs to be glued in place and the hinge installed. I'm also waiting for my neighbor to come over to assist with the hood. I am hoping that everything lines up well.

Using slightly longer bolts than normal to get the bolt started and having someone else pushing or pulling the fender into alignment make this task a bit easier.

The engine compartment is coming along nicely as well. Since the engine and transmission will need to come out to paint the transmission, accessory brackets, and the water pump, I had planned to leave the alternator and the A/C compressor off until final assembly. However, to ensure that everything fits and nothing conflicts, everything needs to be installed at this point. No one wants to alter freshly painted parts.

bolted on, while sheet metal pans can often be welded on if you choose.

Note that at least on the final bed installation, all the bed strips should be installed and all hardware tightened, as some will not be accessible after installation on the truck frame. Typically, four average grown men can install the truck bed onto the truck frame.

The aluminum radiator from PRC includes two Spal electric fans, providing for excellent cooling capacity. On the passenger's side of the radiator is the overflow tank.

Bumper

Begin by loosely bolting the bumper mounts to the frame with the required hardware. Do yourself a favor and measure the distance between the center mounting holes and the bumper mounts to ensure the mounts are installed correctly. On my shop truck, the mounts fit correctly when placed inside the frame rails with the mounting holes toward the outside.

With the aid of an assistant or a floor jack, insert bumper bolts through the bumper and into the bumper mounts. Secure the bumper to the bumper mounts with the lock washers and nuts. Tighten up all the nuts and adjust as necessary until the bumper fits as desired.

The bumper mounts must be in the correct orientation to fit the bumper correctly. Shown is the driver-side bumper mounts. To install the bumper, the bolts must remain slightly loose to get everything to fit together. When all the bolts are installed, they can then be tightened and adjusted, as necessary.

To access the bumper mounts and related hardware, having the truck up on jack stands, roller skates, or wooden planks will make the task easier. However, I know for a fact that with the bumper on, my floor jack no longer has the required clearance.

PLAN AND INSTALL INTERIOR COMPONENTS

The interior of the truck is presumably where you are going to be spending most of your time after it is built. For that reason, the interior requires as much (if not more) planning than any other area of the truck. It needs to be accessible, comfortable, and practical for whatever the overall use of the truck will be.

You are dealing with a finite volume of room, so depending on how the truck will be used and what features are to be included, proper planning is required. Unlike trucks of today, these trucks were designed as work vehicles, and they were therefore very spartan when it came to interiors.

No, this is not the interior of my truck, but I thought it looked very nice, and it is the right color. Unlike mine, this one eliminated the glove box and includes a dash extension to cover the A/C evaporator and provide a mounting location for the vents.

Seats

The stock bench seat is still a viable option in a truck. While the original will most likely require having some foam replaced and being reupholstered, there are plenty of kits available for doing this work yourself. Additionally, custom upholstery work is as close as your local auto upholstery shop. While the price for custom upholstery work may seem expensive, the materials are often much more durable and the work more custom than anything that is mass-produced.

OEM

If you want something better than the stock seat but still desire seating for three, a bench seat out of a newer truck is a good choice. Bench seats from the late 1980s through the 1990s are the correct width and at most might require drilling four new mounting holes for installation. Like a stock seat, upholstery work might be required.

Before committing to paying a salvage yard for a usable seat, check with an upholstery shop to get an estimate of what their fee will be so that you can figure that into the budget. Regardless of how good the seat's condition may be, unless it is exactly the color and material that you want, it still needs to be reupholstered.

With the vast array of pickup trucks and SUVs available today, finding a suitable bench seat, combination split-back bench seat, or bucket seats that meet your requirements is quite high. However, it may take some searching to find exactly what you are looking for, so start early.

If looking for bucket seats, there is now a wider variety of vehicles to choose from. However, one thing to remember when searching for seats is that the floor of these trucks is flat. Some vehicles have floor pans that have contour to them and therefore the seat mounting feet may be curved or somehow different from one side to the other. Like most things automotive, this can usually be overcome, but it may require more creative or fabrication effort than it is worth.

Custom

If you choose to go full custom, several aftermarket upholstery companies offer new seat frames and foam that can be upholstered locally or completely upholstered and ready to install. These come with a higher price than something out of a salvage yard; however, depending on how you plan to use your truck, they may be worth the price.

Bucket Seat Installation

For the shop truck project, I found a pair of bucket seats out of a 2004 Pontiac Sunfire for sale for $100. While the pattern of the fabric was hideous and therefore will be replaced, the seats were in good enough condition as they were to be used for the short term.

These seats are originally from a 2002 Pontiac Sunbird. As with most used seats, they required some new foam and cover material. Longtime St. Louis–area hot rodder and upholstery guru Don Albers covered these for me. The two-tone gray vinyl will be durable and should look great with the Omaha Orange paint.

The existing fabric was in good condition and will make for a good pattern, which will make the reupholstery task easier for the upholsterer. Additionally, they are the same basic seat as what I was planning to buy already upholstered for a much higher price. Lastly, the seat tracks have flat feet, so they will be easy to install.

These seats are from a Pontiac Sunfire and were purchased for a nominal price. They are like the aftermarket seats that I had originally planned to purchase. The existing covers are good enough for an upholsterer to use as a pattern. With some new foam and new covering, they will look great. The headrests will be eliminated.

Positioning

Installing a bench seat is easy. Simply set it on the floor, center it side to side, and then drill the necessary mounting holes and bolt it in place.

Bucket seats are easier in another way, as they can be positioned by one person. Begin by positioning the seat all the way to the back on the seat tracks, then set the driver-side seat in the truck, aligned with the steering column and as far rearward as you would want it. If the seat back can recline, make sure that it is in a comfortable driving position and then mark the rearmost end of the seat tracks on the floor.

Now, adjust the seat so that it is in its most forward position on the seat tracks. Set the seat in the truck aligned with the steering column. In this position, is the seat close enough to the steering wheel and pedals for you and any potential drivers? If it is, mark the front-most end of the seat tracks on the floor. If the seat tracks fit between these two marks, mount the seat anywhere between these

On these seats, all the track feet are flat, which allows for easy mounting to the floor of the truck, whether a riser is required or not. After determining the best location for the seats, simply mark the location on the floor through the openings in the track, and then drill the necessary holes.

two extremes. If the seat needs to be closer to the steering column, move the seat forward to where it needs to be.

When the desired front-to-back position is determined, verify that the seat is still aligned with the steering column, and then mark the necessary mounting holes on the floor. Before drilling any holes, look beneath the truck to verify that you are not going to drill into anything that should not be drilled into. If all is clear, remove the seat and then drill the required mounting holes. With the help of an assistant, secure the seat in place with appropriately sized bolts, washers, and nuts.

After installing the driver's seat, simply match the location with the passenger's seat. Purely as a safety feature, I used plates designed for securing seat belts to mount seats as well. These plates are roughly 4 inches long by 2.5 inches wide with rounded edges and a nut welded onto the bottom side. This plate is substantially larger and stronger than any fender

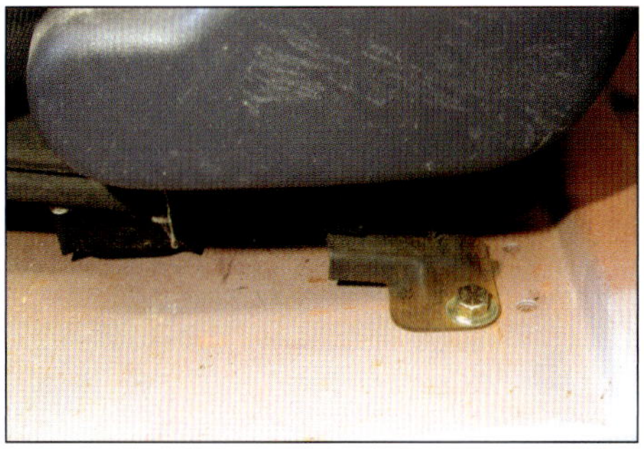

Before drilling any holes, inspect the area below to ensure that you are not going to be creating a big headache for yourself. When all is clear, drill the necessary holes, set the seat into position, then bolt them in place and secure from underneath. Yes, it will require two people to tighten the bolts that secure the seats, at least for the final installation.

These anchor plates are designed for use with seat belts. However, for the same reasons, they are good to use when installing seats. They are larger than any flat washers, which helps to spread any force incurred during an accident over a larger area.

washer and helps to spread any force load that would occur during an accident over a wider area.

Floor Console

Choosing between a bench seat with no floor console and bucket seats with a floor console is really a personal preference. It largely depends on how the truck will be used and who all will use it. My reason for choosing bucket seats and a console was largely based on it providing a convenient location for installing the wiring fuse panel, plain and simple.

The floor console will serve as a mounting location for the satellite radio/CD player/Bluetooth unit and one pair of the related speakers. Additionally, the floor console will house the heating, ventilation, and air-conditioning (HVAC) controls, inboard courtesy lights, cupholders, a few other electrical conveniences, and lastly, some lockable storage. It could be used as a location for the switches for power windows, power seats, or any other switches that may be necessary.

Design

Depending on your skill set and what you plan to put in it, a nice floor console can be made from wood, medium-density fiberboard, aluminum, fiberglass, or sheet metal. Each material will require different design and construction techniques, but what follows is merely one way to build a center console.

With the desire to install the stereo in the console and the narrow distance between the bucket seats, I realized that this console would require something with thin walls. After a bit of redesign, this console will be made from 1/8-inch-thick aluminum.

The overall design is to have the console extend downward from the original dash, fill the area between the seats, and serve as an armrest between those seats. Two vertical panels will serve as the primary walls, which will be tied together internally. An aluminum angle will be bolted to the inside of these walls along the top edge but recessed just enough to have aluminum panels fill the face area of the console.

Use pieces of cardboard or foam core to rough out the profile of the console. The foam core is easier to cut out than the final material but is sturdy enough to be self-supporting for mock-up. After the final profile and width between the vertical panels is determined, measure the length of the vertical panels that will extend all the way to the floor.

To serve as a foundation and to make the entire console removable from the truck, cut a piece of sheet metal this same length or slightly shorter. This piece of sheet metal will need to be the width between the inside of the vertical panels, plus around 1 inch on each side to be bent upward 90 degrees to serve as attachment points for the vertical panels. This channel will later be secured to the floor with four bolts and nuts.

Cut the Material

A plasma arc cutter was used to cut out the profile of the vertical panels, so the foam core pattern was first transferred to a piece of plywood. Any mounting holes or anything else that should be aligned from side to side should also be included in this plywood pattern. Then, cut out the plywood for use as a template to drag the plasma arc cutter along when cutting out the aluminum.

Position the plywood template on the first piece of aluminum and clamp it in place. Cut out the first vertical panel. Reposition the plywood template on the second piece of aluminum, clamp it in place, and cut out the second vertical panel.

Align and clamp the two vertical panels together to ensure that the shapes match. If they do not align and match exactly, correct that now. When the vertical panels match, unclamp them, place the template on the outside of one of them and clamp the three pieces back together. Now drill pilot holes for all the holes that need to be aligned with each other.

Cut the aluminum angles to the required length and clamp them in

Center Console Construction

1 *The actual location of the console was determined while the seats were in place to decide the width and the suitable height of the armrest area between the seats. It is also time to determine locations for anything that you may be using while driving, such as HVAC controls, stereo adjustments, and cupholders.*

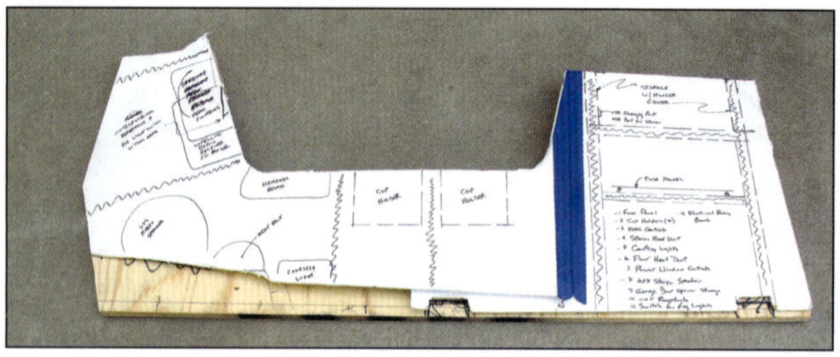

2 *This console is going to be constructed from 1/8-inch-thick aluminum that will be cut using a plasma arc cutter. To ensure that both vertical panels match, the foam core template was transferred to a piece of plywood to be used as a template. Areas to be cut out for speakers and courtesy lights, as well as holes to be drilled will also be included in the template.*

3 *The shiny metal on the bottom of the new panel will replace the transmission hump. As this photo was taken, it still requires a little bit of finessing to fit the toeboard properly. The sheet-metal channel above it is the base of the floor console.*

4 *Using the plywood template as a guide, my neighbor Tom uses his plasma arc cutter to cut out each of the vertical panels from sheets of 1/8-inch aluminum sheet.*

5 *To ensure that both panels are the same size and shape, they were placed one on each side of the plywood template and bolted together in three places. Minor trimming with a file evened up any inconsistencies. These three reference points will also aid in aligning both vertical pieces with the base channel.*

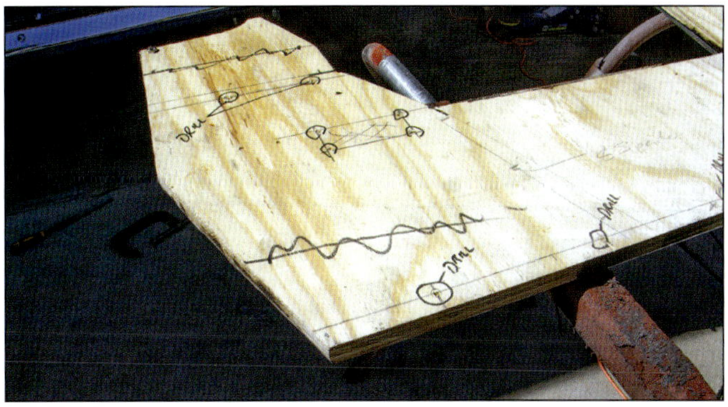

6 *The plywood template also included locations for holes to be drilled for screws to assemble the sides to the base. Holes also indicate the location for the courtesy light and the stereo speaker.*

7 *With all the holes drilled, the vertical panels are secured to the base with 1/2-inch 1/4-20 button-head screws along the lower edge.*

8 *Additional holes around the perimeter will be used to secure a 1-inch aluminum angle to the inside of the vertical panel that will support a 1/8-inch aluminum plate that will mount the stereo receiver, HVAC controls, cupholders, etc.*

9 *Looking through the console front to back, the upper aluminum rails will support a tray for the XM satellite radio. Courtesy lights and speakers are just beyond that. The HVAC controls will take up most of the room in the angled surface below the stereo.*

10 *At the rear (left) of the console will be a hidden compartment beneath a hinged and padded armrest. The angled face will include a USB charging station and a cigar lighter–type power receptacle. Two cupholders will be located in the flat panel that will also be easily removable for access to the electrical fuse panel.*

11 *In place for a trial fit, the console is looking good and is coming out as planned. It will eventually be bolted to the floor and will house the electrical fuse panel.*

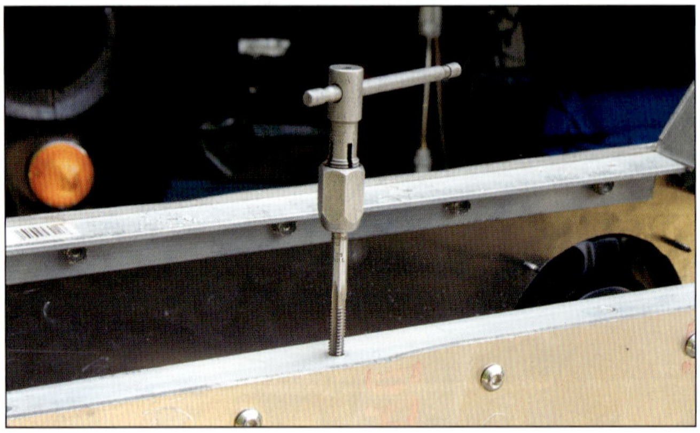

12 *The 1/4-20 button-head screws and nuts were used throughout the construction of most of the console. However, the panel in the middle needs to be easily removable to access the fuse panel. If using sheet metal, sheet-metal screws could be used. Since the panel rests on a 1/8-inch-thick piece of aluminum, holes were drilled and tapped.*

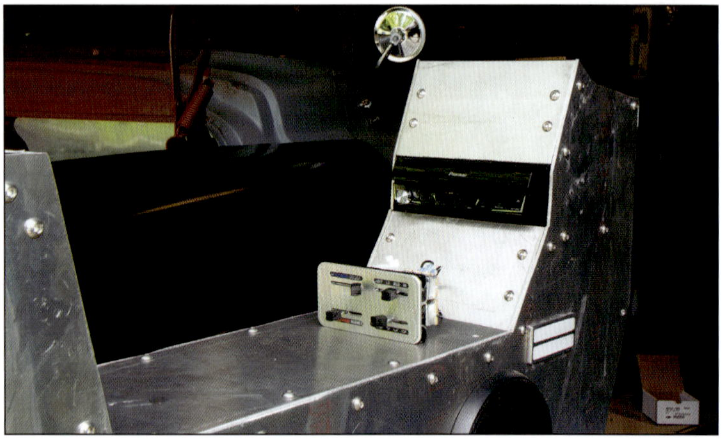

13 *The stereo is shown in its intended position. It includes a display panel that when open will cover the panel above it in the console. The slanted panel below the stereo is where the Vintage Air HVAC controls will be located. Stereo speakers and courtesy lights are already installed.*

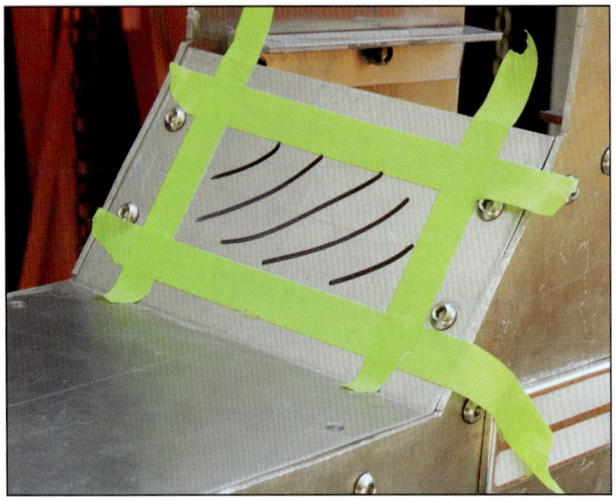

14 *After determining the location for the HVAC controls, the edges of the area to be cut out were scribed in the aluminum panel and then outlined with masking tape for better visibility.*

15 *After using a pneumatic saw to cut out the panel, the edges were smoothed with a file to gain the correct fit and finish.*

16 *After a bit of filing, the control panel slips into place. The control panel is secured in place by fasteners from the back side.*

17 *The aluminum console fits up below the dash and is secured to the floor with four bolts. Below the dash is the satellite radio receiver and the HVAC controls. On either side are courtesy lights and stereo speakers. Farther back on the removeable panel (to provide access to the fuse panel) are two cupholders. The center armrest (that will be padded and upholstered on top) opens to provide access to some storage. In the front of the armrest are a USB charging port and a cigar lighter–type electrical outlet.*

place on the vertical panels. Then, using the vertical panels as a template, drill the mounting holes. Then, use screws and nuts to secure the aluminum angles in place or tap the holes to eliminate the need for nuts.

Cut out the aluminum plate to the correct size to fit in each face position. Clamp each of them in place and drill mounting holes. For any face panels that may need to be removed, these holes will need to be threaded, as you will not be able to put a wrench on the back side for disassembly. At this point, the console is self-supporting. Holes or openings for mounting accessories are now cut out and those accessories installed.

HVAC

Whether you are going old school and merely having a heater in your truck (yes, I know they were optional back in the day) or you plan to have a complete HVAC unit that provides A/C, a heater, and defrost, the unit will require some amount of room. In most cases, either of these units are located behind and below the dash.

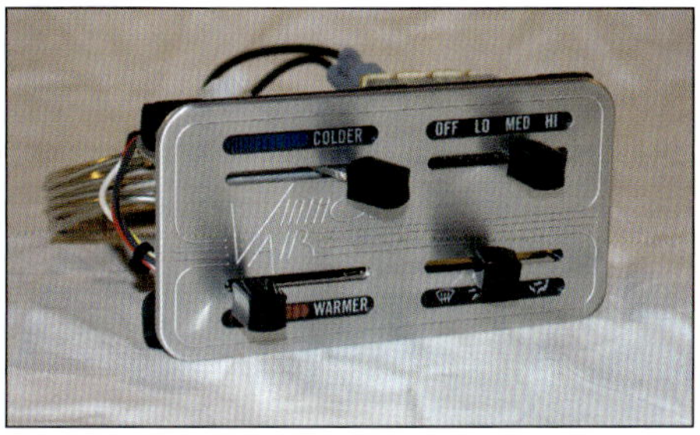

Vintage Air has been manufacturing HVAC units for hot rods and custom car/trucks for quite a while and provides a high-quality product and excellent customer service. In addition to their SureFit units designed to fit specific vehicles, including 1955–1959 Chevrolet and GMC trucks, they manufacture various kits for custom installation. This control panel will be mounted in the floor console within easy reach of the driver or the passenger.

Other than possibly eliminating the room that was previous allocated to the glove box, that is not a problem. However, it needs a location for the controls and the vents, if running A/C. The stock controls were in the dash, approximately in the center. This is still a good location; however, if you are planning to have a stereo along with A/C vents in the dash, the dash can start filling up quickly.

Make sure to also allow for the necessary room behind the controls. You can make most everything fit, but it requires some planning before cutting holes in the dash.

Air-Conditioning

While a licensed service technician will need to evacuate and charge the A/C unit after it is installed, the installation is simple. However, there is some information that you should know beforehand to install the unit properly and get the best performance from it. Most components (compressor, evaporator, condenser, and drier) are capped to prevent moisture from entering the unit.

As moisture in the unit can cause premature failure and reduced performance, they should remain capped until installation. Some units may be charged with dry nitrogen to help prevent the entrance of moisture, so the caps may be under pressure when removed.

Verify which refrigerant is to be used with the A/C unit being used, as an inappropriate refrigerant could become a fire hazard. For this installation, a Vintage Air ComPac Gen II heat/cool/defrost unit is being used and is designed to use only R134a. Be sure to use the correct size O-ring and lubricant on all A/C connections.

Locate and Mount the Components

Prior to installing the evaporator, first determine where to locate the compressor, condenser, and drier, as well as how to route the lines between them. The compressor is driven by one of the engine belts, so that is merely a decision of which bracket to use. The condenser is typically mounted nearby and is sometimes constructed as part of the radiator. The drier can be installed pretty much anywhere but should be installed in the coolest location possible and in a vertical position.

The evaporator location can be anywhere in the truck cab if the location allows for routing of lines and vents for the conditioned air. However, it is commonly mounted behind the dash on the passenger's side. Always mock up the location of the evaporator to verify that connections can be made prior to drilling any holes or cutting any sheet metal.

While the glove box may or may not be useable after the installation of an A/C unit, the unit will be easier to install if the glove box is removed for the time being. If the unit includes the defrost option, go ahead and install the defrost vents.

Secure the mounting brackets to the evaporator with the provided hardware. Verify that there are no obstructions on either side of the firewall where you intend to mount the evaporator. After finding a suitable location with no obstructions, locate and drill the necessary mounting holes in the firewall. For best performance, ensure that the evaporator unit is level.

Route Hoses

Connect the expansion valve to the evaporator. Determine where the refrigeration hoses should go through the firewall, making sure to avoid having any sharp angles in any of the hoses. Determine the location for the drier, keeping in mind that a section of #6 liquid hose will be required between the drier and the bulkhead fitting.

If the compressor safety switch is remote from the drier, find a suitable location for it between the drier and the evaporator. Route #10 suction hose from the evaporator to the suction side of the compressor. Route #8 discharge hose from the compressor to the inlet port on the condenser. Route #6 liquid line to the inlet side of the drier. Yes, the direction through the drier does matter. Verify that the hoses and lines are routed as you want them, and then cut them to length.

If any of the refrigeration hoses require an angled fitting, mark the orientation of the fitting on the hose, as refrigeration hose has little amount of twist in it. Take the hose and fittings to a qualified A/C service technician to have the fittings crimped onto the hose. Remove the evaporator from its mounting location.

Lubricate a #6 O-ring and the threads of the fitting, install the #6 hose onto the expansion valve, and tighten. Lubricate a #10 O-ring and the threads of the fitting, install the #10 hose onto the evaporator and tighten. Insert the capillary tube from the thermostat 4.5 inches into the designated location in the evaporator. Connect and tighten the #6 and #10 hoses to the inside of the bulkhead fitting. Be sure to wrap any exposed #10 fittings located inside the cab to prevent condensation. Attach the duct hoses to their respective locations on the evaporator unit.

Air-Conditioning Installation

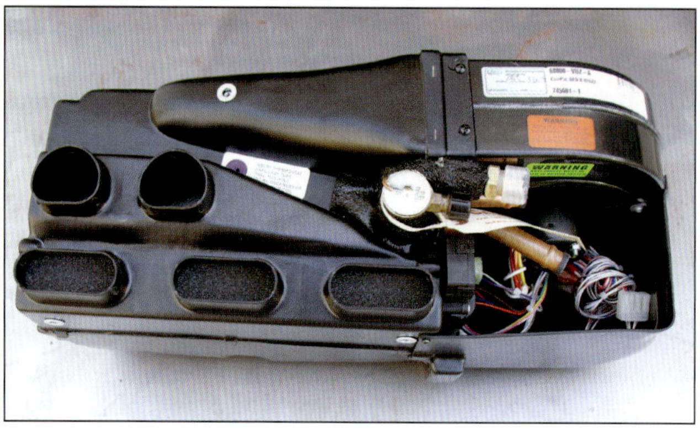

1 ***Looking at the top of the Vintage Air ComPac Gen II heat/cool/ defrost unit, the three oval openings are the A/C vents while the two somewhat rounded openings are the defrost vents.***

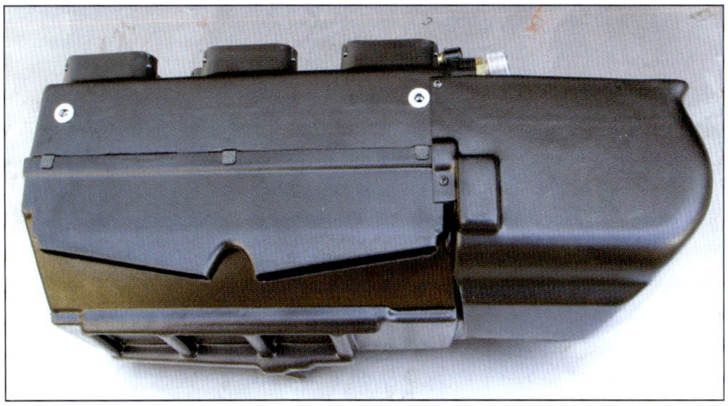

2 *Looking at the unit from inside the cab floor, the three rectangular openings are where the heat will come from when the unit controls are set to provide heat. The nutserts near the top are for additional mounting brackets that may or may not be required for your application.*

3 *Mounting straps are typically included with the A/C kit but can be easily fabricated for a purely custom application. The bracket shown attaches to the forward and top of the A/C evaporator and is secured to the firewall.*

4 *Before getting too far into the installation, be sure to check out your existing defrost ducts to see if they are damaged or even in existence. They will be far easier to access prior to installing the evaporator unit.*

5 *When installation is completed, the cover will be reinstalled to conceal all the wiring.*

6 *The heater control valve is an electronically controlled valve that directs fluid in the A/C system. It is generally mounted on the inside of the passenger compartment, near the evaporator.*

7 *A bulkhead fitting is required when making fluid connections from one side of the firewall to the other. In this model from Billet Specialties, all connections on the outside of the firewall are threaded. On the inside, the heater water lines are push-on fittings, requiring a hose clamp.*

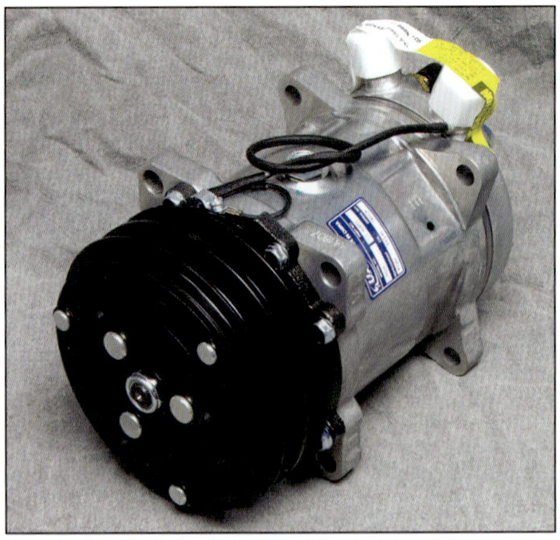

8 *The A/C compressor is driven by one of the engine pulleys, much like the alternator. When purchasing an A/C compressor, be sure to specify whether you will be running a V-belt or a serpentine belt, as the pulleys are different. The four sets of front and rear mounting ears allow the unit to be rotated as necessary to best clear the coolant hoses.*

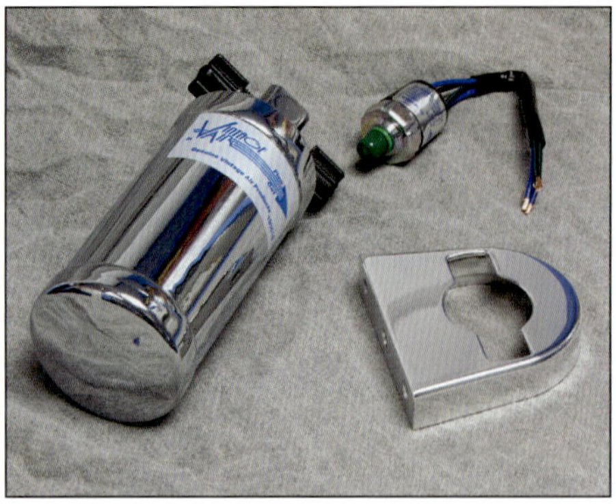

9 *Each A/C unit requires a drier and a mounting bracket. Since refrigerant carries lubrication through the unit, a compressor safety switch is also required. A binary switch disengages the compressor clutch when it senses extremely low pressure or excessively high head pressure (406 psi). A trinary switch (shown) does both and signals an electric fan to begin operation when the unit reaches 254 psi.*

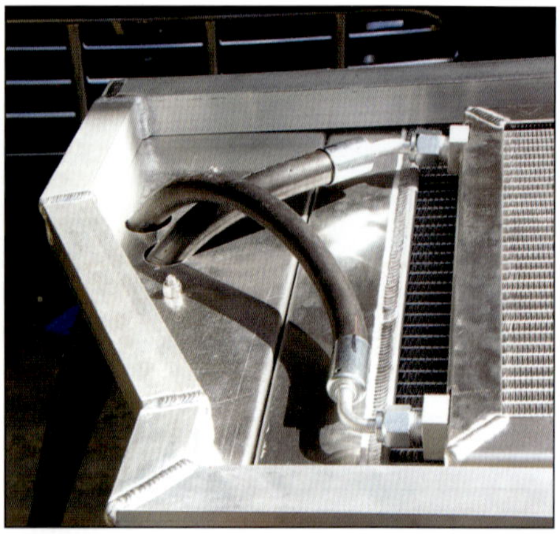

10 *These are the two A/C lines as they connect to the A/C condenser. When the condenser is in front of the radiator, these connections need to be made prior to installing the radiator, and there is not much room between the condenser and the grille. In this application, the #8 hose (top) connects to the compressor. The #6 hose (bottom) connects to the drier.*

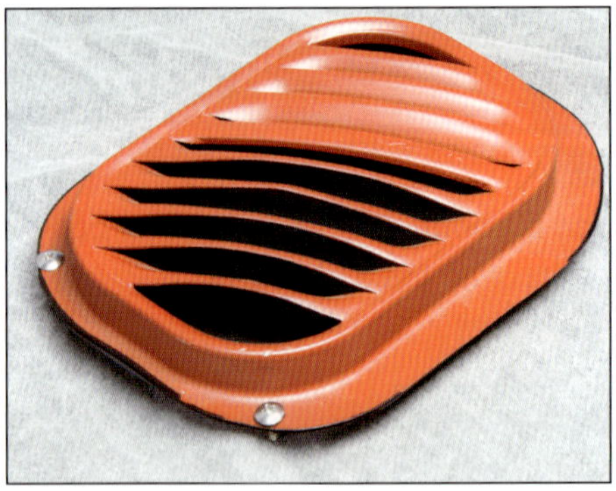

Some thin sheet metal or aluminum, a pair of tin snips, and a can of black spray paint is all that is needed to clean up the look of the cowl vents. They will be painted body color but will not have the grungy look behind them. Merely a quick and easy detail that is often overlooked.

Since the project truck will become my daily driver, I want it to have most of the creature comforts of my current daily driver. Of course, that means tunes and hands-free telephone service. Satellite radio, Bluetooth, navigation, and the option to install a backup camera are all included. The display screen retracts into the unit when it is not in use.

With all connections tight, lift the evaporator unit back into position and secure with the mounting hardware. Route 5/8-inch heater hose from the heater tube on the evaporator to the heater connection on the engine's intake manifold. Include the heater control valve in this line somewhere convenient. Route another 5/8-inch heater hose from the evaporator to the suction connection on the water pump.

Install Vents

Install the A/C vents where you want them. Route duct hose to each vent. To ensure maximum airflow, stretch the duct hose tightly and avoid sharp bends or kinks. Make the electrical connections according to the wiring diagram provided with the unit. Be sure that the unit is correctly grounded.

To test the unit, fill the radiator with a blend of antifreeze and water appropriate for your location (50/50 minimum), start the engine, and

Although the center console will contain a couple of stereo speakers, I chose to add kick-panel speakers as well. Not only does this provide additional speakers but it also provides a panel for this open area. It can be painted, upholstered, or left as is. I have not yet made up my mind on what to do with it.

let it run until it reaches the normal operating temperature. Place the control switch into the heat position and the desired fan speed. This will heat the truck.

Allow the engine to continue running long enough to thoroughly circulate the antifreeze/water mixture through the heater core. Place the control switch to the cool position and the desired fan speed. This will cool the truck.

If installing A/C, it is quite possible that you will no longer plan to use the stock vents. If that is the case, you may want to remove the hardware and seal off the vents. A simple and easy way to do this is to cut out a piece of sheet metal to match the shape of the vent covers. Paint this new piece of sheet metal black, and then sandwich it in between the stock vent covers and the kick panels. This is much simpler than welding in a block-off plate.

Stereo

Not only does the stereo take up valuable real estate on the face of the dash (or wherever it is mounted) but, like the HVAC controls, it also takes up quite a bit of room behind the scenes also. Both should be well within the driver's range of accessibility while driving. This is sometimes another cause for including a center console into the truck's interior design.

In addition to the head unit, speakers and antennas must also be figured into the equation. Before drilling any mounting holes for a radio antenna, verify that the required wiring can be routed between it and the receiver.

Hands-free telephone and backup cameras are all part of the stereo system. These features will also involve additional controls and/or cameras to be placed somewhere. Planning for and placing these items where they will be most convenient will make them more user friendly and worth the effort in the long run.

Electrical Conveniences

Even though you can appreciate the classic styling of trucks from the late 1950s, chances are that you will also appreciate some modern conveniences. I am sure the designers of these trucks never thought that they would someday be equipped with Bluetooth capabilities, navigational software, chargers for mobile phones, and power windows. For these electrical conveniences to really be convenient, they need to be located at your fingertips. Unless you always have a passenger, stashing something in the glove box is not convenient, unless it has a remote control. And then, how do you keep the remote from sliding down between the seats?

Power windows are typically controlled by remote switches located somewhere on the door panel, in an armrest, or centrally located in a console located between bucket seats. The doors of these trucks provide a lot of area and switches are not big, so power window switches can easily be used as a design element in the interior door panels.

Phone chargers, although they should be easy to access, do not need to be as convenient as the stereo or the A/C controls when driving. Not that phone chargers or 110-volt power outlets need to be hidden, but they can still be usable even if they are not as accessible.

These are USB charging ports and a cigar lighter–type receptacle that will be installed in the dash or most likely in the center console somewhere to provide various conveniences such as charging a cell phone or powering a flashlight. Note that these types of conveniences require planning. The housing behind the mounting surface is 1 inch in diameter and requires more than 1.5 inches of clear depth.

Safety

In addition to creature comforts, there are some safety items that will reside within the interior of the truck, and they need to be planned for. You and your passengers need to be able to see out of the truck and stay in it until you want to get out, making a dependable windshield wiper and seat belts a must.

For ease of installation and reliability, the New Port Engineering Clean Wipe wiper motor is arguably the best on the market. There is nothing universal about these wipers, as they have a model that is specific to the 1955–1957 trucks and another that is specific to the 1958–1959 trucks.

Electric Wiper Motors

Anyone who has ever driven a vehicle equipped with a vacuum-powered windshield wiper knows that they leave a lot to be desired in some instances and are downright useless in others. And yes, that is what these trucks were equipped with from the factory. For those who do not know, the vacuum wipers worked great when the vehicle's engine was not under a loaded condition. So, if you were just cruising around town, driving down a hill, or coasting, the wipers worked. However, if you were driving up a hill or

Electric Wiper Motor Installation

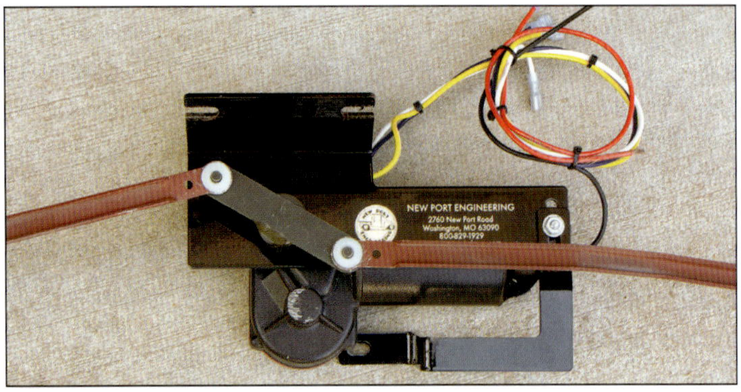

1 *The New Port Engineering Clean Wipe wiper drive mounts in the original location with two screws and an additional support bracket. Slip the linkage arms with the new bushings over the wiper motor transmission arms.*

2 *Route the opposite end of the linkage arms to their respective openings in the cowl and secure each in place with a bezel nut. Install the wiper arms and blades, then make the electrical connections.*

3 *Mount the switch in the desired location in your truck. Connect the power wire to an accessory circuit on the fuse panel, along with a dedicated ground wire to a suitable ground. Connect the remaining wires to the wiper switch according to the wiring instructions provided with the kit.*

4 *Install the windshield washer fluid reservoir in a location that is convenient to fill and the washer pump in a convenient location that is out of the way. Note that the washer pump has an inlet and an outlet. The inlet on the washer pump should be connected to the washer fluid reservoir. The outlet on the washer pump should connect to the nozzles near the windshield.*

at highway speed, they simply did not work.

Of course, the cure for vacuum wipers is an electric windshield wiper motor. If the wiper motor is wired correctly, it does not care how fast or slow your engine is running. The better versions of these for Chevrolet trucks are simply a bolt-in replacement that uses the original wiper transmission arms and some quite simple wiring.

When replacing the original wiper motor, make note of how it is installed, and of any vacuum lines that are attached to it. The vacuum lines must be plugged, as they will no longer be used. The New Port Engineering Clean Wipe wiper drive bolts into the original location. The original wiper switch and the rubber bushings from the end of the linkage arms must be removed.

Mechanical

Remove the existing wiper blades and wiper arms. Install the nylon bushings provided with the kit into the linkage arms. Install the wiper drive mounting bracket directly to the cowl where the original wiper motor was originally located. Do not fully tighten the mounting screws until the support bracket is attached. Attach the support bracket to the factory mounting hole and then tighten all three mounting screws. Connect the wiper linkages to the wiper motor transmission.

Electrical

Install the switch in the desired location. Connect the power wire to an accessory circuit on the fuse panel and the remaining wires to the switch according to the diagram provided with the kit. Be sure to run a dedicated ground wire to the wiper motor. Run the wiper motor on the low speed while watching for any binding or flexing.

Return the wiper motor to the park position and then install the wiper arms and wiper blades. Spray a bit of water onto the windshield to prevent scratching the windshield and then run the wiper motor through several cycles. Check the park position of the wiper blades. If it is not as desired, adjust by removing the wiper blades from the wiper transmissions and repositioning them.

Seat Belts

While there are undoubtedly people who would not wear their seat belts if not legally required to do so, seat belts are a good idea. And as the owner/builder of a vehicle, you

Seat Belt Installation

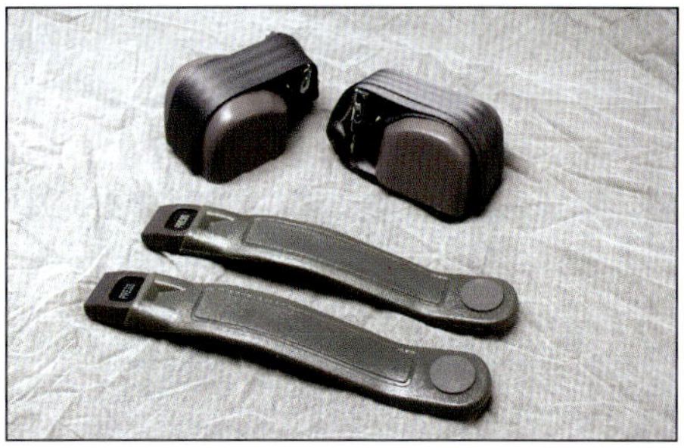

1 *Shown are the three-point retractable seat belts purchased from Juliano's Interior Products. The retractor with the belt wrapped around it mounts at the floor to the exterior of the seating position. The third point will mount to the car in a position above the shoulders. The receptacle for the belt mounts at the floor to the interior of the seating position. The hard-back covers are for use with bucket seats, while a bench seat would not require the covers as the belt would pass between the seat and seat back.*

2 *After checking for clearance on the underside of the floor, I determined that the most suitable location for the seat belt retractor was at the edge of the floor at the door step and in line with the rear seat mounting bolt. The angle bracket is secured to the floor with a 7/16-inch grade-8 bolt that threads into an anchor plate as used for the seats.*

3 *Secure the seat belt retractor to the outside of the angle bracket and the opposite end of the seat belt to the inside of the angle bracket with the same bolt. The loop around the belt and the plastic cover are the third point and will be mounted above the shoulder.*

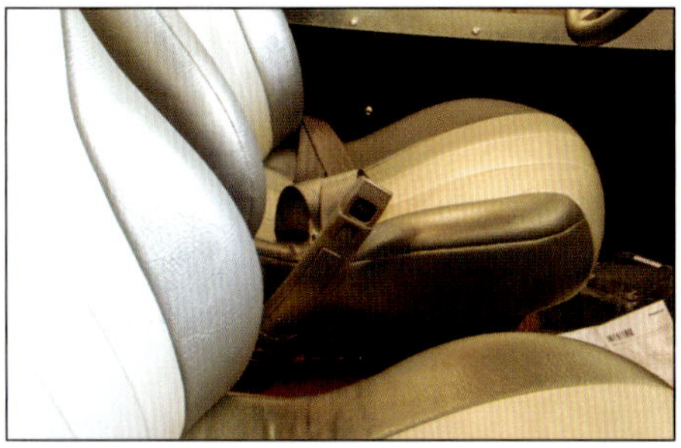

4 *If your seats have the provision for it, the receptacle for the seat belt can be mounted to the seat. The driver's seat in the shop truck has this provision, but the passenger's side does not. They are both secured to an angle bracket that mounts them to the floor with an anchor plate beneath the floor.*

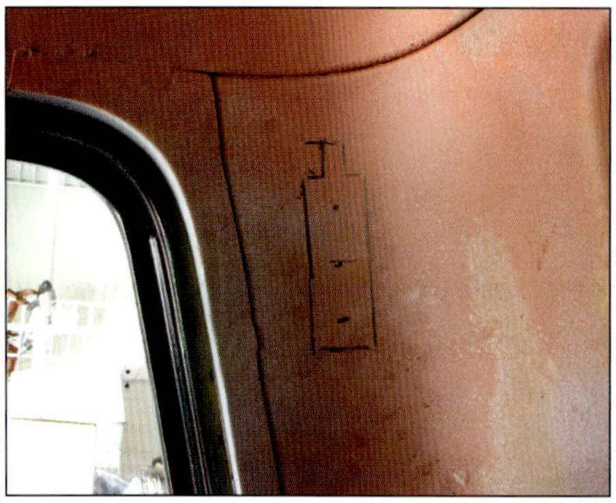

5 *With the seat in place and yours truly sitting in the driver's seat, the location for the third point of the three-point shoulder belt was determined. The perimeter of the mounting plate was outlined on both sides of the inside of the cab.*

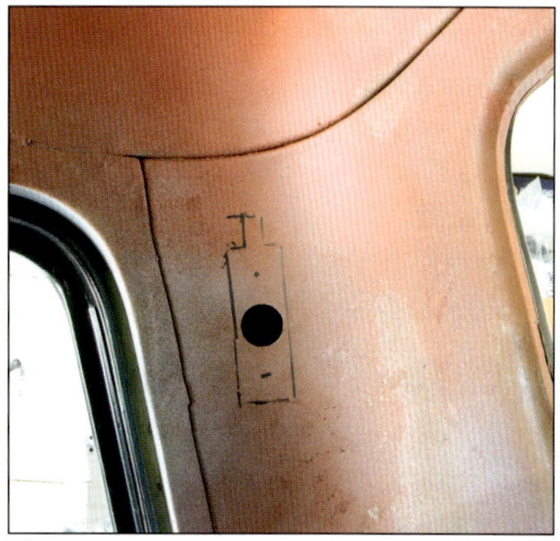

6 *To allow for the length of the mounting bolt a 1¼ inch hole saw was used to drill a recess in the cab's interior wall. The backing plate will be welded in place.*

7 *After welding the third point mount in place, it still needs some grinding before a bit of body filler will be added to smooth up the installation. It admittedly looks pretty rough in this photo, but it will be cleaned up quite a bit prior to being painted.*

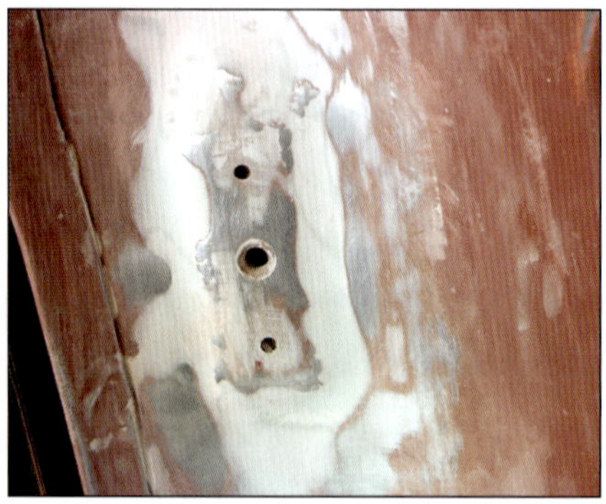

8 *With some body filler, sanding, and tenacity, the B-pillar and seat belt mounting point look considerably better than before. Installing two-point lap belts is much easier, but I personally felt that the increased safety factor of the three-point shoulder belt was worth the effort.*

would simply be remiss by not providing them to anyone driving or riding in your truck.

Seat belts are available in a variety of colors to match or contrast with the interior. Plus, they are easy to install. Avoid buying seat belts from a salvage yard, as you have no idea what conditions the belt fabric has been subjected to or how fatigued it may be. They are priced new at about $100 per seat for a three-point shoulder harness and less for simple lap belts, so they are not expensive.

For lap belts, it is necessary to drill just two holes in the floor pan, slightly behind the back of the seat cushion and the approximate width of each driver's or passenger's seat. On a bench seat, squeeze the middle position a little bit if necessary to make the outer seating positions wide enough to be comfortable. However, the seat belts should not be mounted too far apart, as that could allow some lateral movement

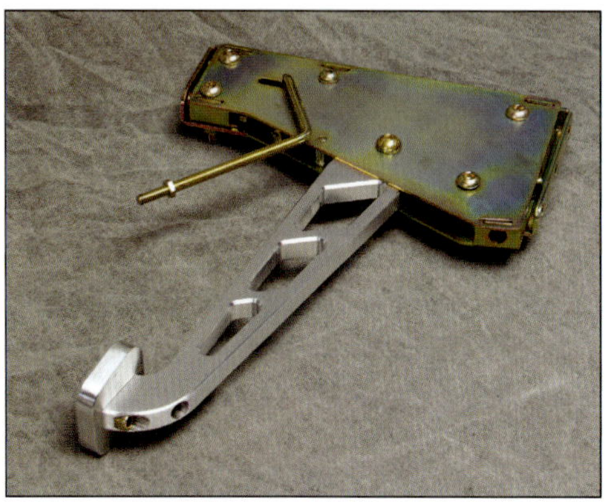

This is the right side of the Lokar underdash emergency brake pedal mechanism. The aluminum arm and pedal pad match the brake and throttle pedals that will be used in the truck. The threaded rod emerging from the slot in the housing is the release mechanism. It must be mounted so that it can slide in the direction of the slot to release the e-brake.

The opposite side of the Lokar underdash emergency brake pedal mechanism shows the adjustable mounting brackets. These mount to the firewall in the front and the dash in the back. With both brackets being adjustable, the actual pedal position can be adjusted also.

of the wearer in the event of an accident. A three-point shoulder harness requires a third hole to be drilled in the "B" pillar just behind the seat that the belt is intended for.

To keep the bolts from pulling through the floor (or door pillar), do not simply attempt to thread the mounting bolts into the floor pan. The floor on these trucks simply is not thick enough to be threaded for use as an anchor for seat belts. Instead, use an anchor plate mounted beneath the floor pan to spread potential stress over a larger area.

Emergency Brake System

While today's brake components, especially disc brakes, are less likely to fail than the stock drum brakes on these trucks, installation of an emergency-brake system is definitely a good idea, even if it is never used for anything more than a parking brake. The emergency brake system is comprised of three basic compo-

Emergency Brake Component Installation

1 *Using the front mounting bracket as a template, locate and drill the three mounting holes in the firewall. Double-check everything on the outside of the firewall to ensure that the mounting bolts will not interfere with anything on the opposite side.*

2 *The triangular-shaped bracket is designed to be mounted to the dash and has a curved mounting slot to allow for different applications. Since the dash is relatively flat in this area, that does not really matter. However, there is a second piece of metal in this area behind the dash, which complicates installation a little bit.*

3 *The next step is to mount the release mechanism. It must move parallel to the mechanism. After designing and fabricating a new bracket to secure the release mechanism, the connector cable can be installed. The cable may be installed with the mechanism installed, but having it out of the truck allows for a much clearer photo of how the connector cable is installed.*

4 *Remove the C-clip retainer from the end of the connector cable, insert the cable into the bottom of the mechanism, and then secure the outer cable to the mechanism by reinstalling the C-clip. With the emergency brake in the OFF position, pull the inner cable out enough so that the ball end can be placed into the clevis.*

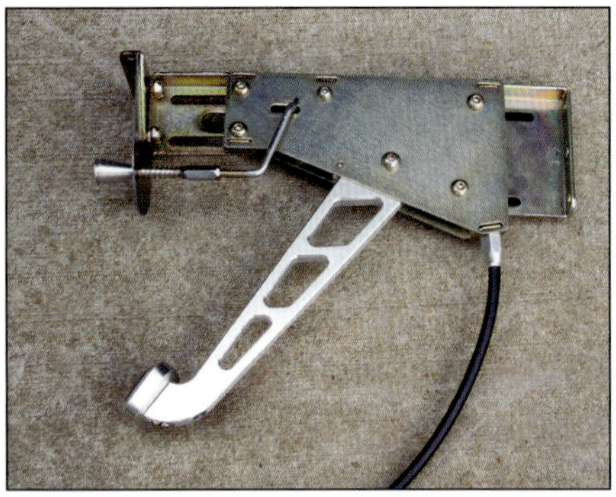

5 With the connector cable, side cover, and release mechanism bracket reinstalled, the e-brake mechanism is ready to be installed in the truck. Three bolts secure the front of the mechanism to the inside firewall with one bolt securing the rear of the mechanism to the underside of the dash.

6 Drill a hole near the dimmer switch location in which to route the connector cable outside of the cab. It will run downward along the front of the cab and then beneath the cab. It will then connect to the single connector cable bracket that is mounted to the frame. There are two individual cables, one to each rear brake.

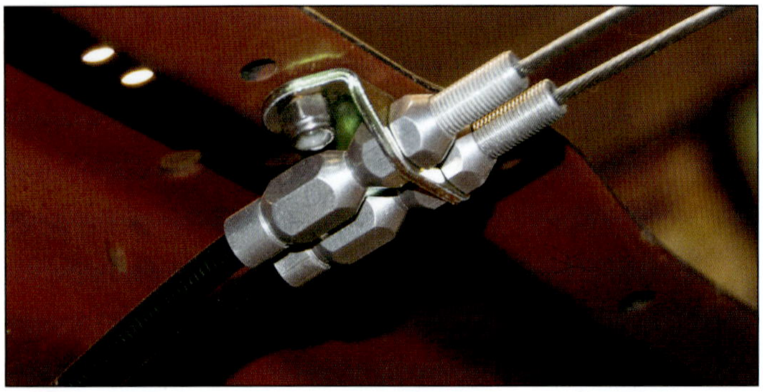

7 Mount the single connector cable bracket to a convenient location on the frame. It must be located so that the pull from it to the double cable adjuster bracket is a straight pull.

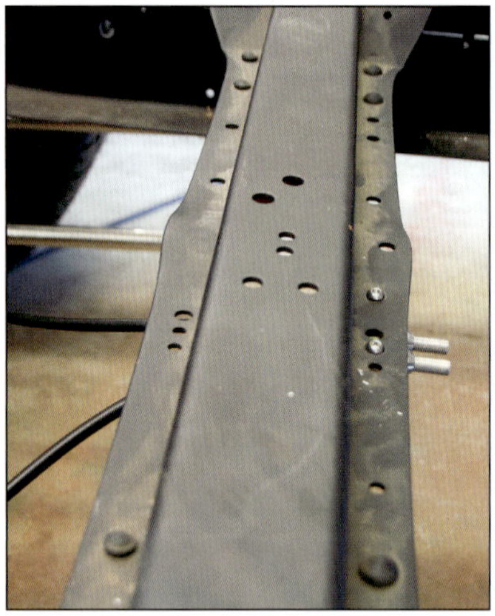

8 Mount the double connector cable bracket to a convenient location on the frame. After slotting the holes just a bit, I was able to install both the single and the double connector cable brackets in the stock holes on different crossmembers, slightly offset from the driveshaft.

9 Remove the inner wire and connect one rear cable to each of the rear brakes and secure with a nut. Route each cable housing to the double cable adjuster bracket and cut the cable housing to the correct length.

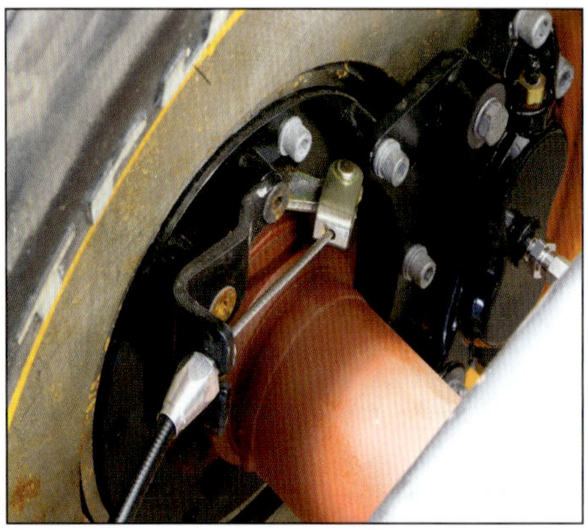

10 This application uses Wilwood disc brakes, which require an additional clevis to connect to the lever that actuates the e-brake. Slip the inner cable through the small holes in the front of the clevis and then run the inner wire through the cable housing.

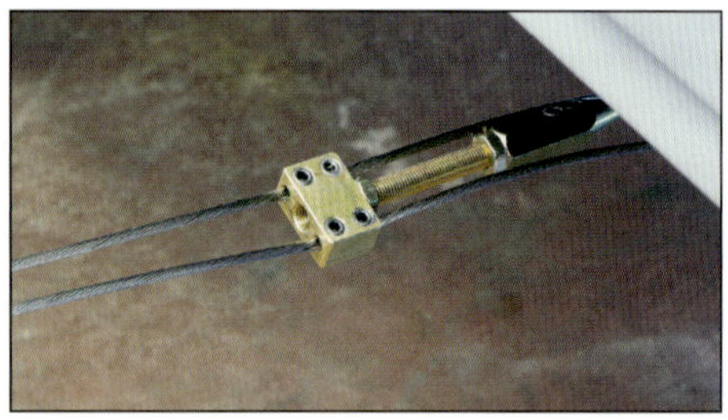

11 Loosen the setscrews in the cable union block, then run each inner wire through it. Pull the inner wire taut and then tighten the setscrews. When you are assembling this for the last time, the inner wire will need to be trimmed in front of the cable union block. This truck will still need to be disassembled for paint and then reassembled, so the inner wires are left plenty long to pull them tight during reassembly.

Making some progress, but there is still plenty to do.

nents: e-brake mechanism, cables, and the actual e-brake apparatus.

The e-brake mechanism is the apparatus used to apply the brake and is usually a pedal or a lever with a release mechanism. If it is actuated via a pedal, it commonly mounts to the firewall somewhere under the dash where it can be reached with the driver's foot. If it is actuated via a lever, the location can be most anywhere, if it is within easy reach of the driver.

The e-brake cables connect the e-brake mechanism to the actual e-brake at the rear wheels. Typically, one cable connects to the mechanism and is routed from inside the cab to some point on the chassis. It then attaches to two separate cables: one for each wheel. There may be additional fittings required to adapt the cables to the e-brake components.

The e-brake apparatus is usually integral to the rear brakes. However, some versions apply a caliper to a disc that is mounted to the pinion yoke of the drivetrain.

Begin the installation by determining just where to install the e-brake mechanism. The Lokar universal version (used in this project) is foot operated, so it must be mounted to the left of the steering column. It will mount to the firewall in the front and to the lower edge of the dash in the rear. The mounting brackets are adjustable, so not only can this mechanism be used in a variety of vehicles but it also allows for horizontal adjustment. This allows the mechanism to be located farther from the driver or closer.

After mounting the mechanism securely in the truck, some adjustments had to be made to the release mechanism. For the release mechanism to work correctly, it must be pulled parallel to the locking mechanism. This called for shortening the threaded rod and then fabricating a mounting bracket that will mount to the lower edge of the dash. You can bend the threaded rod in a couple of places to fabricate a short bracket to hang from the dash or use it as is and fabricate a longer bracket. Of course, this all depends on exactly where you located the e-brake mechanism in the truck.

With the mechanism and release situated, route the single e-brake connector cable beneath the cab toward the rear emergency brake cables. The single cable adjuster bracket must be mounted approximately 9½ inches in front of the double cable adjuster bracket and aligned so that the cables are being pulled in a straight line, rather than at an angle.

Mark the connector cable where it aligns with the cable adjuster. Remove the inner wire prior to cutting the cable housing. Then, cut the connector cable at this mark. Insert the cable housing into the cable adjuster at the single cable adjuster bracket.

Reinstall the inner wire into the cable housing from under the dash. Verify that the brake is in the OFF position and then insert the cable ball into the slot in the clevis on the e-brake mechanism. This will get the front portion of the emergency brake cable to about the middle of the truck.

Cables are now run forward from each rear brake. Actual connections will vary depending on the rear axle housing used, drum brakes versus disc brakes, and other variables. This installation is for Wilwood disc brakes with an integral e-brake. The front cable will ultimately connect to two rear cables.

CHAPTER 6

DRIVETRAIN

This truck is going to be a daily driver, so I will not be afforded the time to keep an engine compartment sparkling. Still, I want it to be detailed. The engine block is painted silver to contrast with the Omaha Orange sheet metal. The valve covers, air cleaner, water pump, and pulley brackets are black to contrast with the engine block. Still, the old gal needs some jewelry, thus the polished aluminum accessories.

If you have not yet decided which engine to install in your Task Force truck, the time has come to decide. Straight six, V-6, small-block, big-block, old school, or modern, all are available and at a variety of price points.

Are you looking for economy, brute horsepower, or something in between? Is your budget a few hundred dollars, a few thousand, or several thousand? There are lots of choices and therefore lots of decisions to make. Most (if not all) of these decisions revolve somewhat around how you will use your truck.

Engine

For those merely wanting some inexpensive transportation, a straight six or a V-6 is a good choice. Depending on the transmission selected to go with it and the rear-end gearing, a smaller-displacement engine can become a very economical commuter or a stump-pulling workhorse. However, a running small-block can probably be purchased just about anywhere for less than a six banger, simply due to the quantity that is available.

If high horsepower is what you are looking for, nothing beats cubic inches. However, small-blocks can probably hold their own if your budget allows for that. From a reliability standpoint, a small-block V-8 probably cannot be beat. They may not be different, but they are everywhere.

Short versus Long; Small versus Big

Two terms to understand when shopping for an engine are "short-block" and "long-block," and they should not be confused with "small-block" and "big-block." A short-block includes the actual block with crankshaft and pistons, while a long-block includes these items plus the heads and valvetrain. Typically, intake and exhaust manifolds and accessories, such as starters and alternators, are not included.

The terms small-block and big-block literally depend on the size

Small-Block Engines			
Engine Displacement (ci)	**Bore (inches)**	**Stroke (inches)**	**Years**
265	3.770	3.000	1955 (no oil filter), 1956–1957
267	3.500	3.480	1979–1982
283	3.875	3.000	1957 (no side motor mounts) 1958–1967 (with multiple versions and casting numbers)
302	4.000	3.000	1967–1969
305	3.750	3.480	1978–1980
307	3.875	3.250	1968–1973
327	4.000	3.250	1962–1969 (with multiple versions and casting numbers)
350	4.000	3.480	1967–1979 (with multiple versions and casting numbers)
400	4.125	3.760	1970–1980 (with multiple versions and casting numbers)
Big-Block Engines			
Engine Displacement (ci)	**Bore (inches)**	**Stroke (inches)**	**Years**
348	4.125	3.250	1958–1964 W-Series (AKA Mark I)
366	3.935	3.760	1960s–2004
396	4.094	3.760	1965–1972
402	4.097	3.760	1970–1972
409	4.310	3.500	1961–1965 W-Series (AKA Mark I)
427	4.310	3.650	1962–1963 W-Series (AKA Mark I)
427	4.250	3.500	1966–1969 Mark IV
454	4.250	4.000	1970–1976 LS, 1991–1995 Generation V, 1996–2000 Vortec 7400
496	4.250	4.037	2001–2009 Vortec 8100
502	4.466	4.000	1991–1995
572	4.560	4.375	1998–2009

Note: Specific casting numbers, stock head information, and original applications for engine blocks are available in several different sources, and therefore are beyond the scope of this publication.

of the basic block that the engine is based upon. A small-block has smaller-diameter cylinders than a big-block, which allows them to be positioned closer together. Therefore, when compared side by side, the size of the block is easily noticeable. Changing the cylinder bore diameter and/or the piston stroke is what allows for the different displacements.

Salvage Yard or Parts Vehicle

When you are merely looking for a running engine to install and get on the road quickly, purchasing a parts vehicle that has the desired drivetrain or purchasing a drivetrain from a salvage yard may be the way to go. A donor vehicle that has been totaled in a collision may have a good drivetrain with low mileage, which would be ideal. It would most likely also have all the necessary brackets, pulleys, and other related items included, which when purchased separately quickly begin adding to the overall cost.

Before purchasing an engine, start it up and look and listen, regardless of what the person selling the engine may have to say. Worn rings or other oil consumption issues are indicated by blue smoke, which is the result of engine oil getting into the combustion chamber. White smoke indicates that a bad head gasket is allowing coolant to get into the combustion chamber. Main bearing or rod wear is indicated by rhythmic noises. These things can be resolved, but they will cost some additional time and money, which may or may not be within the budget.

Compression Check

Running a compression check will also help evaluate the condition of the engine. Begin by running the engine long enough to reach normal operating temperature, then shut it off. Remove all the spark plugs and examine them for obvious signs of burning oil or water getting into the combustion chamber. If the spark plugs are wet or rusty, pass on that engine.

Refer to the appropriate shop manual for the correct compression specification. Then, check the compression by threading the hose of the compression tester into the spark plug hole and attach the hose to the gauge. Crank the engine over and make note of the compression reading. Repeat this process for each cylinder. Compare the readings with the specs in the engine shop manual and proceed as recommended.

If the compression levels are significantly low on all cylinders, the engine needs an overhaul. Low compression in two or more adjacent cylinders indicates a cracked block or head. If the low compression is limited to one cylinder or two non-adjacent cylinders, the issue could be associated to bad rings, valves, or the head gasket.

To determine whether the issue is with the rings or the valves, squirt a bit of oil into the suspect cylinder and check the compression again. If the rings are bad, the compression will come back up to spec temporarily because of the oil that was added. If the valves are bad, the compression reading will stay the same.

With this bit of testing, you can better assess whether the engine is enough for your needs or if potential repair expenses make it beyond economical repair. This also depends largely on your abilities as an engine rebuilder and the associated resources for the work that you cannot perform yourself. This might come into play if you are looking for some nostalgic engine that might be a bit out of the ordinary for your truck project, such as a 500-ci Cadillac, Oldsmobile Rocket, or a Buick Nailhead engine.

Rebuilt Engine

Depending on what is available in your area, a rebuilt engine might be a good choice. It might cost a bit more than an engine from a salvage yard or a donor car. However, why pay for a complete donor car if all that you need is the engine and drivetrain? In some instances, especially with homeowner's associations these days, getting rid of the unneeded parts may negate any potential savings.

Other than some accessories and dress-up items, a rebuilt engine should be complete and ready to run. However, do not let a freshly painted engine sitting on an engine stand get the best of you. Just as with any engine purchase, listen to it run. Again, watch for smoke and leaks while listening for anything that sounds odd. If things get iffy, a compression check as described previously will answer some questions.

Of course, purchasing an engine directly from a reputable rebuilder is the best bet, whether that is a nationwide company or a local rebuilder. However, answering a classified advertisement in the local newspaper or community bulletin board could potentially be a risky deal. The engine might be freshly rebuilt, but that does not mean that it was rebuilt properly. Do not hesitate to ask some questions, such as where the parts are from and the name of the machine shop that may have done any machine work.

Crate Engine

With an automotive aftermarket that is flourishing and the resultant competitive prices on crate engines, this option is probably as good as it gets. Everything from short-blocks to complete engines are available in a wide variety of displacements.

If available finances dictate how much can be spent at one time, a short-block will be less expensive to purchase up front. Then, add the heads and other required items as finances allow. This also allows you to purchase the specific items that you want for your engine. It simply does

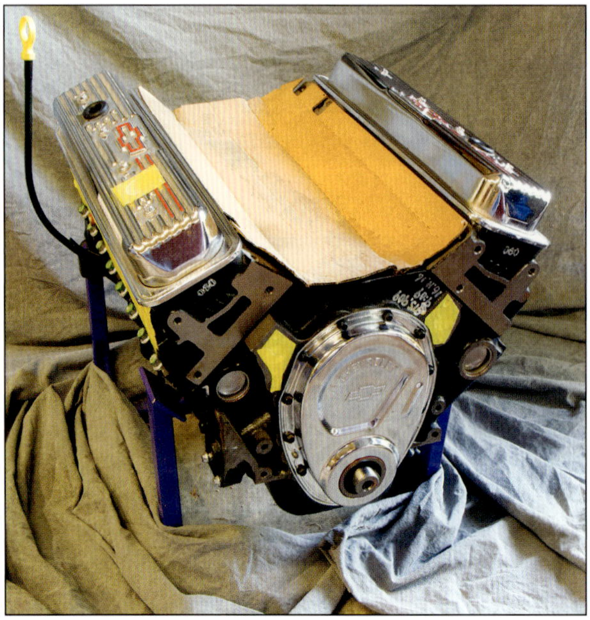

After I purchased a 290-hp Chevy 350 for the shop truck, I had the good fortune of winning a 330-hp Chevy 350 in a raffle. Thank you, Shelby's Way! Other than an extra 40 hp, this crate motor includes the newer Vortec heads along with chrome valve covers and timing chain cover. This one will ultimately go into a 1940 Chevrolet Business Coupe project.

not make sense to buy a complete engine, to then replace the heads, intake, aspiration, and dress-up items.

The engine for my shop truck is a 290-hp 350 long-block directly from GM Performance Parts for a price of $2,300. To complete the engine, I purchased an intake manifold, carburetor, headers, an alternator, a distributor and coil, a harmonic balancer, pulleys, a starter, water pump, spark plugs, and filters and gaskets, which brought the total to around $5,600.

Regardless of how pretty or shiny the parts are, with almost any engine, additional parts are going to be required. If not for the glitter, the required parts could be purchased for about $1,000 less. It's your choice. That price does include some nicer-looking components to dress up the engine substantially. While the truck is not going to be a show vehicle by any means, I still want the engine to look nice when I open the hood. That does not mean that everything needs to be chrome.

As a magazine photographer, I will tell you that an engine decked out with chrome or polished aluminum everything is very boring and shows little initiative. A very nicely detailed engine will get more sincere compliments from most folks who know anything about hot rods. Again, good taste works wonders toward dressing up the engine compartment.

Cleaning

Unless you buy a complete engine, you will most likely need to install some of the components on it. Even if they are already installed, many of them will need to be removed to paint the engine.

Speaking of which, to have a nice, clean, beautifully detailed engine compartment, you need a nice, clean, and painted engine. Many engines have simply been taken to the local car wash, shot with the degreaser cycle, rinsed off, and treated to a fresh paint job with the spray bomb color of the owner's choice. While there may be a right time for that (such as when buying a salvage yard motor), there is a better way.

The first thing to do is remove any accessories or other components that are not going to be painted. Then, seal off any openings in the engine. With a pressure washer (if available), spray the entire engine, and transmission if attached, with a degreasing solution from the local auto parts store. Start spraying from the bottom and work up so that no areas are missed.

After applying the degreaser, allow it to soak a little bit, and then rinse it off. If this does not get the block clean, repeat the process. Stubborn areas may require some scraping or brushing to remove stubborn grease and dirt buildup.

When the engine looks clean, mount it on a suitable engine stand for paint and assembly. Pour some wax and grease remover into a spray bottle, and starting at the bottom again, spray the wax and grease remover onto the entire engine block and/or transmission. Using paper shop towels, wipe off the surface and then use a second towel to wipe it dry. You will be surprised at how much dirt will be on the first towel. Then, use an air hose with a nozzle to blow away any wax and grease remover that may remain.

Engine/Transmission Prime and Paint

While the engine and transmission must withstand hotter temperatures than the truck's sheet metal, today's automotive primers and paints are up to the task. A great thing about this is that the paint on

This is a 290-hp Chevrolet 350 crate motor that has just received two coats of epoxy primer prior to being painted. Regardless of what you are looking for from an engine, new GM crate motors are a great value. From basic long-blocks to complete engines, the prices are certainly competitive with having an engine built.

the engine can match the paint on the truck if you desire. The important part is getting the engine and transmission clean before applying primer and paint.

With that task done, mask off anything that should not be primed or painted with automotive paint–grade masking tape. Apply two or three coats of epoxy primer, following the specific instructions for the primer product being used. After allowing the appropriate flash time for the epoxy primer, apply two or three coats of paint in the color of your choice.

Engine Accessory Installation

Even complete long-block engines typically do not include an intake manifold, so that makes a good place to start. Besides, the intake manifold will need to be installed prior to the distributor and carburetor. Verify that the intake manifold bolt holes, cylinder head flanges, and end seal surfaces are all clean.

A new crate motor will typically be clean in these areas, but a used motor will need to be checked to ensure that any previous gasket material is removed. Using a light and a wire, verify that all internal passages are not obstructed.

Intake Manifold

Set the intake manifold gaskets in place, just to verify that mounting holes line up and nothing is amiss. When that all checks out, remove the gaskets. Then, apply a bead of red RTV sealant to the mounting surface of the cylinder head and to the bottom side of the intake manifold gasket. Allow the RTV sealant time to become tacky.

Set the intake manifold in place, then loosely install all the mounting bolts to verify that the intake and engine still align properly. If using stainless-steel bolts, be sure to dab on a bit of anti-seize compound on the bolts before starting them.

After all the bolts are started, following the correct sequence, tighten them to the appropriate torque specification. This information will be provided with the intake manifold. Use Teflon tape on any pipe plugs and fittings.

Thermostat

Install the thermostat by merely setting it in place at the water inlet. Verify that the thermostat is installed right side up and then install the thermostat housing. Some housings require sealant while others have an O-ring and do not require sealant. Apply sealant if required and then secure the thermostat housing to the intake with two bolts.

Carburetor

If not present, install four carburetor studs. Note that these have different threads on each end. One end specifically goes into the intake manifold, while the other end is specifically for the nuts that secure the carburetor. Install a new carburetor gasket, set the carburetor in place, and secure it with a nut on each stud.

Distributor

If you are replacing a distributor in a used engine, first determine which cylinder is at top dead center (TDC) and how the distributor is positioned. Match that with the new distributor. There will be instructions for doing that with the new distributor; therefore, to avoid any confusion, they will not be included here.

On a crate motor, cylinder number-1 will be at TDC. For all intents and purposes, the distributor can be installed at any position, if the spark plug wire is run from the rotor's current position to cylinder number-1. Install the supplied gasket over the shaft of the distributor, apply the supplied lubricant to the gear, and then insert the distributor into the engine block until it fully seats.

The distributor will rotate slightly as the gears mesh. If the distributor does not fully seat, it may be necessary to use a long, thin screwdriver to rotate the oil pump shaft

While they may be commonplace and boring to some, a good 4-barrel carburetor will get you home, unless you just flat-out run out of gas. I went with the electric choke, merely out of convenience. Another common alternative is electronic fuel injection (EFI), which may replace this carburetor in a few years.

The standard GM high energy ignition (HEI) distributor is huge since it encloses the coil inside the top of the distributor cap. For the same benefits (getting rid of points and condenser) in a more condensed package, I chose the MSD Pro-Billet Ready-to-Run Distributor. The smaller distributor cap will also provide a bit more clearance near the firewall.

Yes, it must be a small-block if the carburetor reaches almost side to side. Several openings in the intake manifold allow for hose routing options. Unused holes will need to be capped with pipe plugs. Do not forget to wrap them with Teflon tape first.

The distributor must be adjustable to achieve the proper timing, but then it must be clamped down to retain that timing. The polished aluminum yoke that fits around the distributor shaft is the distributor hold-down clamp. It does not have to be shiny to work, but it is pretty.

Unlike a GM HEI distributor that has an integral coil, the MSD Ready-To-Run uses a standard-style coil. It will be mounted on the firewall in a vertical orientation. Power from the ignition switch and the red wire to the distributor both connect to the coil's positive terminal. The orange wire to the distributor connects to the negative terminal.

slightly, then reinstall the distributor. Repeat as necessary until the distributor fully seats. Then, install a distributor hold-down clamp by pressing the concave portion against the distributor shaft and then securing the clamp to the block with a bolt. If installed, remove the distributor cap to determine where the rotor is currently located.

Using a permanent marker, make a small line on the distributor housing for reference when installing the spark plug wires. While it may be easier to install the spark plug wires while the engine is on the stand, it may be better to wait to install them after the engine is installed in the truck. You do not necessarily need extra stuff in the way when lifting an engine with a hoist.

Spark Plug Wires

Whenever the spark plug wires are installed, refer to a repair manual for the engine being used to verify the firing order. Begin by verifying the gap of the spark plugs is correct for the application and install the spark plugs in the engine.

Route the spark plug wire from

the cylinder currently at TDC to the current location of the distributor rotor. Then, route a plug wire from the next firing position of the distributor to the appropriate cylinder. Repeat until all cylinders have a plug wire to the correct location in the distributor.

Unless you purchased spark plug wires that require being cut to length and then crimping on the terminal, the plug wires will all be different lengths. Use the longest wire to go the longest distance between cylinder and distributor.

It is probably easiest to then use the next-longest wire to connect the next-farthest cylinder to the correct terminal on the distributor. However, remember that the next-longest plug wire cannot simply connect to the next position on the distributor. The spark plug wires must connect to the correct cylinder in the correct firing order. A plug wire will also need to connect the center stud on the distributor to the coil. This wire will have a different type of terminal on the end that connects to the coil.

Valve Covers

Although a long-block engine comes with valve covers installed, this is usually the first thing that people replace purely for aesthetic reasons. However, the original valve covers do come in handy when priming and painting the engine. Remove the existing valve covers and gaskets. Verify that all gasket material is removed.

Lay the new gaskets and valve covers in place to verify that all mounting holes line up. Remove the valve cover, then apply a bead of RTV sealant to top side of the valve cover gasket and to the lower side of the valve cover. Set the valve cover in place and secure with the correct hardware.

Harmonic Balancer

When purchasing a crate motor and some rebuilt motors, the harmonic balancer is not included, so one will need to be installed. Clean the threads in the end of the crankshaft and use a tap to chase the threads if necessary. Install the replacement harmonic balancer according to the instructions that come with it to avoid causing any damage to the crankshaft.

Lubricate the threads of the bolt, including the area under the head of the bolt. Then, lubricate the front face of the balancer where the washer contacts it. Slide the washer onto the bolt, thread the bolt into the crankshaft, and then tighten to the specified torque specification.

Water Pump

Another necessity is the water pump, but it is an easy installation. However, if you are using a small-block Chevy engine, decide early on whether you are using a long pump or a short pump. Either one will work fine, but pulleys and brackets for accessories such as the

Close scrutiny will reveal that the water pump in this photo is a long pump, meaning that it sits away from the engine about 3/4 inch. That should not present a major problem; however, I meant to purchase a short pump. I did not notice my mistake until I began mounting the brackets for the alternator and A/C compressor.

In keeping with a simple but good-looking engine, these valve covers from Billet Specialties made the cut. The black finish will contrast nicely with the silver paint of the engine block.

With a little bit of jewelry in the form of polished aluminum breathers, the black-and-silver color scheme is not looking bad. This breather will be completed by connecting a vacuum hose to the back of the carburetor.

The harmonic balancer (AKA damper) mounts to this front end of the crankshaft. When installing, be sure to use plenty of lubricant and avoid getting the harmonic balancer on crooked. Avoid using a hammer to drive it on directly. If a hammer is required, use a block of wood or something that is larger than the balancer.

With the harmonic balancer and water pump installed, it will not be too long before an alternator bracket, pulleys, and belts can be installed. Just do not get too carried away tightening the upper bolts of the water pump, as they commonly secure the alternator and A/C compressor brackets as well.

alternator and A/C compressor are not interchangeable.

Since the long pump sticks out from the engine roughly 3/4 inch farther, most hot rodders go with the short pump just to be on the safe side regarding overall engine length. While the front fenders are far enough apart to install just about anything, the firewall-to-radiator distance can fill up quickly.

Since a lot of accessory brackets mount off the water pump, have those brackets in hand when installing the water pump. Depending on which aftermarket brackets are used, they may go on in a different order to obtain the correct belt alignment.

External Engine Assembly

1 *The Edelbrock intake manifold offers several optional locations for a water temperature sensor. Do not forget to install block-off plugs in any openings that are not used. The A/C compressor and alternator brackets are from Alan Grove Components and will be painted black to follow the paint scheme for the engine.*

2 *These brackets will install their respective components in close to the engine. With the wide berth of the engine compartment in a Task Force truck, an option would be to use brackets that space things a lot farther to each side.*

3 *The alternator fan is secured to the alternator with one bolt from the factory. If the pulley should ever need to be changed on the alternator, such as the pulley for a serpentine belt and you are running V-belts or vice versa, the simplest way is to use an impact wrench with the correct-size socket.*

4 *Another option is to install an aftermarket pulley, such as this one from Billet Specialties. Small details like this do as much or more to dress up an engine compartment than polishing a bunch of large, high-dollar items.*

5 *Of course, an aluminum alternator pulley calls for an aluminum nose cone. Do not go just halfway when it comes to detailing. Do not forget to dab a bit of anti-seize on the stainless-steel fasteners.*

6 *Although they may be a bit more expensive, if purchasing pulleys for a rebuilt or salvage yard engine, you might as well buy ones that are indeed round and balanced. Not all, but many aftermarket dress-up components are not balanced.*

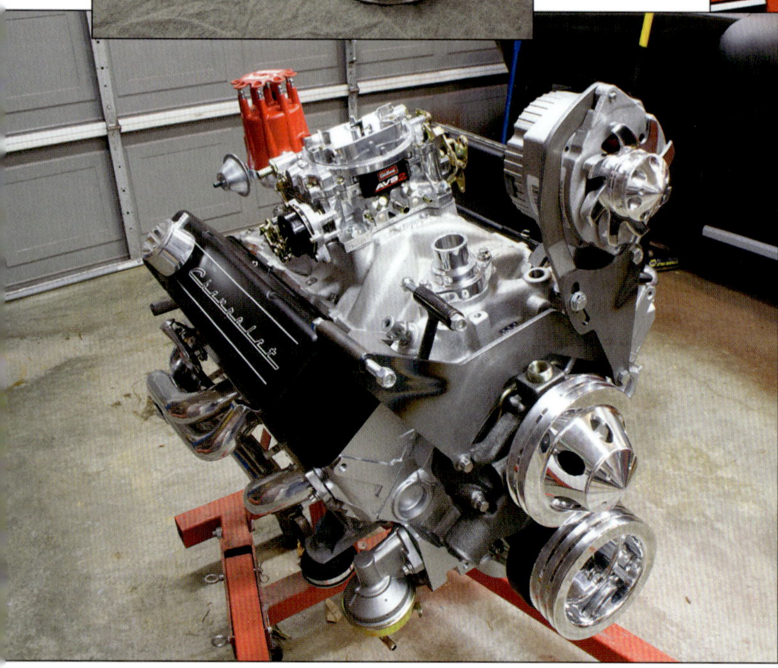

7 *The future installation of the A/C compressor will ultimately balance out the looks of the engine. With the installation of belts, spark plug wires, and connection to a radiator, we would not be far from hearing this engine run.*

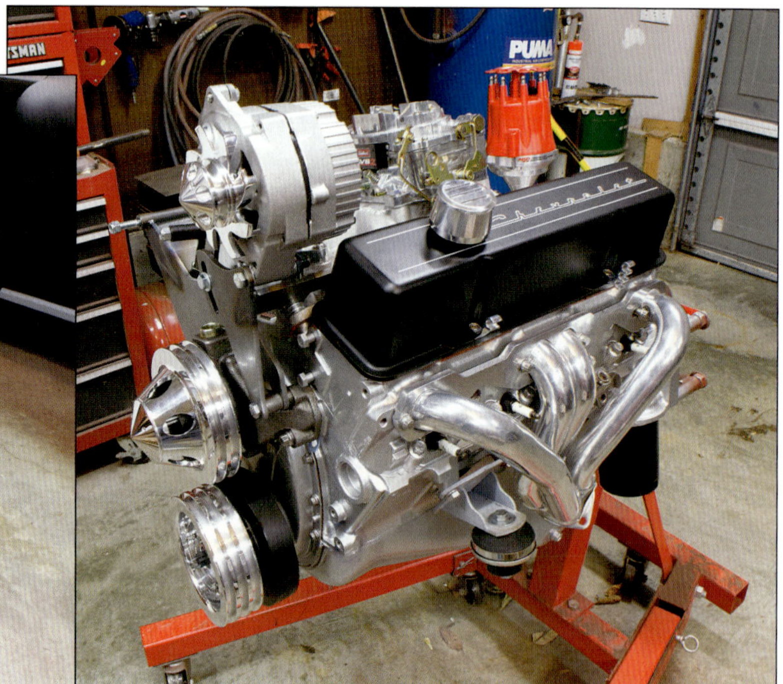

8 *The headers are from Sanderson (model CC56) and are designed specifically for these trucks with a small-block Chevy engine. Unlike years ago, the automotive aftermarket has realized that trucks are cool and are strongly supporting those of us who are building them.*

9 *The mounting holes for the power steering pump bracket required being chased with a tap to clear the threads. This should be done to all mounting holes on a painted engine block.*

10 *Using a belt left over from another project, I checked the alignment of the pulleys. When all the pulleys are installed, a collection of belts will be checked for the best fit. If you have a good rapport with your local auto parts store manager, he or she may let you bring a collection of belts home and then return the ones that do not fit.*

11 *This is the power steering pump that will be used in the shop truck project. It is for a 1986–1993 S-10 4-cylinder and is what works best for the Billet Specialties power steering bracket and reservoir that I chose to use. Compact size is a good thing.*

Transmission

Purchasing a transmission for your truck project is along the same lines as purchasing an engine. The big difference is that you cannot "hear it run," unless it is in an operable vehicle. Therefore, you cannot really determine how well it shifts, which is really the sole purpose for having a transmission.

Salvage Yard or Parts Vehicle

Perhaps the best deal for a salvage yard purchase is one where the engine and the transmission come as a matched set. If you are able to inspect the vehicle that the drivetrain came out of, you stand a better chance of knowing how many miles are on it and perhaps how well (or poorly) it may have been maintained.

While you do not run a compression check on a used transmission, there are other things for which to look. Begin by visually inspecting the transmission, looking for any cracks in the case or broken mounting locations. If the donor vehicle was in an accident, there could be physical damage to the case that would make it impossible to use or repair.

Look for buildup of fluid around the pan gasket. Pull the transmission dipstick and then look at and smell the transmission fluid on the end. If the fluid looks clean, it is probably okay. However, if the fluid is thick or smells burnt, it needs to be rebuilt.

Even if there is no engine connected to the transmission, you can shift the transmission through the gears, whether it is a manual or an automatic. Verify that the shifter will go into all gears smoothly. Just remember that transmission repair work is expensive. So, if you install a used transmission in your truck and then break down away from home, it is going to be an expensive repair.

Rebuilt

A better alternative might be to purchase a rebuilt transmission from the get-go. However, while you may be able to purchase the transmission that you are looking for, it might not be built specifically for the way that you drive or how you plan to use your truck. It may be sufficient but not necessarily optimal. Whether the rebuild was designed for a four-door sedan or a hot street car, it probably is not exactly what you would want for your truck.

If you consider this rebuild route, check with a transmission shop before buying anything to see how much a rebuilt transmission will cost. They will ask about the kind of vehicle it is going into, the type of engine and horsepower, and other questions regarding how you plan to drive your truck. If they have a case available, then a transmission can be essentially custom built for your truck for a lot less money than a new transmission.

However, the shop may not have a case for the specific transmission you want. Then, you will need to find one to be rebuilt. If the transmission requires a rebuild, the case can usually be purchased relatively cheaply. Then, take it to a transmission shop to have it rebuilt.

Most shops that specialize in transmission rebuilds can probably complete it in less than a week, presuming that it is out of the vehicle. The labor of removing and reinstalling the transmission in the vehicle is what takes the most time and therefore is the most expensive.

New

While a new transmission may sound ideal, it will most assuredly be more expensive than a rebuilt transmission. Also, it will be built to the factory specifications, not to what you may specifically want or desire. A rebuilt transmission from a reputable transmission rebuilder will typically be every bit as good as a new one but less expensive.

Motor and Transmission Mount Installation

There are motor mounts of some kind mounted on each frame rail, either welded in place or bolted on. There is also the corresponding portion of that mount that bolts to the engine with a cushion in between the two when fully assembled. In similar fashion, there is a transmission crossmember that spans from one frame rail to the other. It too has a corresponding cushion that bolts to the transmission.

For ease of installation, secure the motor mounts to the engine before it goes into the truck. This allows better access for tightening the bolts. Since the transmission crossmember typically has slotted holes, secure the cushion to the transmission. After installing the engine and transmission, the transmission can be bolted tight to the transmission crossmember where it best fits.

I was able to find and purchase a 700R4 transmission core for $80. For an additional $900, two days later I had a completely rebuilt transmission and a new torque converter. The case can use a bit of additional detailing, primer, and paint.

Engine and Transmission Installation

Some instances and situations may require installing the transmission to the engine while the engine is already in the truck. However, in a complete buildup, it is probably easier to connect the transmission to the engine and install them as one assembly.

Whether the connection is made out of the truck or in, to marry the engine and automatic transmission together, first secure the flexplate to the engine and the torque converter to the transmission. Verify that the torque converter is fully seated on the transmission shaft. For manual transmissions, the torque convertor is essentially replaced by the clutch plate and bellhousing.

Since the shop truck is a frame-off rebuild and to make drivetrain installation much easier, the front sheet metal and radiator were removed. There was no need to take a chance on damaging expensive parts. Still, it is a good idea to have an assistant

To align the engine and the transmission, I used two of the long bolts from the engine stand. They served as an extra set of hands to pull the two components together until the other bolts were started. Just in case anybody wonders, the flexplate and torque converter were not installed at this time. I had the wrong flexplate and could not get the correct one in time for the photos. It all must come back out later for primer and paint, so all is good.

I took my time and used a floor jack beneath the tailshaft of the transmission to guide the way to install the engine and transmission. Note that the frame is up on jack stands to provide plenty of clearance beneath the truck.

The small-block fits great with the stock firewall; however, a big-block installation might require some modification to the firewall.

Using a set of Sanderson headers designed for these trucks and a similarly designed steering column from ididit, there is no interference between steering and exhaust.

or two during this operation. One to raise or lower the engine hoist and one person on each side to guide the engine/transmission into position.

Since the drivetrain is going to be suspended from a cantilevered hoist, swinging engine weight should be limited. Safety is important. That said, I was able to install the transmission onto the engine block, and then install the combined assembly into the truck myself with an engine hoist and two floor jacks. Having at least one other person would have made the task much easier.

Shifter Linkage

Connecting the shifter linkage to the transmission will vary depending on the location of the shifter: column mount or floor shifter. Typically, a floor shifter is easier to connect, as the component parts are physically closer together and move in the same general direction: forward or backward. For a column shift, it gets a little more complicated. Movement of the shifter rotates about the steering column and must ultimately turn a shaft that rotates 90 degrees in a different direction.

Throttle Cable and Pedal Assembly

To install the throttle cable, the throttle pedal must first be installed in a location in the cab where it will be comfortable for the driver. Since this is essentially a custom-built vehicle, there is a bit of latitude for this loca-

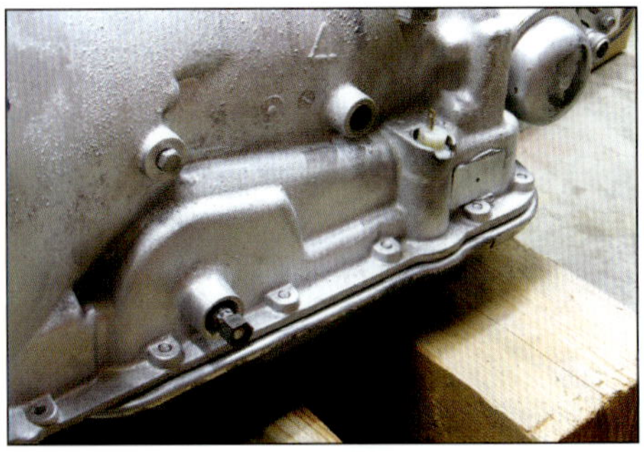

Two important connections are located on the driver's side of the 700R4/4L60 transmission. The horizontal shaft with the nut on it is where the shift lever connects. Multiple types of connections are available for both column-shift and floor-shift applications. The vertical cylinder with the electrical spade is for connecting 12-volt power.

Two important connections are also located on the opposite side of the transmission as well. The small hole on the left of the photo is where the kickdown (AKA a tv cable) connects on the transmission. The larger hole at the right is for the transmission fluid dipstick.

tion. The throttle cable between the throttle pedal and the carburetor does not and should not be in a direct line. However, the throttle cable must exit the cab where the pedal mechanism aligns with the front of the cab. If the cable connection of the pedal is at a different level than where the cable exits the cab, that cable will begin to saw through the sheet metal.

Mount the pedal assembly so that the pedal arm where the throttle cable connects touches the front interior of the cab. Then, drill a hole in the cab's sheet metal for the throttle cable to pass through. Make the necessary connections to the fuel induction system.

Install the throttle and/or kickdown cable brackets to the fuel induction system. In this application, cables are from Lokar and are designed for use on a 700R4 automatic transmission and a carbureted engine. Lokar has great instructions with their products, so follow them as written and it will work great.

When using an automatic transmission, a kickdown cable is also required. The lower end of it connects to a stiff wire in the transmission and then slides into the transmission much like a dipstick. Be sure to secure the kickdown cable to the transmission.

Kickdown Cable

Prior to connecting the kickdown cable, the throttle cable must be properly adjusted. Verify that the throttle is indeed wide open when the throttle pedal is fully depressed. With the throttle adjusted correctly, slide the kickdown throttle body fitting onto the kickdown cable and connect it to the throttle linkage. With the throttle wide open, pull the kickdown cable as tight as possible, slide the cable end stop against the kickdown throttle body fitting, and tighten the setscrew that secures it in place.

The kickdown cable is then routed to the induction system, where it ultimately ties into the throttle mechanism. A cable end stop is required at the end of the kickdown cable.

Driveshaft Measurement and Installation

It is obvious that the driveshaft connects the transmission to the rear axle housing. What is not so obvious is that it should possibly be the last major component to buy for your soon-to-be-drivable Task Force truck. While aluminum is a little more expensive, it is lighter, which will help to minimize any driveline vibration.

The driveshaft is bolted solidly to the pinion of the rear axle third member and is allowed to slip somewhat into the transmission. This slip fit is necessary to allow for suspension travel while driving. For this reason, it is essential to have the full weight of the vehicle on the

Transmission shafts have different diameters and splines from one model to another, so it is necessary to know which transmission you have when purchasing a driveshaft.

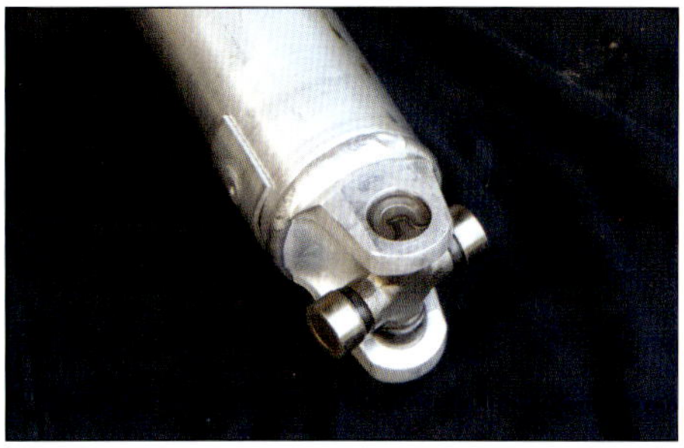

Pinion yokes are different sizes also, so the shop building or modifying your driveshaft must know which rear axle housing and differential is being used.

suspension when measuring for the driveshaft.

Support the rear axle with jack stands or ramps to raise the rear axle housing enough to accurately measure. If you have a transmission yoke, slide it all the way into the transmission and then pull it back out 1 inch. Then, measure the distance between the centerline of the front universal joint to the flat surface where the universal joint retaining bolts mount to the pinion yoke.

If you do not use a transmission yoke, measure from the end of the transmission case to the flat surface where the universal joint retaining bolts mount to the pinion yoke. In either situation, exactly where you measured to must be communicated to the person building the driveshaft. The shop making the driveshaft must also know the width and cap diameter of the universal joint at the pinion yoke on the rear axle housing.

To install the driveshaft, slide the transmission yoke into the transmission. If the universal joint U-bolts are installed on the pinion yoke, remove them. Position the rear universal joint in the pinion yoke and secure with the universal joint U-bolts. Do not overtighten the nuts that secure the U-bolts, as this often leads to universal joint failure. Also, be sure to lube the grease fittings on the universal joints.

Exhaust Mounting

A major consideration in the design of the exhaust system is where to terminate the exhaust tips. There are three basic locations, each with their own variables. These basic locations are out the rear, to the side in front of the rear wheels, and turned down below the bed.

For the rear exit, the exhaust should be routed up and over the rear axle housing. This can certainly be done, but it may be a bit more complicated, especially if you are creating a custom exhaust. The choices also include the tips to be spaced close together or farther apart. To exit behind the wheels, route the exhaust up and over the rear axle housing, which will result in several sharp bends close together.

To exit in front of the wheels is simple. Merely come back out of the exhaust manifold or headers, through the mufflers, then out to the side at an angle or perpendicular. Even simpler yet is to mount turndowns right after the mufflers.

A must, however, is that the exhaust tips be to the rear of any openings in the cab to prevent any exhaust fumes from entering the passenger compartment. For instance, on a pickup truck, the exhaust could terminate anywhere under the bed. On a panel truck or Suburban, the exhaust tips would be required to terminate somewhere beyond the rear doors.

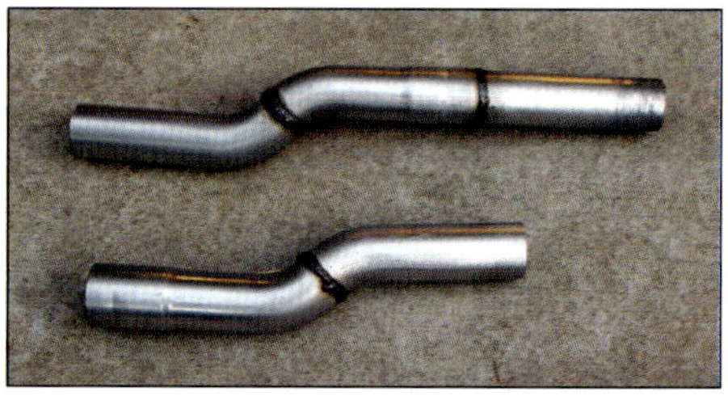

Using a universal exhaust tubing kit, 2.5-inch tubing was used to connect the Sanderson headers to the mufflers. The S-curve was created to get beneath the transmission crossmember.

Magnaflow mufflers were chosen for their sound. These pass straight through, making routing convenient for a home installation. They will be clamped to the exhaust tubing on both ends.

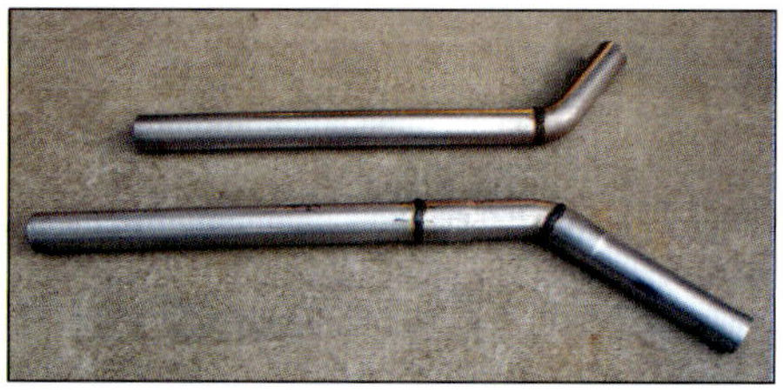

To the rear of the mufflers, exhaust pipe will run straight back and then turn approximately 45 degrees to exit in front of the rear tires. After installation, the pipes will be cut to the exact length, thermal coated, and reinstalled.

CHAPTER 7

ADDITIONAL SYSTEMS

We all know that the engines in our trucks require fuel. That means that they also require a fuel tank, a supply line to the engine, and a pump to move fuel to the engine.

Fuel System

On a simple carbureted engine, a single fuel line from the fuel tank to a mechanical fuel pump that is driven by the engine works well. Quite simply, if the engine will turn over, it will pump fuel. A second fuel line continues from the fuel pump to the carburetor.

On fuel-injected motors, the fuel system usually calls for two lines between the tank and the engine: a pressurized supply line and a non-pressurized return line. An electric fuel pump, commonly mounted in the tank, is used to push the fuel.

Two other things are worth mentioning regarding the fuel system. One applies specifically to the fuel level gauge, while the other applies to the fuel pump. Ensure that the fuel level gauge and the fuel level sender are compatible. Long story short: if they are not compatible, you will get incorrect readings.

An electric fuel pump and an electric fuel gauge must be grounded to work properly. Ground studs will be discussed later, but you should know that an inadequate ground is a common culprit with the poor operation of either of these components.

Stock Fuel Tank

When using the stock fuel tank, verify that it is not full of rust and debris. If it is full of rust, discard it, as it is impossible to get all the rust out of it. If it is not full of rust, dispose of any fuel that is in it. If it is a completely empty tank, check it for leaks.

A simple process for checking any fuel tank for leaks is to place the tank on sawhorses or something similar so that you can see all around it. Squirt a bit of dishwashing liquid into the tank and then fill the tank with water. If you do not see any leaks within about 15 minutes, direct compressed air into the tank. If no leaks appear, the tank is acceptable for use. If the tank has leaks but you are still set on using a stock-style tank, they are available new from a variety of sources.

Aftermarket Fuel Tank

Two different aftermarket fuel tanks are commonly used in these trucks and fit nicely between the frame rails behind the rear axle.

Whether constructing a custom gas tank or testing an old tank for leaks, a proven method is to fill the tank with water. If it has major leaks, you will know right away. If it passes this first test, squirt a bit of liquid dish soap into the tank, and then use an air hose and nozzle to force air into the tank. If there are leaks, the dish soap will cause them to bubble.

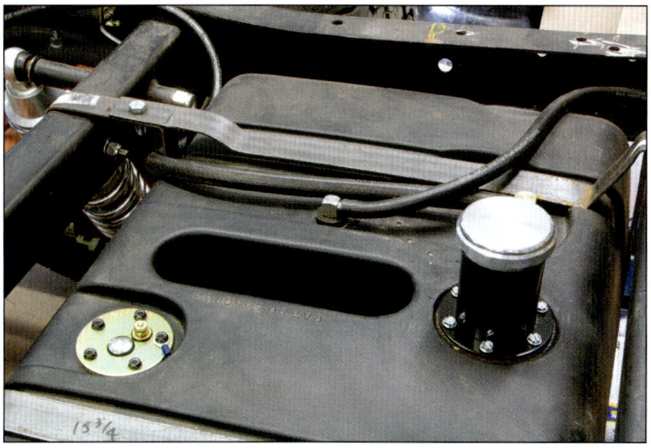

A variety of fuel tanks (OEM and aftermarket) have been used successfully to replace the original behind-the-seat gas tank. Aftermarket tanks that work include some made of steel and some made of molded plastic. Regardless of what type of fuel tank you use, it will require three additional items: a filler neck, a fuel gauge sender, and a supply line (and sometimes a return line) to the engine.

This is a fuel level float and sender mechanism for an electric fuel gauge. The black float is affixed to an adjustable arm. The arm adjustment is to compensate for the depth of the tank. The extra length of the arm has been removed.

The top of the fuel level float is typically secured to the tank with five or six screws that also secure a gasket. The wire that provides a signal to the electric fuel gauge connects to the stud near the middle that has two nuts on it. The mounting stud with the electrical connection will eventually connect to a ground wire. For the gauge sender and electric fuel pump (if used) to work properly, they must both be grounded.

If you are adamant about using a steel tank, one from an early Mustang works well, as it has mounting flanges that make for an easy installation. Various universal-fit steel or plastic tanks are available, but these usually require fabricating your own mounting straps.

Fuel Tank Installation

When mounting the fuel tank, there are two things to keep in mind. First, the tank and fuel filler should be located so that it can be filled easily. If the filler neck requires excessively tight bends or any areas that do not slope adequately, the tank will be difficult to fill. Especially in the case of the tank being mounted under the bed, the filler must be within reach of whomever may be filling the tank. Second, remember that the tank will expand slightly depending on the temperature, fuel level, and other variables. So, be sure to allow some extra room around the exhaust components.

Most (if not all) of the plastic aftermarket tanks include recessed areas designed specifically for locating the mounting straps. Use 3/8-inch-diameter (or larger) bolts to secure the mounting straps to the truck crossmembers. Verify that none of the tank sits below the scrub line in the event you have a tire blowout. The scrub line is an imaginary line between the driving surface under one tire to the wheel rim on the opposite end of the axle.

Fuel Line Routing

To provide ample fuel to the engine, 3/8-inch line is typically used. For the most part, 3/8-inch hard (brake) line was used with 3/8-inch rubber hose at some of the connections. The use of braided stainless lines with AN fittings can eliminate rubber hose. Aside from being slightly more difficult to bend initially, 3/8-inch line is like working with brake line and requires the same tools.

Fittings and Lines

The fitting supplied by Tanks with the universal poly fuel tank is a barbed hose fitting. A piece of rubber hose slides over and the connection is secured with a hose clamp. This rubber hose was used to run up to the hard line nestled within the passenger-side frame rail, where another hose clamp was installed to

As the fuel line moves forward from the gas tank, it transitions from a rubber fuel hose to a 3/8-inch hard line to run along the frame rail. Be sure to run the hard line into the rubber hose at least 1 inch and secure it with a hose clamp.

Simply to avoid any interference with the Panhard bar, the hard fuel line has been bowed out away from the frame rail slightly in this area. This will allow for service of either component without affecting the other should the necessity arise. After the frame is painted, the rubber hose will be secured in place with a rubber hose clamp.

After following the contours of the frame rail, the hard fuel line is bent to be clamped to the boxing plate for the front suspension. After entering the engine compartment, the fuel line transitions to rubber fuel hose to connect to the mechanical fuel pump mounted on the engine. From the outlet side of the fuel pump, the fuel line will be routed to an inline fuel filter and then on to the carburetor.

prevent the hose from becoming disconnected from the hard line.

The hard line is then bent to conform to the profile of the inside of the passenger-side frame rail as it runs forward toward the engine. Another section of rubber hose is used to connect to the mechanical fuel pump. Just like on the brake line, rubber-coated line clamps were used to secure the fuel line to the frame. From the fuel pump, a section of hard line will be bent and routed to near the carburetor. Rubber hose will then connect to the fuel filter and continue to the inlet of the carburetor.

When routing fuel lines, be careful to avoid pinching the line, allowing it to rub against anything that may rub a hole in the line, or allowing it to touch exhaust pipes. If connecting two pieces of hard line, both lines should be double flared, just like brake line. When connecting a piece of rubber hose to a piece of hard line, the rubber hose should be slid over the hard line by at least 1 inch with a hose clamp used to ensure that the hose does not slide off. Be sure that the hose clamp is tight against the hard line inside of the hose and not just against the hose.

Brake Fluid Reservoir

A benefit of installing the brake master cylinder beneath the floor is that it gets that large, ugly monstrosity off the firewall. The downfall is that filling it or even checking the fluid level is virtually impossible. Everything automotive is a tradeoff.

The remote brake fluid reservoir is mounted on the driver-side inner fender at approximately the middle of the inner fender. The line to the master cylinder still needs to be run at this time. The power steering reservoir is mounted slightly forward. Both reservoirs will be within easy reach from the front of the truck when the hood is opened. This makes it very convenient for adding or checking brake fluid and power steering fluid.

However, a remote-fill master cylinder reservoir can be placed in a convenient location. A potential location is under the hood near the front of the truck, where it is easy to access, rather than back on the firewall.

Remote Reservoir Mounting

If it does not come with one, the reservoir will require a mounting bracket of some sort. The Wilwood reservoir used on the shop truck came with a nice bracket that was mounted to the driver-side inner fender panel by merely drilling two holes for the two bolts included.

To connect the remote reservoir, simply run the line of choice to the master cylinder. Use braided stainless line with AN fittings on each end or bend the brake line. Just be sure that the master cylinder has the appropriate cap for the type of line that is run to it.

Cooling System

Whether running a stock straight six or a blown big-block engine beneath the hood of a Task Force truck, that engine needs a cooling system. And if having heat in the winter, air-conditioning in the summer, and a defrosted windshield is appreciated, be thankful for that cooling system. The radiator serves as a reservoir for the antifreeze/coolant that is constantly flowing through the engine due to the operation of the water pump.

Radiator

The coolant is heated as it flows through the engine's cooling jackets. Then, it returns to the radiator, where it is cooled by air passing over the radiator fins. A mechanically driven fan located behind the radiator helped pull more air across the stock radiator to keep the engine cooler. Most vehicles now use electric fans, as they are more efficient and can be controlled by sensors to turn on when needed and shut off when not required.

Radiator Hoses

To provide a method for coolant to move between the radiator and the engine, radiator hoses are required. While every auto parts store in the world carries radiator hoses, finding the one that is needed may be difficult if you are building anything other than the stock engine and radiator configuration.

The first step toward finding the correct radiator hoses is to ask the company that manufactured the radiator. It may have a database of application info for part numbers that a local auto parts store may be able to cross reference. If that doesn't work, and you do not want to use flex hose, make a template of the shape that is needed and then search the hoses at the parts store until something usable is found. Using some heavy-gauge electric cable works well, as it can be bent into shape easily but maintains that shape.

Transmission Cooler Mounting

Excessive heat is tough on automatic transmissions, therefore two fittings for connecting a remote transmission cooler are located on the passenger's side of the automatic transmission. A transmission cooler is often integral to the radiator, but

The aluminum radiator for the shop truck is from PRC and is all-aluminum construction. It includes its own core support, A/C condenser, and overflow recovery tank. On the backside are dual Spal electric fans that will operate via the thermostat to pull plenty of air through the radiator. The two holes on the passenger's side were drilled to allow for the A/C lines to reach the condenser.

To find a suitable radiator hose, use a piece of heavy copper electrical wire to form the basic shape and length, then take it to your favorite auto parts store. Realize that custom applications may require modification to a radiator hose to get it to fit.

This is the finned transmission cooler that comes with the PRC radiator. Since this will be mounted rigidly onto one of the frame rails, and the transmission could have some vibration, hard line will come off the transmission. However, it will have a short section of rubber hose installed at the transmission cooler to eliminate any damage from fatigue.

Two inlets on the passenger's side of the automatic transmission provide for connection to a remote transmission cooler. On this transmission, the connections are for 5/16-inch hard line. Two pieces were bent to span the area between the transmission and the cooler.

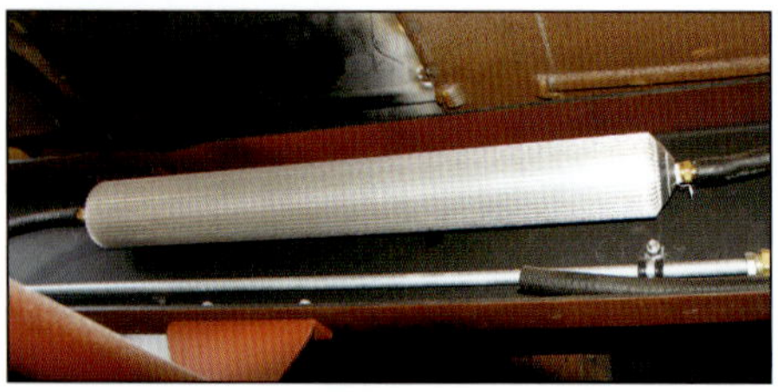

After the transmission cooler is mounted to the truck's frame, rubber fuel hose is used to connect to the hard lines. The flexibility of the hose will minimize any fatigue damage possibly caused by vibration between the transmission and the cooler.

the transmission fluid should not be anywhere near as hot as the engine coolant. Therefore, a separate transmission cooler mounted away from the radiator is a better design.

There are various designs for coolers, but the concept is the same. Run transmission fluid through a finned reservoir that is cooled by airflow and then run that back to the transmission. Some coolers have two fittings located on the same end, with the fluid making multiple passes through the cooler. Others have a connection on each end and the coolant just makes one pass through the cooler. Regardless of which type is being used, it should be situated so that it gets airflow through and around it.

For the shop truck, the finned transmission cooler was mounted inside the passenger-side frame rail, near the transmission. This required drilling two holes, inserting the mounting bolts that slide along a track on the back of the cooler through the frame rail, and securing each with a lock nut. To position the cooler a bit farther away from the frame rail to gain some airflow, two 1/4-inch nylon spacers were installed on each mounting bolt.

The 5/16-inch hard line was bent as required to connect from the transmission to the hose barb fittings in the transmission cooler. A short length of rubber tubing was then installed between the hard line and the transmission cooler to minimize any possibility of vibration-induced fatigue in the connections. Be sure that hose clamps are used to secure the rubber hose in place.

Steering System

The steering system requires a steering wheel, a column, and steering shafts to connect the steering box (or rack-and-pinion) as its major components. Additional components are a steering column drop or support and U-joints to connect everything below the end of the steering column.

Steering Wheel

A steering wheel should be comfortable, as you will be holding it most any time that you are driving. It should also somewhat match the décor of the truck's interior as well. You should also choose a steering wheel that does not totally block the driver's view of the instrumentation.

Steering Column

For a steering column, first decide if the transmission shifter will be on the floor or on the column. If the shifter is not going on the column, then that part does not matter. Do you want/need a tilt column? I do not believe many people change the tilt of their steering wheel very often once they set it, but a tilt column may be necessary to get the wheel where you want it.

While it may seem pricey for some, ididit makes a tilt steering column specifically for these trucks. It is a bolt-in replacement for the stock column. It is made of all new components and includes the internal wiring for plug-and-play connections to the wiring system. It also includes the column drop for securing the column to the dash. Besides the choice of shifter or not, you can also choose a chrome steel column or a paintable steel column.

Steering Column, Column Drop, and Wheel Installation

Sacrificing budget for simplicity and ease of installation, I opted for the paintable steel column with col-

In similar fashion as the stock steering column, the vehicle-specific steering column from ididit mounts to the cab toeboard with three nuts and bolts. The steering column is available with or without the shifter and in a chrome finish or paintable.

Different drops are available, but again, the steering column drop for this specific vehicle from ididit works great. It mounts to the underneath side of the dash.

umn shifter from ididit for the shop truck. With the stock steering column removed and out of the way, this product is quite easy to install. Slip the base of the column through the floor plate provided with the kit and bolt it to the toeboard with three bolts and nuts. Assemble the column drop onto the column and then secure it to the underneath side of the dash.

Depending on the steering wheel used, a column adapter may be required to fit between the steering column and the steering wheel. Remove the nut from the top of the column, install the wheel and then secure it with the nut just removed. It does not get much easier than that.

Steering Shafts, Universal Joints, and Shaft Supports

Steering shafts and U-joints are available as splined, smooth-bore, or DD, and in various sizes. The steering system will require one U-joint at the steering box and one at the end of the column, at a minimum. The U-joints must match the input and output shafts of these two components. The opposite end of the U-joint must match the steering shaft that connects the column and box.

If two separate pieces of steering shaft must be used, one of them must be secured by a support bearing (AKA shaft support) that is typically attached to the vehicle's frame. Steering shafts and U-joints are commonly available in mild steel, stainless steel, and polished stainless steel. Note that if a support bearing is required, it will slide onto an unpainted stainless or polished stainless shaft much easier than one that has been painted. And yes, mild steel will rust if not painted.

Perhaps the biggest challenge with installing the steering is getting around the obstacles created by the exhaust manifolds or headers and the motor mounts. To determine the best fit, use some 3/4-inch wooden dowel rods to mock up the steering. U-joints should not be used at more than a 30-degree angle, so placement of the U-joint is also important. Avoid attempting to install the steering system without the exhaust installed, as you will be wasting your time.

Electrical System

With the growing number of high-quality do-it-yourself wiring kits available and the relative ease of wiring a vehicle, knowing how everything is wired may mean the difference between being able to limp home after a side-of-the-road repair and being forced to hire a tow truck. A pair of crimping pliers, some electrical tape, and some spare fuses should be in the glove box of every truck.

You may not be able to lay down a smooth-as-glass paint job or weld with the beauty of a painter on canvas, but wiring tasks are simple. They must be done correctly, but they are easy enough to learn.

Fuse Panel

Most of the wiring kits currently available include a fuse panel and a fair amount of color-coded wire. The fuse panel will have a predetermined number of circuits and the necessary fuses. Some kits are rather basic with fewer circuits, while others have several circuits including those for optional electrical accessories such as power windows, power seats, and power radio antennas.

Having a good idea of what you want your truck to include will be your guide toward choosing a suitable fuse panel. Some specific questions to answer when purchasing a wiring kit is whether the ignition key is in the column or on the dash, the dimmer switch is on the column or

With the ididit steering column and Sanderson headers, only one section of steering shaft and two U-joints are required to connect the steering wheel and the rack-and-pinion steering. A clean setup that can often be extremely complicated.

The Wiremaster Power Panel from Affordable Street Rods has provided great performance on multiple projects for me in the past. Its compact design allows for a variety of installation locations. It also allows you to wire as many or as few circuits as needed, with room for expansion later.

Being able to repair or at least temporarily bypass an electrical issue will often prevent a call to the local towing company when you are out enjoying your truck. Having the tools to cut and strip electrical wire and temporarily tape it back together will be very handy. Of course, sometimes just having a spare fuse will save the day. The long pliers are electrical crimping pliers, while the shorter ones cut and strip. Combination units are also available.

the floor, and if it is using an electric fuel pump. Also specify if you are using one of the newer fuel-injected engines.

To make these kits even easier to install, many of them printed the use for the wire directly on the wire, so even if you are color blind, the wire tells where it is to be connected. The basic steps to wiring the truck are to mount the fuse panel inside the cab, route the wires to their destination, cut the wire to the correct length, crimp on the correct connector, and secure it to the destination. A few steps may be a bit more difficult than that, but not by much.

Some kits have all the wires preconnected at the fuse panel, so you must only crimp on the terminal end. In other kits, the terminals are already crimped on the fuse panel end, but you are required to make the connection. My personal preference is to use this latter type and simply deal with the circuits that I plan to use, rather than have a bundle of wire that I have no intention of using in the way. Regardless of how you do it, running one wire at a time keeps it simple.

Other than wires, connectors, and crimping tools, there are a few other electrical components that you should have some awareness of: relays, master disconnect switch, neutral safety switch, and ground studs.

Relays

Simply put, a relay is a low-current device to control a high-current accessory. When the circuit will have current exceeding 10 amps, a relay will prove to be more reliable than a standard switch. Relays are commonly used to switch headlights, fog lights, a hydraulic brake light switch, or an electric fan, but many other uses exist.

Typical relays have two circuits: one that carries the large amount of current from the battery to the accessory and a second circuit that switches the flow of current. When the relay is switched on, electrical current from the power source (battery) passes through the relay to operate a switch within the relay. Electric current then flows directly to the accessory, without passing through the entire wiring harness.

Just as a regular switch, relays can be of the single-pole, single-throw (SPST) or single-pole, double-throw (SPDT) variety. An SPST would be used in an ON/OFF application, while an SPDT would be used in an ON/OFF/ON application, such as turn signals where one ON position would be for right and the other ON for left.

Most relays have a number near each terminal and a wiring schematic printed on the side. An SPST relay will have terminals labeled 85, 86, 30, and 87. An SPDT relay will have those same terminals but will also include a terminal marked 87a.

Relay Terminal	Connection
85*	Coil input (+12VDC)
86*	Coil input (to ground)
30	Common
87	Normally open
87a	Normally closed
* Terminals 85 and 86 can be interchanged.	

To provide a practical example of how to wire a relay, consider an electric fan. A terminal on the fuse block has two wires running from it. One of those connects to terminal 85 to provide 12 volts of power to the relay's coil. Somewhere in this wire, a switch will need to be installed so that you can manually turn the fan on or off. An inline fuse for 2 or 3 amps can be installed to protect the switch.

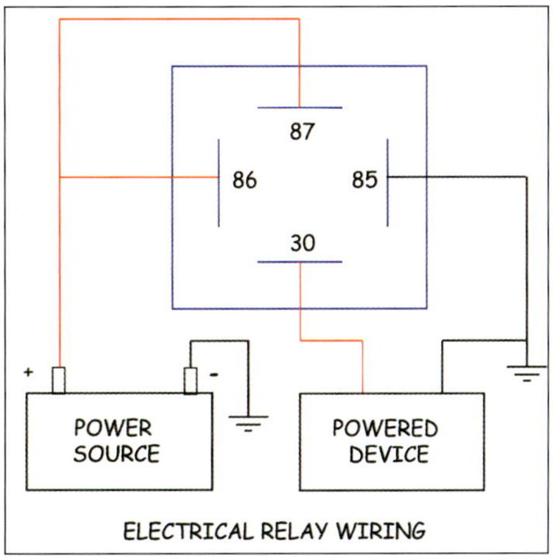

Regardless of the device being powered by an electrical relay, the wiring connections are basically the same. In some instances, additional items such as fuses or diodes may be needed.

Automotive electrical relays are about 1 ci in size, but they serve a huge purpose with any electrical system. Their use allows for the use of components that require high current, without requiring huge wire.

The second of these power wires will connect to terminal 30, which is the common terminal in the relay. This wire should be fused (at the fuse panel) for the load of the fan (or whatever accessory the relay is used on).

A third wire connects terminal 86 on the relay to a suitable ground.

The fourth wire connects terminal 87 of the relay to the power side of the fan. Note that the fan will also require its own ground wire.

Master Disconnect Switch

Depending on how often the truck will be driven and where it is parked, consider installing a master disconnect switch. Often referred to as a kill switch, a master disconnect switch opens or "kills" all electrical circuits, which shuts down all electrical power to the vehicle. If the truck will not be driven frequently, this device will prevent the battery from running down if there is some sort of draw. If the truck is ever parked in a questionable area, having a master kill switch may prevent you from having to fill out a police report. Of course, the kill switch is only as good as your memory to turn it off.

To work properly on a street-driven vehicle, the master disconnect switch should be installed between the battery and the starter. Obviously, this type of switch should be positioned within easy reach of the driver, so that it can be turned on easily when you are simply going for a drive.

Many master disconnect switches are a two-position rotary switch that simply has an ON and an OFF position. If the battery runs beneath the floor and under the passenger (driver) compartment, the switch can easily be installed in the floor, just under the front of the driver's seat. This makes it convenient for the driver, yet somewhat unobtrusive to legroom or to a typically crowded dash panel.

Neutral Safety Switch

A neutral safety switch is not a required component to an ignition system. However, it is a particularly good idea. This is the mechanism that allows a vehicle's engine to start only when the automatic transmission is in park or neutral or a standard transmission–equipped vehicle to start only when the vehicle is in neutral or the clutch is depressed.

Neutral safety switches vary from different manufacturers, but they are all designed to activate based on

A heavy-duty master kill switch is commonly mandatory on competition vehicles, but it can also be used as a theft deterrent on any vehicle. Electrically, it must be mounted inline between the battery and the starter. As a security device, it should be mounted in an easily accessible location but not out in the open. Remember to turn it on or off at the appropriate times for it to function as designed.

the position of the shifter linkage. Located electrically between the ignition switch and the starter solenoid, the neutral safety switch typically has two electrical contacts. One contact is for "park start" and the other being "neutral start." On some vehicles, the neutral safety switch may be part of a larger switch that also controls backup lights.

To create a "poor man's" theft deterrent system, an SPST (ON-OFF) toggle switch can be installed in line with one of the wires connected to the neutral safety switch. Since this would not be installed in a heavy wire that is connected to the battery, the switch can be physically smaller and more easily hidden.

If this switch is chosen, do all of the wiring and verify that the engine starts and runs properly first. Then, install the switch later to minimize troubleshooting a new build that may not start. Since this toggle switch might very well be installed out of sight, it may take some getting used to for turning it on to drive or off when walking away from your truck.

After mounting the neutral safety switch to the underside of the automatic transmission pan, one of two different arms are secured to the shaft of the shifter mechanism. When using just one arm to contact the switch's detent ball, the switch is configured to operate when the transmission is in reverse. This is used to power a backup light switch or a backup camera. A power wire from the fuse panel or the headlight switch is connected to one terminal on the switch, while a power wire for the backup lights or camera is connected to the other terminal on the switch.

When using the arm that provides two contacts with the switch's detent ball, the switch operates when the transmission is in park or neutral. This is a safety feature, allowing the engine to start only when in park or neutral. In either configuration, the appropriate wiring connects to the two electrical terminals. When a fuse panel includes a neutral safety switch, each of the two wires connect to the separate terminals on the switch.

Ground Studs

While there are legitimate mistakes in wiring that can cause problems, probably the most common electrical wiring issue is an improper or insufficient ground. Some components will not work at all if not grounded, while others will work sporadically.

Everyone probably knows that it makes sense to ground the battery to the engine block or transmission (typically a bellhousing or transmission mount bolt) by way of a large battery cable. For all the other electrical accessories in the vehicle to work, they must be grounded also. An incredibly good way of doing this is by using grounding studs.

Determine suitable centralized locations near the front, rear, and interior of the truck to mount the grounding studs. A 10-32 x 3/4 stainless-steel screw, a 10-32 brass nut, and a 10-32 wing nut will be required for each ground stud. Different sized hardware can be used if desired, but this size is suitable without being obnoxiously large.

Drill the appropriate-sized hole for the hardware being used in the truck's chassis at the front and rear, and in the interior near the dash. Run 12-gauge wire from the negative side of the battery to each grounding stud and terminate the wire with a #10 ring terminal. Insert the stainless-steel screw through the ring terminal, into the hole in the chassis (or dash), and secure with the brass nut. It now has a convenient ground location for lights and accessories.

Terminate each ground wire with a ring terminal and then slide it over the ground stud and secure with the wing nut. Yes, you can use

Placing grounding studs at convenient locations will provide adequate grounding. Multiple grounding studs help minimize lengthy ground wires, which cleans up the appearance of your wiring.

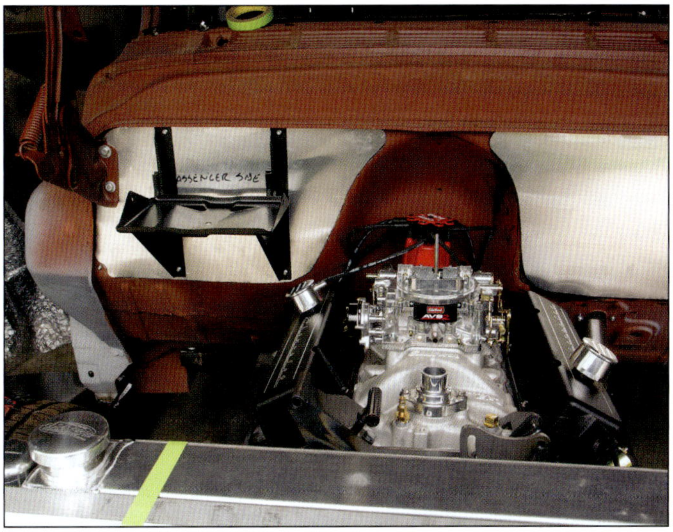

While the stock battery location is not pretty, it is convenient for both installation and service. Any other location, such as between the frame and the doorstep or in the truck bed, would be served well by a set of remote terminals should the truck ever need a jump.

a regular nut if you would like. Several ground wires can be connected to a common grounding stud. This method will prevent you from having multiple ground wires running throughout the length of the vehicle and will also eliminate sporadic electrical problems caused by improper grounding.

Battery Locations

The stock battery location on these trucks leaves a bit to be desired. It is nice to have a smooth, clean firewall, but to hang an ugly battery on it with a couple of battery cables dangling off to the side just does not seem right.

However, for a truck that gets driven on a regular basis, the location is not bad. It requires a relatively short positive cable to reach the starter and one of similar length as a ground cable. Other locations might be suitable but would be significantly less than desirable when the battery needs to be replaced or serviced. Wherever the battery is mounted, ensure that it is properly secured and will not move around.

Frame Rail

A few alternate locations for the battery location are mounted to a frame rail beneath the floor or in the bed of the truck. Depending on the exhaust routing, inside the frame rail on the passenger's side (opposite the master cylinder) is a good choice.

The street rod industry has been doing this for years, so there are multiple versions of remote battery boxes available. This would greatly minimize the length of wiring required to connect to the starter and the ground. If going this route, you may consider incorporating a pair of easily accessible remote terminals, just in case the truck ever needs a jump-start. After all, if you are going to the trouble to move the battery, you are probably going to lower the truck.

The Bed

Putting the battery in the bed can be done easily and conveniently. However, in this location especially, it would be wise to mount the battery inside some type of enclosure. You do not want it to be easy for a scoundrel to simply walk away with your battery. Additionally, you do not want to run an unnecessary risk of a piece of cargo inadvertently making contact with the battery terminals or sliding into the battery case. Creative methods of storing the battery in the truck bed are in a portion of a larger storage chest or disguised as a case of motor oil or your favorite beverage.

Wherever the battery is located, just be sure to mount it securely. A battery rolling around in a vehicle is not a good thing. Also, be sure to use rubber grommets on the battery cables anytime they pass through metal or any other material that might abrade them.

Fuse Panel

Most commercially available automotive fuse panels allow for a limited number of circuits. Any manufacturer will typically have a standard panel with dedicated circuits for the essentials, along with an extra one or two circuits for whatever you want to use them for. They will then have a deluxe panel that includes a few extra dedicated circuits, typically for power windows, power door locks, backup lights, and an electric fuel pump, plus two or three extra accessory circuits.

Number of Circuits

A big difference from one kit to another is that the essentials in one kit may be contained in a 10-circuit kit, while those same essentials make up 20 circuits in another kit. Quite simply, this means that with fewer circuits, more items are being powered by that same circuit. Not saying that is bad, but it is something to consider, especially if you plan to drive the truck a lot.

Before you begin wiring is the time to determine what is needed or wanted as far as electrical components for the truck. Even if the plan is to merely get the truck running now, but foresee adding A/C, power windows, heated seats, and who knows what else, do yourself a favor and start with the additional circuits.

Location

Install the fuse panel where it is convenient to access when you need to replace a fuse, but out of the way so that it does not get kicked around or mashed. It needs to be in a safe environment, otherwise wires could become disconnected, which would be a bad thing.

Countless vehicles have the fuse panel located on the inside of the firewall, up behind the dash. Trying to work around clutch and brake pedals while standing on your head does not make for an enjoyable fuse-changing experience. Nor is it real convenient for the person doing the wiring, be it you or someone else. For the shop truck, the fuse panel is in the bottom of the floor console. It is safely tucked in between the seats and easy to access for service by simply removing one aluminum panel.

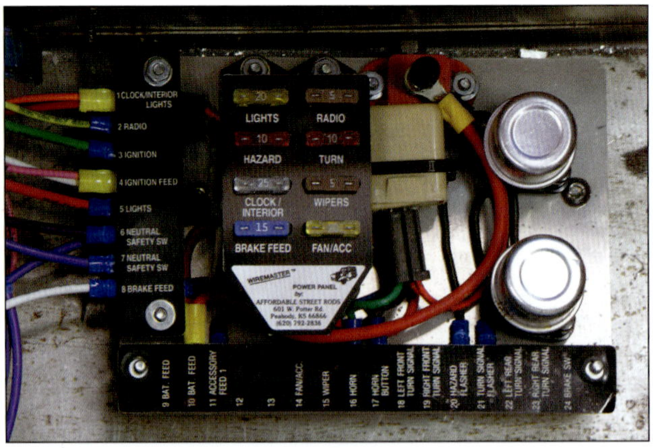

While the wires for the electrical system all start at the fuse panel, they all branch out into one of about four different areas of the truck. Depending on the exact location of the fuse panel, the best routing to each of these locations will be different for each branch. One branch of wiring will be to the engine and transmission area. Another will run to the front of the truck, while another will run to the rear. Lastly, one branch will remain in the interior.

Gauge Wiring

To make the installation task much simpler and more convenient for service later, consider wiring the dash panel out of the truck, running all the wires to a quick-disconnect plug. This will allow you to wire the gauges at the convenience of a workbench, a kitchen table, or an easy chair. This will also allow you to remove the dash panel if need be to access anything behind the dash.

In addition to the wire from the specific sender (or mechanical sender) for the gauge, all gauges will require 12-volt power as well. This power wire is what serves as a sender to the voltmeter and can be continued to the rest of the gauges as well. Dash or gauge lights will also require a power wire. The gauges and the lights will also require a ground. The high-beam indicator and turn-signal indicator will also require a sender and a ground.

Standard Gauges

The voltmeter is fed by the ignition switch and receives power only when the ignition key is in the RUN or START position.

The fuel level sending unit includes a float, an arm, and a variable resistor, all of which are connected to a bracket that is inserted through an opening in the top of the tank. The float is attached to one end of an arm that also connects to a

I have used these trailer electrical connectors in the past to be able to quickly and easily disconnect the gauge panel. After passing the wire through the rubber boot, the bare end of wire is simply slid into the terminal and secured with a small screw on each terminal. Connections for one terminal of the connector are reversed to allow for proper orientation.

variable resistor that is connected to the mounting bracket.

As the float rides up or down with the level of the fuel, it moves a wiper along a strip of bimetallic metal that is grounded on one end. When the float moves so that the wiper is closer to the grounded end of the bimetallic strip, there is less resistance; and when the float moves so that the wiper is farther away from the grounded end, there is more resistance. This amount of resistance (small or large) is what causes the fuel level gauge to operate.

Some gauges are designed so that a small amount of resistance indicates a full tank and a large amount indicates an empty tank, while other gauges are designed just the opposite. Verify that your gauges and sender are compatible so that your fuel gauge reading is correct. The fuel level sender must be grounded. If your fuel level gauge begins operating erratically, that is a good sign that it has a faulty ground. Additionally, the arm length must be adjusted during installation to compensate for the depth of the tank.

An electric oil pressure gauge reads an electrical voltage output directly from an oil pressure sensor that is threaded into the engine block. When the engine is not running, the oil pressure gauge should read zero, but it should rise immediately when the engine is started.

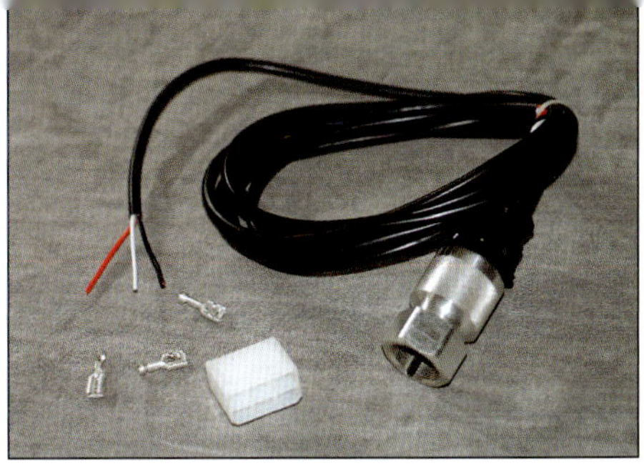

Some speedometers are mechanical, while others are electric. This speedometer cable is electric, which allows for easy calibration. The fitting threads into the transmission, just as a mechanical cable does; however, the three wires then connect to the gauge.

The water temperature gauge reads the temperature of the coolant that is flowing through the engine block and the radiator. This temperature will vary depending on where it is measured, therefore the most accurate location for a water temperature

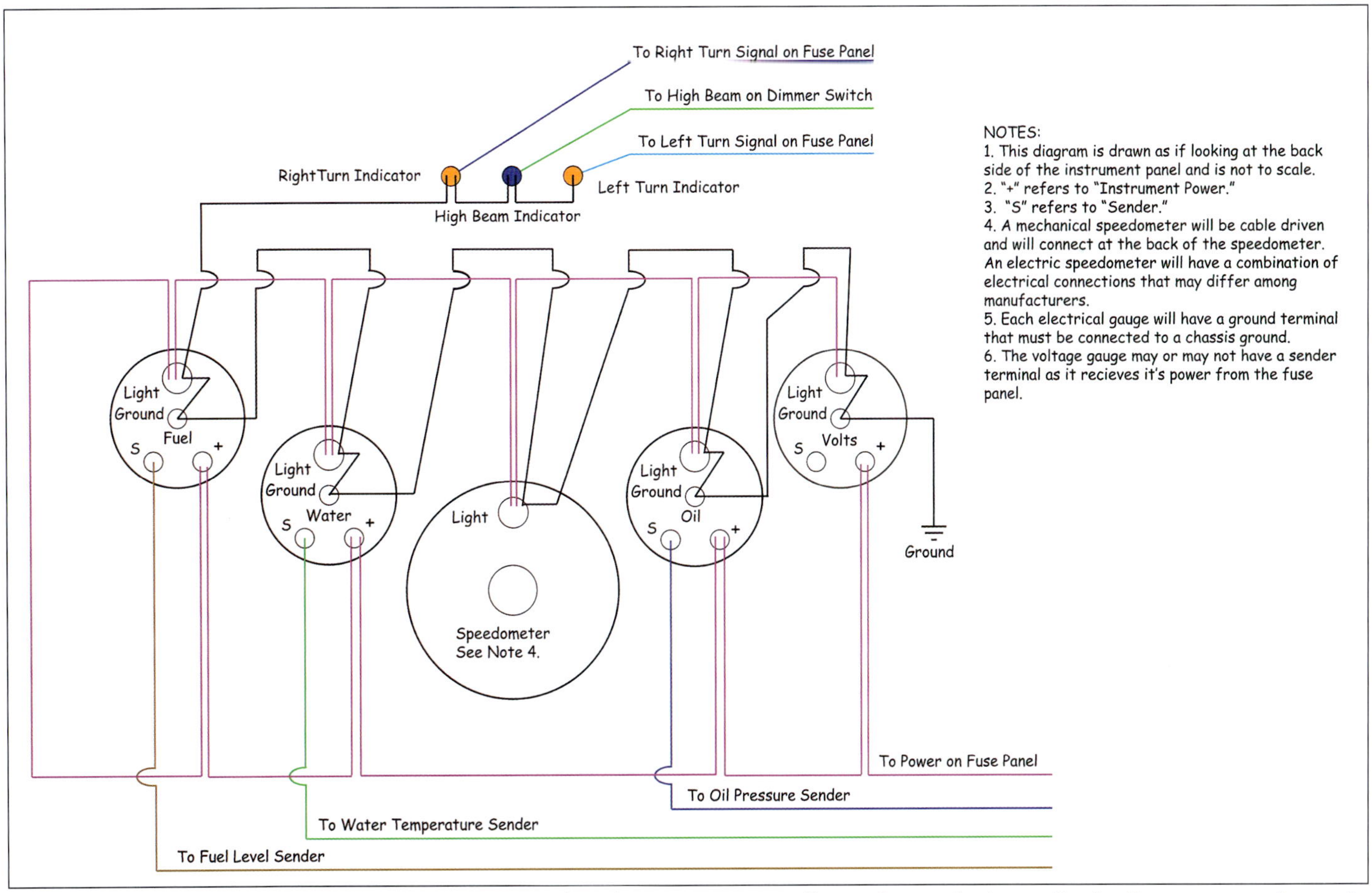

This wiring schematic should work for most any electric gauges, regardless of manufacturer. Basically, a power wire and a ground wire goes to each gauge and light, along with the sender for each specific gauge or indicator light.

Gauge Installation

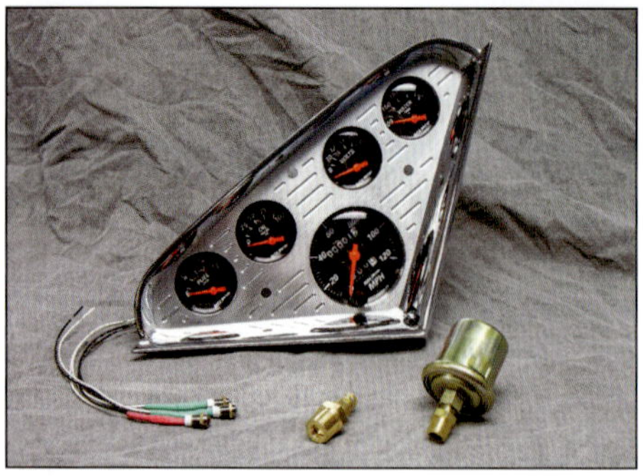

1 *If you have tried to put analog gauges in your Task Force truck, you may have already found out that at least one aftermarket dash panel does not fit from Boese Engineering. I had to return my first-choice panel and gauges but was able to find these that fit because the bezel mounts behind the dash panel. Also shown are the water temperature sender and the oil pressure sensor. Sadly, the fuel level sender is not included in this kit.*

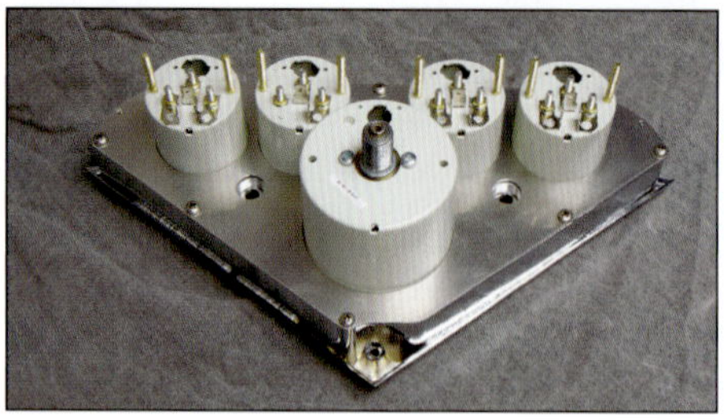

2 *With the removable back panel, the small gauges can be rearranged if desired. A light bulb goes into the hole in the back of each gauge. In addition to a wire from the specific sender for each gauge, each gauge and each light require a power wire and a ground wire.*

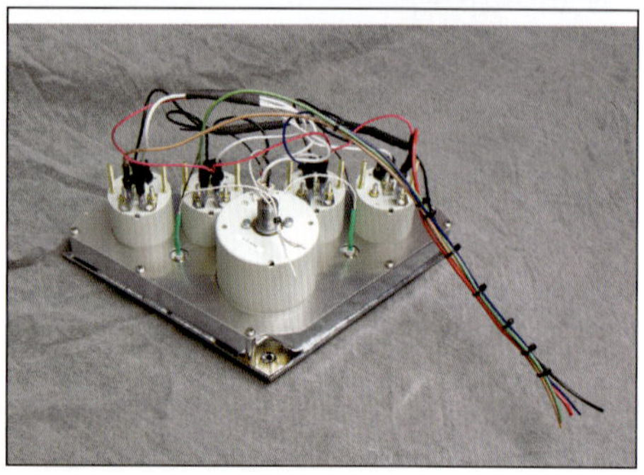

3 *In less than an hour's time, the gauge panel can be wired and connections sealed with heat-shrink tubing. All the wires will be terminated at a quick-disconnect plug, making for easy removal of the gauge panel if ever required.*

4 *Whenever using a quick-disconnect plug, ensure that the wires are in matching locations. While you do not want excessive amounts of wire stashed behind the panel, there should be enough to easily remove the gauge panel when required.*

5 *The speedometer sender cable connects to the transmission at this threaded fitting. Depending on the gauges, signals are then sent mechanically or electrically, allowing for calibration of the speedometer, such as when changing rear tire sizes or rear-end gears.*

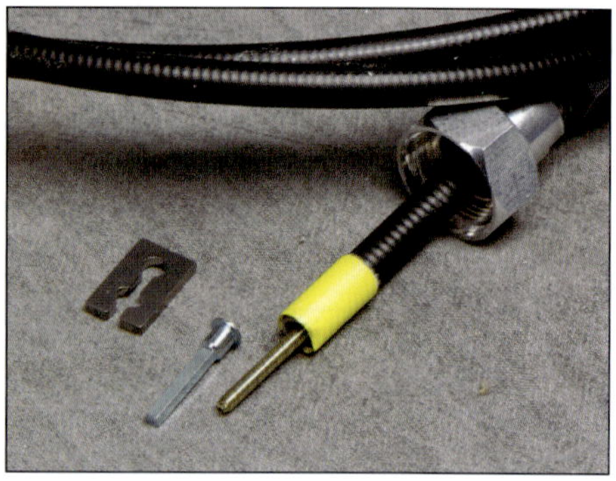

6 *For the Autometer gauges used in the shop truck, the speedometer signal is via a mechanical cable. After cutting the cable and cable housing to the correct length, the square end is crimped onto the inner wire. The transmission drives the square end of the cable's inner wire.*

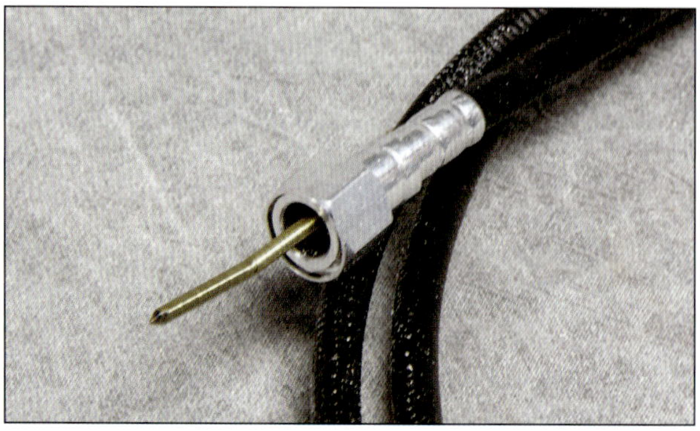

7 *The speedometer end of the inner wires is already square at the end. It is merely inserted into the back of the speedometer and then secured by threading the nut onto the speedometer.*

8 *The water temperature sensor threads into a bung in the cylinder head or intake manifold. The sender wire to the gauge attaches to the sender with a ring terminal. The sensor is shown near the front of the intake manifold, but it has since been moved to a different location at the other end of the manifold to hide some wiring.*

9 *The oil pressure sensor threads into a bung in the engine block. The sender wire to the gauge attaches to the sender with a ring terminal. Since the oil will be under pressure, wrap the threads of the sender with Teflon tape. Note that an angled fitting may be required for proper fit.*

sensor to be placed is in the cylinder head since that is where the temperature is most critical. The sensor threads should be wrapped with Teflon tape prior to installation to prevent leakage of coolant.

Speedometer

The speedometer provides the driver with the speed of the vehicle and, depending on the make and model of the vehicle, will display in miles per hour (MPH), kilometers per hour (Km/H), or both. Although exact wiring of speedometers will vary from one manufacturer to the next, they will be somewhat similar. Each speedometer will require a connection to a fused power source, a suitable ground, and input directly or indirectly from the transmission. The input from the transmission may be through a Hall-effect sensor, an inductive sensor, or an electronic control box.

Many aftermarket gauge kits offer mechanical or electrical speedometers, even if the rest of the gauges in the kit are electric. A benefit of an electric speedometer is that it can be easily programmed by the driver. While this may not be of interest to everyone, it is of great benefit if you ever change tire sizes or rear-end gears. It would go through a relatively simple recalibration process, rather than be required to change the drive gear in a mechanical speedometer.

Calibration of a programmable speedometer will vary depending on the manufacturer, but the simplest procedure is to drive the vehicle in question to a stretch of highway that has an exact 1-mile distance marked. Either measure this 5,280-foot distance yourself or use the mile markers often found along the highway.

Go through a preliminary set of instructions to begin the calibration, then drive the exact 1-mile distance, stop, and then follow some ending instructions. This process would then calibrate the speedometer and therefore the odometer. You can also adjust the speedometer with the vehicle on a dynamometer.

Tachometer

A tachometer (tach) indicates the revolutions per minute (RPM) the engine is turning. Just like the speedometer discussed previously, wiring for a tachometer will vary by manufacturer. However, the tach will require a connection to a fused power source, a suitable ground, and input from an electronic ignition control box, the ignition coil, or from the tach signal from the alternator. With all gauges, consult the installation instructions provided with the gauges for more detailed information.

Installing the gauges is always a bit of a milestone in a build as the gauges are typically the largest visual object in the dash. Additionally, it also means that you are a step closer to hearing the engine run. That will be a good thing.

Some instrument clusters are comprised of the gauge panel that the gauges are installed in and a separate V-shaped bezel. Others assemble these components so that they are assembled as one unit. The out-

Anytime that electrical wires pass through sheet metal, fiberglass, or any other component that could abrade the wire, an appropriately sized rubber grommet should be installed in the panel. Since the grommet should be installed prior to the wire, plan how thick the wire or group of wires will be and drill a hole the correct size prior to installing the grommet. Grommets are available in different diameters, as well as for different panel thicknesses.

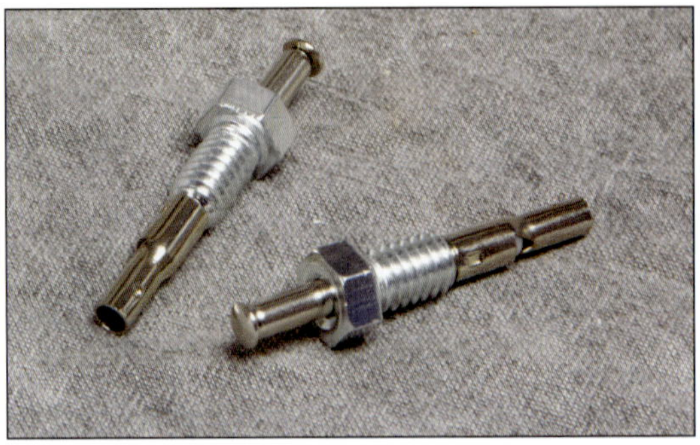

Besides the dome light in the stock location, white courtesy lights will be mounted on each side of the center console, with red/white courtesy lights mounted on the interior of each door. For these lights to illuminate when a door is opened, each door will be equipped with a GM-style jamb switch. The threaded housing threads into the doorsill of the cab, while the door pushes into the plunger when closed. Closing the door opens the circuit, turning off the courtesy lights.

A pressure-activated brake line switch threads into a T-fitting in the brake line. One electrical connect goes to ground, while the other provides signal power to the brake lights. This latter power signal should include an electrical relay to provide optimum performance.

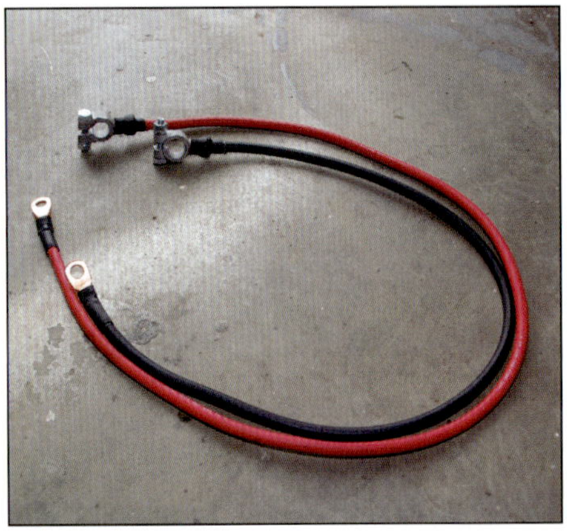

To provide power to the entire electrical system, a power cable from the positive terminal on the battery must connect to the engine's starter. Likewise, a ground cable must connect to a substantial ground, such as a bolt between the transmission and the engine. Standard-length cables are available at local auto parts stores, but some stores will make custom-length cables for you.

Just as any electrical component, the electric choke requires a power wire and a ground wire. For the choke to be able to start the engine, power should come from a circuit that is hot at all times.

The dimmer switch for the headlights includes three connections. The single connector is for power coming from the headlight switch. The two other connections are for the low-beam and high-beam lights, whether they are a single light (1955–1957) or dual lights (1958–1959).

A heat gun (available at local auto parts stores) works great for sealing electrical connections with heat-shrink tubing. The connections look more professional, as well as being more secure. The heat gun is much safer than using a cigarette lighter or a match to complete the task.

come is the same, but you should investigate the instrument panel prior to installing it just to avoid any glitches. Once the panel is assembled to the bezel, three screws secure the assembly in place in the dash.

Wiring

Wiring may not be considered a safety item, but the safe installation of it is. The fuse panel should be mounted in a location where it is safe from road debris and weather, meaning that it should be mounted inside the cab. This is merely common sense. What might not be as obvious is that the fuse panel should be mounted to something relatively solid that is not going to vibrate. You do not want any of the electrical connections to the fuse panel coming apart due to vibration.

For these reasons, fuse panels are very commonly installed on the inside of the firewall, up behind the dash. That location does meet the criteria, but it is not a convenient location for wiring the truck or replacing a fuse, especially along the side of the road at night.

As mentioned previously, the fuse panel for the shop truck will be in the base channel of the floor console. To access the fuse panel, simply remove a few screws that secure the aluminum cover panel. Additionally, the console serves as a mounting location for several electrical relays, making most electrical repair service accessible in one location. Anyone who has ever basically stood on their head between the seat and the steering column to merely replace a fuse should certainly be able to appreciate this.

Braided ground straps are useful for grounding the cab sheet metal or the truck chassis to the main ground of the engine/transmission that typically connects to the ground terminal of the battery. Most electrical issues are due to insufficient ground. Therefore, remember to ground the battery to the engine/transmission. Then ground the chassis to this same location. The cab can then be grounded to the chassis.

Test Components Beforehand

Something that I have learned over the years is that prior to wiring a vehicle, use a 12-volt battery charger to test each light. If the light doesn't work before (due to a bad bulb or other issue), it is never going to work after the wiring is installed, which may cause you to pull your hair out troubleshooting the issue.

When all of the wiring chores are done, the best way of testing them is to simply use them as designed. However, when they are not working as designed, the first step of diagnosis is to determine if they are receiving electrical current or not. A multimeter will provide that info. Knowing if the electrical device is not receiving power, or not enough, will often diagnose the electrical problem.

Group Wires by Destination

When wiring the truck, connect each wire to the fuse panel, if not already connected from the manufacturer. Prior to completely unrolling each strand of wire, determine where the wires will finally end up. Some will run toward the front of the truck, some to the rear, and some will remain inside the cab. Of those

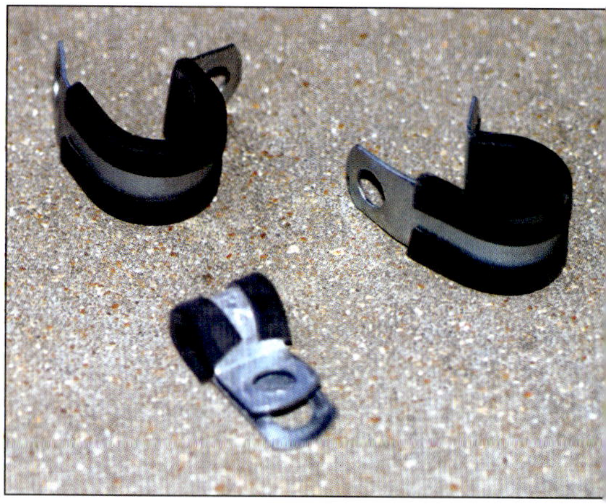

Although they are not fancy, these rubber-coated clamps serve very well for securing not only bundles of electrical wires but also fuel and brake lines. Wrapped around the lines, they can be secured to the surrounding area with either a self-tapping screw or a bolt and nut as desired.

going toward the front, some may need to go through the firewall into the engine compartment, while others may be run along the frame rails toward their destination.

When you have the wires divvied into their respective areas, you can better determine what size hole will be required for all the wires to pass through. Be sure to allow for and use a rubber grommet in any location where wires pass through sheet metal. While the holes should not be significantly larger than necessary, avoid drilling holes that are too small, just to be required to pull the wires back through just to enlarge the hole.

The antenna for the XM satellite radio is relatively small (approximately 1.5 x 3 inches) and has a magnetic base, so physically mounting it is not a big issue. However, short of drilling a hole in the roof, a fair amount of cord is going to be exposed. Now that I realize the issue, I will search for an antenna that could be mounted on the back of the cab but have a vertical mast that could extend above the roof.

Route the Wires

Determine the main route to the destination for the longest wire in the group. Route the wires so that they are protected as well as can be. Avoid hot surfaces and moving components, all the while keeping service in mind. Do not locate any wiring so that it will prevent other components from being serviced. Run the wire to its destination, but do not cut it yet.

Now run the second-longest wire along this same route until it needs to branch off to its destination. Place some wire ties around these two wires, but do not pull the wire ties tight yet. Continue running the wires to their destinations, following these same steps. As you add more wires, add more wire ties. When all wires for a group are routed to their destination, take a step back and see if the routing makes sense or if there is any part of it that should be different.

When satisfied with the routing of the wire, begin cutting the wires to length and adding the necessary connections. Be sure not to cut the wires too short, and remember that during the life of the truck, you may need to replace a terminal for some reason, so having some extra slack in the wire will be a good thing.

Taking your time and paying attention to details will make for a good-looking wiring job that you will be proud to say that you did yourself. With each crimp-on connection made, give it a slight tug to ensure the connection is indeed secure. It is much better to find that out now, rather than on some back road at night.

Install the Antenna

Perhaps a good transition between wiring and bodywork is the installation of the antenna for the satellite radio. Sure, it is a wiring issue plain and simple, as there is the receiver on one end and a plug that goes into the receiver on the other. However, unlike an FM antenna that can be hidden inside the truck, XM reception requires an exterior antenna. Of course, the stereo is located in the interior. The big question is where to breach the cab. I, for one, am hesitant to drill a hole in the roof of the cab.

If the antenna cable came straight out the bottom of the magnetic base, it would be easy enough to drill a small hole and then apply some sealant around the base of the antenna. However, the unit that I purchased has the cable coming out the side. After doing some head scratching, I realized that some amount of the cable will be visible no matter what. Therefore, I will place it near the rear window, atop the roof, and route the cable beneath the rear window rubber. After that, it is a simple matter of running the cable down the rear interior panel and into the console.

CHAPTER 8

PAINT, GLASS, AND UPHOLSTERY

If you have made it this far on your truck project and have not yet thrown in the towel, you are doing better than many. All too often, hot rod projects in general do not get finished for one of two reasons: lack of money or lack of desire. Both are understandable and something that we can all relate to in some regard. There is still much work to do, but we are getting close at this point, so do not give up.

Building a truck requires a certain skill set, and few of us have mastered everything. Most of us can turn wrenches and beat on metal, some more successfully than others. The emphasis of this chapter is on paint, glass, and upholstery, and each aspect requires specialized talents and skills.

Obviously, these skills can be learned, and I have written books on two of those subjects. However, here's the kicker: unless you plan to do this type of work on a regular basis, it may or may not be worth learning to do yourself. Bodywork, painting, and upholstery all require specialized equipment in addition to manual labor. What this boils down to is that there is no shame in paying to have these tasks done by a professional.

However, the bulk of this chapter will provide insight as to why this type of work is so expensive. Whether you do it yourself or pay a professional, this is how it is done.

Depending on the heat and humidity in your shop, in addition to various other circumstances, you may find yourself getting ready to spray primer or paint early in the morning or late at night. This, of course, applies mainly if you are working in your home shop.

Final Bodywork and Surface Preparation

Prior to beginning final bodywork, you must first have the body components fitting as good as they can be. No amount of block sanding is going to make sheet-metal panels magically align with each other or provide consistent body gaps. It is imperative to obtain the best fit possible prior to even touching a can of body filler.

Shims

Shims may be required to properly align panels and one side may

This is the front cab mount beneath the passenger's side of the cab. Traditional body shims are available in various thicknesses and are U-shaped to allow them to be easily inserted or removed as required. While this is good for mockup, many builders choose to replace these with washers of the necessary thickness to eliminate the possibility of a shim working its way out.

If necessary, shim the back of the cab above the black bracket that attaches to the frame. It would make sense to not place any shims between the cab and the frame and then shim other locations as required. However, shims may need to be used to get the cab to sit square on the frame.

This mount is very commonly replaced due to being damaged by collision or rust. Without it, the portion of the front fender that is to the rear of the front wheel merely flops about. While the threaded hole on the backside of the fender accepts a 3/8-inch bolt, the access hole is quite large, allowing for quite a bit of adjustment and the need for a large fender washer.

need more shims than another. Remember, tolerances on the 60-plus-year-old trucks were not great to begin with, and now we are including reproductions of those new ill-fitting panels in with the old.

Four bolts secure the cab to the frame: two in the floorboard area and two behind the seat. Upon setting the cab on the frame, verify that it sits squarely on the frame and does not rock. If there is any movement of the cab prior to securing it to the frame, add the necessary shims between the frame and the cab.

With the cab secured to the frame, install the doors if they are not already on the truck. They should be centered in the door opening. Open and close each door multiple times to ensure that the doors operate as they should.

The front fenders are secured to the cab at the upper cowl. This is a likely place where shims will be required. As you install the front fenders and related sheet metal as described previously in chapter 4, remember that the front fenders are also secured to the radiator, which is secured to the frame. How the body line aligns from the door to the fender will give some indication of what must happen at the cowl location regarding shims. The table "Cab and Front Fender Shims" provides some basic guidelines for aligning the cab and front fenders.

The front fenders are also secured to the cab between the wheel opening and the lower cab with one bolt on each side. This bolt can be shimmed a bit to adjust the gap between the fender and the door both front to back and in/out.

Cab and Front Fender Shims

Fender Position	*Condition at Rear of Fender/ Front of Door*	*Door Position*	*Action Required*
Opposite end of fender is correct	Body line matches and line is straight	Opposite end of door is correct	None required
Opposite end of fender is high	Body line matches	Opposite end of door is high	Front of cab should be raised
Opposite end of fender is low	Body line matches	Opposite end of door is low	Front of cab should be lowered
–	Fender line is higher than the door	And gap is close	Remove fender shims at the cowl
–	Fender line is lower than the door	And gap is close	Add fender shims at the cowl
–	Fender line is higher than the door	And gap is larger at the bottom	Front of the cab should be raised
–	Fender line is lower than the door	And gap is larger at the bottom	Add fender shims at the cowl
–	Fender line is higher than the door	And gap is larger at the top	Remove fender shims at the cowl
–	Fender line is lower than the door	And gap is larger at the top	Front of the cab should be lowered

Filling Holes

Most old trucks are going to have some holes somewhere in the sheet metal that are no longer needed or wanted, and you may never be able to figure out why they are there in the first place. When the hole is no more than approximately 1/4 inch in diameter, you can simply weld up the hole, grind away any excess weld that is above the surrounding surface, and then sand it smooth.

When the holes are larger than that, cut slugs to fit inside the hole and weld them in place. In locations that will not be exposed, weld a small piece of sheet metal in place on the backside. Either of these situations may require a small amount of body filler.

Filling Low Spots

Whether it is filling a hole that was welded shut or a minor repair to a parking-lot dent or errant golf ball, judicious use of body filler will most likely be required somewhere in the final bodywork. If the area to be filled is painted, scuff the surface to bare metal. If the surface is in EDP primer, such as reproduction sheet-metal panels, scuff it with a red Scotch-Brite pad. If the surface is in epoxy primer, apply the body filler directly to it.

Reproduction front fenders are made of two pieces, which creates a seam in the front. To resolve this, the front fenders will first receive a couple coats of epoxy primer and then a bit of body filler.

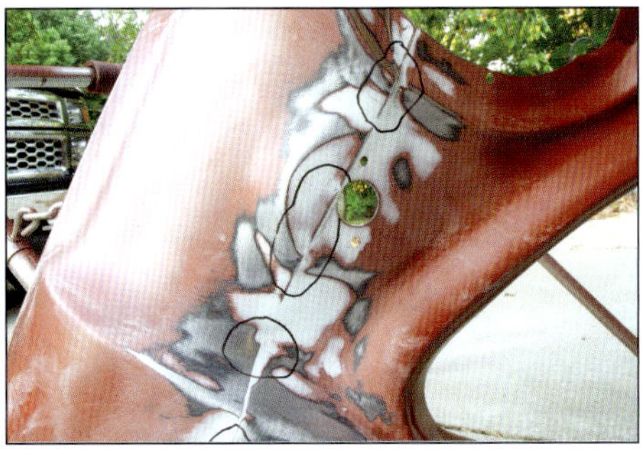

I had not mixed any body filler in quite a while, so I got it a little hot, which resulted in needing to do more sanding than required. After sanding off the excess with 80-grit sandpaper, there are still some slightly low spots within the circled areas. They do not look bad, but a coat of primer would magnify the imperfections and paint would make them stand out greatly.

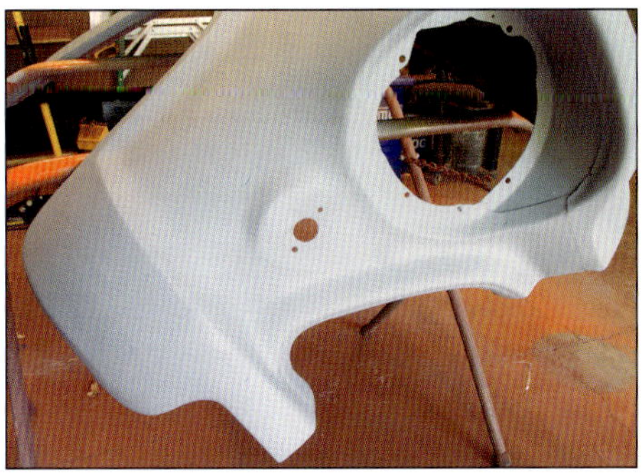

The right front fender still requires some small amounts of filler in a couple of spots and block sanding all over prior to paint. At least it no longer has the obnoxious seam right in the front.

Cleaning Metal

Prior to applying any primer or paint to a surface, that surface must be clean for the primer or paint to stick to it. Use air pressure to blow off layers of sanding dust from body surfaces, as well as between panel gaps, door edges, and doorjambs. Then, dampen a clean cloth or heavy-duty paper shop towel with wax and grease remover and use it to thoroughly wipe off all surfaces.

After merely letting the bedsides dry overnight after applying filler primer and then cleaning with wax and grease remover, the towels were very dirty. Any wax, grease, dirt, or debris on the surface to be painted is going to be a detriment to high-quality paint adhesion.

The mild solvents in wax and grease removers loosen and dislodge particles of silicone dressings, oil, wax, polish, and other materials embedded in or otherwise lightly adhered to surfaces. To assist the cleaning ability of wax and grease removers, follow the damp cleaning cloth with a clean, dry cloth in your other hand. The dry one picks up lingering residue and moisture to leave behind a clean, dry surface. Use a new towel on every panel, wipe wet, and dry thoroughly.

Epoxy Primer

With trucks that are 60-plus years old, you are undoubtedly working with some original sheet metal, probably some new sheet metal, and some of unknown age or surface condition. Some of it may have been media blasted or EDP coated. To get all these metal components to the same condition, applying epoxy primer is a recommended starting point. Epoxy primer, unlike other primers, does not absorb moisture, which will eventually cause rust. An application of epoxy primer also helps to promote adhesion of other primer and paint products.

These are new Dynacorn front fenders that came with an EDP coating. They were first cleaned with wax and grease remover to avoid pressing any contaminants into the surface during the scuffing process. The next step was to scuff the EDP surface with a red Scotch-Brite pad. The fenders were then sprayed with two coats of PPG's DPLF epoxy primer.

When the sheet-metal or chassis components have been stripped to bare metal, the surface should be cleaned with wax and grease remover prior to applying epoxy primer. When any surface rust has been allowed to form on these parts, it is necessary to use sandpaper, a wire brush, or a dual-action sander (DA) to remove the rust prior to applying epoxy primer. For panels that have been coated with EDP primer (typical on reproduction patch panels), the surface should be scuffed with a red Scotch-Brite pad, cleaned with wax and grease remover, and then sprayed with epoxy primer.

Scotch-Brite pads are extremely useful for scuffing the surface slightly on panels that do not require sanding. A common occurrence of this is reproduction panels that typically have an EDP coating on them. Without scuffing this coating slightly, there is a distinct possibility of not having good adhesion. However, you do not want to use sandpaper and cut through the EDP coating.

Plastic Body Filler

When you have straightened or modified any sheet metal or installed any patch panels, you will probably need to apply at least a skim coat of body filler. Whether filler is applied to bare metal, to fiberglass, or to a primed surface, some amount of filler material is spread onto a mixing board or a mixing sheet and then mixed thoroughly with a proportionate amount of hardener, using a flexible spreader.

The amount of hardener used depends on the shop conditions regarding temperature and humidity. As a start, add a proportionate amount of hardener to the filler (i.e., a quarter tube of hardener to a quarter of the container of filler). If it is mixed a little too cool, the curing process can be sped up slightly by placing a portable heater or a heat lamp nearby. If the filler begins to "kick" before it is spread out, scrape it off the mixing board and throw it away, as it won't spread properly.

Since the body filler is one color and the hardener a different color, when the mix is the same color throughout, it is well mixed. If there are streaks of color, keep on mixing. Apply the thoroughly mixed filler with a flexible spreader, but never more than 1/8-inch thick total. If necessary, make a couple of light passes over the area with an empty spreader to even out the filler.

Filler, like most auto body repair products, cures as its various chemical components react and escape from the material that is left. If the filler is applied too thick, it will quite often cure on the outside before all the chemical reaction has taken place on the inside, trapping uncured material inside the repair. When this happens, the repair will not last like it should and will ultimately show up in the finished paint job.

Use 80- or 100-grit sandpaper to knock off the high spots before the filler gets rock hard, but not too soon or you will easily gouge out more material than you really want to. Continue with 80- or 100-grit sandpaper to smooth the entire filled area, then switch to 200- or 240-grit to blend the filler into the surrounding area. When you are finished sanding with 240-grit, you will have a good idea if more filler is required prior to applying primer.

When finished sanding, blow all the sanding dust away with an air nozzle. If there are low spots remaining, lightly rough up the area to be

The new bedsides were EDP coated from the vendor, so they were scuffed with a Scotch-Brite pad, sprayed with two coats of epoxy primer, then two coats of filler primer. The bedsides were pleasantly surprising, as they were very straight with crisp lines. That is not the case with all reproduction panels.

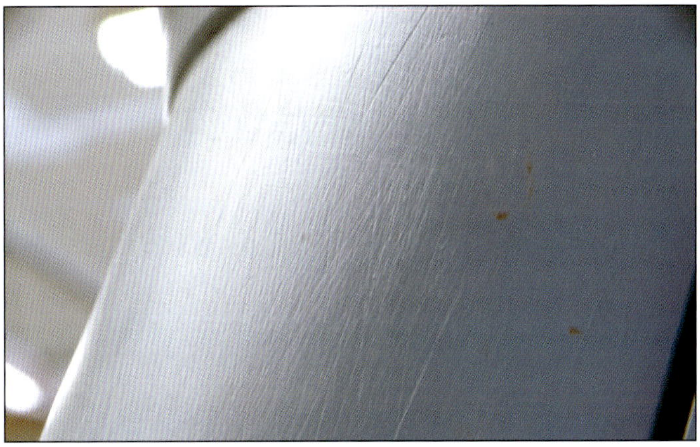

This is the area between the passenger-side door and the rear window. A lot of bodywork has been done in this area as part of the rear panel replacement. While it is solid, it still requires a lot of block sanding to remove the sand scratches prior to being anywhere near ready for paint.

On the smaller, more curvaceous panels, a smaller sanding block will be necessary. Regardless of what size sanding block is used, the same grits will be necessary on all panels. Avoid sanding in the same area continuously. Move the sanding block around in different directions. Also avoid pressing down on the sanding block; let the sandpaper do its job as it glides across the surface.

filled with the previous grit of sandpaper, mix an appropriate amount of body filler, and apply it as before.

Primer-Surfacer

Primer-surfacer includes a high solids content, making it useful for covering slight imperfections such as sanding scratches. While it is commonly referred to as high-build primer, it is not designed or intended to be used as body filler. When localized low spots are encountered, they should be filled with body filler, presuming they are not deep enough to require hammer and dolly work.

A uniform coat of primer-surfacer will provide great visual evidence of how well the bodywork has been done, as it will show most every high or low spot, along with any other blemishes. Clean the area with wax and grease remover, and then use a tack rag to remove dust particles and lint. Mix the primer-surfacer and reducer per the mixing instructions on the label, and then apply two or three coats to all areas where bodywork has been done. Allow the proper flash time between coats.

When several localized spots of repair are on one or adjacent panels, apply primer-surfacer to the entire panel rather than just the spots where repair work has been done. This will allow you to better blend the surfaces during the block sanding process.

Primer-surfacer will be the last undercoat that will be sanded. Therefore, look over the entire surface thoroughly when the last coat of primer-surfacer has dried to ensure that the surface is as uniform, as smooth, and as flat as you can get it.

Block Sanding

After allowing ample time for the primer-surfacer to dry, block sand the entire surface with 320-grit sandpaper. When high or low spots appear, address those now. Repeat this process as required until the surface

After allowing the filler primer to dry the recommended time, it can be sanded. The longer and larger the panel, the longer and larger the sanding board or block can be. Sand all surfaces with 240-grit sandpaper and then 400-grit sandpaper at the minimum. Preparation is what makes or breaks a paint job.

is uniform. Apply a second coat of primer-surfacer, allow it to dry, and then spray on a light dusting of a contrasting color from a spray can enamel.

This guide coat does not need to cover, it merely needs to be somewhat uniform. When the guide coat has dried, sand it with 320-grit sandpaper. The guide coat will quickly disappear from high spots but not from low spots. When low spots appear, fill them as required and apply another coat of primer-surfacer. When the surface is at the proper contour, apply another coat of primer-surfacer, sand with 400-grit sandpaper, then 500-grit, and finally 600-grit sandpaper.

Sanding with finer sandpaper grits will focus on texture smoothness and the removal of sanding scratches and very shallow imperfections. Using the longest sanding board or block available with progressively finer sandpaper is the key to achieving the straightest and flattest surface upon which to apply paint.

Getting It Flat and Smooth

In addition to getting panels aligned and smooth, also strive to get them "flat." This does not mean to remove all the body lines. It means to eliminate all waves or imperfections that distort the reflections off the surface.

Water in a lake or a reflecting pool is flat, providing a perfect reflection. A slight breeze or throwing a pebble into the water temporarily disrupts the flatness, distorting the reflections that it provides. Many amateurs waste their sanding efforts simply by not using a sanding block or sanding board. They use the palm of their hand instead of spending $10 for a sanding block. For sanding to be done efficiently, the sandpaper must make full, even contact with the surface. Being harder and softer, the knuckles and palms of your hands create waves in the panel being sanded.

Another method to sanding is to move the sanding block in different directions. Sanding back and forth in a straight line will merely create a series of grooves and high spots, with the final surface being wavy.

Surface preparation (especially sanding) plays a more important part of the high quality of a finished paint job than most people realize. Having body surfaces that are flat will yield the most brilliant paint and allow for the brightest shine. Any imperfections that you can find now will be greatly magnified after applying a new coat of paint.

Seam Sealer

Seam sealer is available in forms that can be brushed on, but it is typically dispensed from a tube. It is used to seal seams in sheet metal, such as in floorboards, toeboards, or the step area inside the door where the step meets the floor.

Any location that is prone to collecting and trapping moisture is a good candidate for an application of seam sealer. Its application is much easier and less expensive than replacing rusty sheet metal. Most seam sealer products can be applied directly to bare sheet metal or over primed surfaces, but they are usually applied prior to paint.

Sealer

Sealer has multiple purposes, including to prevent top coats from seeping into the under coats and vice versa, to add maximum adhesion, and to ensure a uniform color. If it were not for an application of sealer, areas that received significant bodywork and filler would appear different from those that did not receive bodywork, regardless of the paint color. The sealer provides a uniform surface so that the final paint can appear uniform.

Sealer is typically not sanded; however, sometimes there is a run in the sealer, just as with any other primer or paint product. When this happens, allow the sealer to dry and then use fine sandpaper to remove

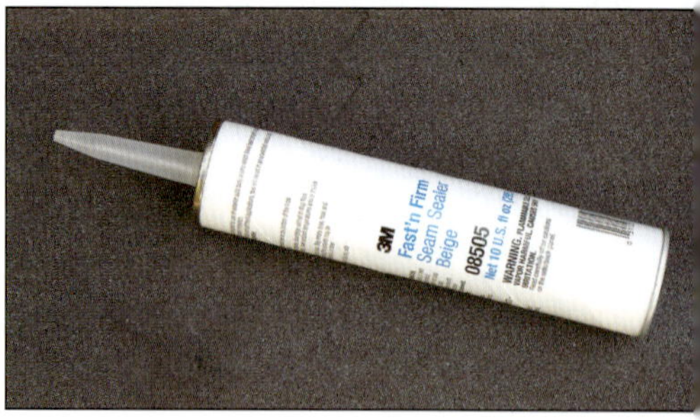

Using a standard caulking gun is probably the easiest method to apply seam sealer. Prior to application, clean the area well by blowing it out with an air hose and then wiping it clean with wax and grease remover.

the blemish. To prevent this blemish from "shadowing," apply spot putty over the area that you just sanded and sand it off. Then, respray this area with sealer. After the sealer has cured in accordance with the label directions, paint can be applied.

Masking

When it comes to masking a truck for primer and paint, use only masking paper and automotive paint–quality masking tape. To use newspaper or hardware store masking tape will cause you more trouble than the money that you may or may not save. When masking large areas, use plastic masking material that is available at retailers of automotive paint products. Understand that less-than-meticulous masking will almost always result in obvious spots of overspray. Some paint overspray can be cleaned off, but proactive masking is much easier than reactive cleaning.

The truck will be easier to paint before the glass is installed. However, situations sometimes call for painting with the window glass already installed. If the roll of masking paper is wide enough, cover the glass with one piece of masking paper.

Begin by masking the weather stripping or metal trim around the window edges with masking tape. Cover the glass with masking paper, folding it as required to fit around the perimeter of the glass. When the paper bulges in the middle, fold it over neatly, then tape the loose edges. Always run lines of tape along the length of paper edges to completely seal off underlying areas. This is especially important when the edge of one piece of masking paper is lapped over another.

When you are painting a truck that is already assembled, do not forget to mask doorjambs before spraying primer and paint. When bodywork calls for priming and painting of door edges and doorjambs, paint these edges first and allow to dry. After they have cured sufficiently for masking tape and paper to be applied, the inside portion of the door and the doorjamb can be masked. The door can then be closed and the exterior primed and painted.

This same procedure should be used if the doors are being replaced. It is much easier to paint the interior side and the perimeter edges of doors while they are off the vehicle. The doors can then be installed on the vehicle, the door edges and doorjambs masked off, and then the exterior panel painted along with the rest of the body.

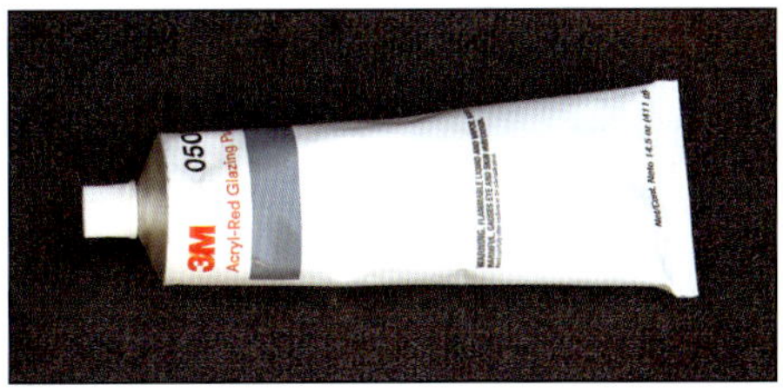

Spot (or glazing) putty comes in a tube and is typically used when there is a small sand scratch or dimple after having applied sealer. Allow the sealer to dry, apply the spot putty, then sand smooth. After allowing time to dry, apply sealer to the affected area.

Different paint systems use different sealers. Some use specific sealers, while others use epoxy primer mixed with a different mixing ratio. For the best results, be sure to use the sealer recommended for the paint system you are using. There is no need to play chemist. One or two coats of sealer is usually all that is required.

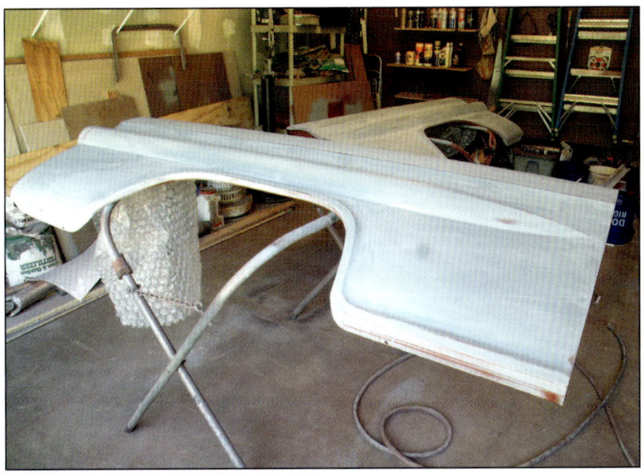

After the final block sanding is completed, use an air nozzle to blow away any sanding dust. Then clean again with wax and grease remover. The wax and grease remover and paper towels are cheap when compared to redoing a paint job because the surface was dirty.

Paint Application

Before painting a truck, decide if a single-color, two-tone, or graphics will be part of the paint scheme. This all fits in with the overall style and use for the truck but should be included in the plans way before you start painting. To a lesser degree, this will also help determine the type of paint that should be used.

When planning on driving the truck on a regular basis, where it may be prone to rock chips and bug splatters, a single-color or stock-type two-tone paint scheme would be appropriate. Using a single-stage acrylic enamel or acrylic urethane, this would be easy to spray and take care of. Since no clear would be involved, it would be easy to touch up if necessary, and would be significantly easier to color match if involved in a collision.

When you plan to drive your truck just to shows or include multiple colors, a base coat/clear coat paint system may be more appropriate. This paint may require a little less effort to maintain the shine due to the clear coat. The clear coat also adds protection to the first color in a multicolor paint scheme if there is an error when spraying or masking for the second color.

Regardless of which type of paint product or the brand, refer to that product's specific instruction sheets for the best performance. Each product may be slightly different, so there is no way to provide completely accurate information for these products here.

Different paint companies may call them different things, but they all provide technical data sheets for their entire line of paint products, primers, color, and clear. They are usually available where paint products are purchased, but you may have to ask for them. These information sheets are usually available through the manufacturer's website as well. Technical data sheets usually provide the following information:

- Required additional products (what else is required to make it work)
- Compatible surfaces (what it can be applied over)
- Compatible top coats (what can be applied over it)
- Surface preparation (how to prepare the surface)
- Mixing ratio (how much of what)
- Pot life (how long it will last before being applied)
- Spray gun setup (what size spray gun tip and how much air pressure)
- Number of coats (how much to apply)
- Flash time (how long to wait between coats)
- Dry times (how long to wait to touch, to handle, to tape)

Other information is often included, but that typically describes more of the chemical aspect of the product that is required for compliance to safety and health regulations.

For the first few coats of epoxy primer, the cab was still mounted to the chassis. To protect the frame, wheels, tires, and suspension components from overspray, they were covered with masking film. It is very thin, but can be used to cover large areas quickly and easily. It can be taped into place or merely weighted down to the floor, hence the upside-down chassis dolly in the front.

Single-Stage Paint

When using acrylic enamel or acrylic urethane, several coats can be applied, if there is proper flash time between coats. This allows more color to be put on the vehicle. With more color, rock chips and other debris are less likely to go all the way down to primer. This is a good thing, as chips that go deeper in the paint, if left alone, will eventually begin to rust.

Additionally, more layers of color allow for more wet sanding and buffing to bring out the shine, which comes from a smoother surface. However, to maintain that shine, the vehicle should be waxed on a regular basis. Many painters also believe that a single-stage paint system that is wet sanded and buffed provides a better color.

Base Coat and Clear Coat

When using base coat/clear coat, the painting process requires a somewhat longer time frame, as the clear coat must be applied within a certain time after the base coat has been applied. Typically, two or three coats of the base coat are applied to obtain coverage, allowing the proper flash time between coats.

After the designated dry time, multiple clear coats are added and allowed to dry. After the proper drying time, the clear may look milky, but that will go away after the surface is wet sanded. Using exceptionally fine sandpaper dipped in water and a light touch, imperfections are removed, providing a glossy finish.

These are the ingredients for PPG's Delfleet Essential HS Polyurethane Single-Stage paint. Left to right are: ESX510 standard activator, ESH200 single-stage hardener, and ESSS in the color of your choice. The recommended mixing ratio is 6:1:1. Mixing sticks, strainers, and mixing cups are also required.

Prep Before Spraying

When it comes to painting, you cannot have too much room or too much light. Whether the truck is painted as a completed assembly or as individual pieces, have adequate room to maneuver about before, during, and after spraying. Also have adequate lighting to avoid missing spots in the paint coverage.

Always mix paint products according to label instructions and apply them at the recommended air pressure. Hold the tip of the spray gun about 6 to 8 inches away from the surface, moving parallel to the surface, and overlapping each pass slightly. See how that works for you, then move closer or farther away, depending on your results. Avoid moving the spray gun in an arc, as this will result in heavy and light applications of paint.

If you do not spray paint regularly, hang a large piece of paper on the wall or use a scrap hood or something to do some practice passes on so that you can get accustomed to the spray gun.

Clean the surfaces to be painted with wax and grease remover to remove any contaminants that may interfere with good adhesion of the paint. Then, use a tack cloth to remove any tiny pieces of dust particles, lint, or anything else that could cause an imperfection in your painted surface.

Color Application

Other than during the original manufacturing process, two schools of thought exist when it comes to painting vehicles. The choice depends largely on how much of the truck is going to be painted, how much room is available, and how much time you have. There is no right or wrong, so whichever method you choose is right for you.

On a complete, frame-off rebuild, the builder usually assembles all the sheet metal to ensure that everything fits. Everything is then disassembled, primed, painted, and reassembled. This requires a lot of space to spread everything out for painting. It also requires extreme care during reassembly, as any scrapes or scratches will require touch up.

The other option, one that is perhaps better suited to the use of single-stage paint, is to prep and paint the cab interior and underside, as well as the inside and edges of the hood, doors, fenders, and tailgate. Then, reassemble the entire front half of the truck.

Mask off the previously painted surfaces and paint the rest of the truck. This should minimize any paint touch-up work and will provide uniform color on adjacent panels. The truck bed will typically be easier to paint while off the truck frame.

Clear Application

Other than clear not having any pigment, it is applied just like color, and according to the specific instructions for the specific product. However, since it has no pigment, more care is required to ensure that the coverage is even. Perhaps the most important difference is the required flash time between the last color coat and the first application of clear in a base coat/clear coat paint system.

Wet Sanding

Although wet sanding (color sanding) is not required on single-stage paints, it does provide a smoother surface, which provides

After allowing the sealer to dry for the recommended amount of time, color can now be applied. When using a base coat/clear coat system, two or three coats of color are typically required to provide coverage. Additional coats of clear are applied to allow for wet sanding to obtain a slick, glossy finish. With a single-stage paint system, more color is applied so that it can be wet sanded to provide that same glossy finish.

Whether wet sanding the clear coat of a base coat/clear coat paint system or the color of a single-stage system, the process is the same. Do not remove any layers of color or clear, but simply smooth the surface. Using 2000-grit or finer sandpaper, a light touch, and plenty of water to remove the slightest of imperfections will greatly improve any paint job.

a more reflective and shinier surface. Single-stage or base coat/clear coat paint wet sanding is done using the same process. As a basic rule of thumb, most paint products that are catalyzed (meaning that reducer and hardener is added when the paint is being mixed) can be wet sanded and buffed. However, not all paint is suitable for wet sanding, so verify with the paint dealer if unsure.

Many clear coat products designed to be used with base coats can be wet sanded as soon as 24 hours after application, while single-stage paints should be allowed to cure for 60 days or longer prior to wet sanding. Wet sanding will bring out a much deeper shine and gloss when followed by controlled buffing and polishing.

A couple of things must be mentioned when it comes to wet sanding. The intent is not to remove paint (or clear), but merely to make it as smooth as possible. You must apply extra coats of material if you plan to wet sand.

Just like other sanding chores, use a sanding block. Begin with 800- to 1000-grit wet-or-dry sandpaper. Fill a clean bucket with water and a small bit of car wash soap to aid in lubrication. Let the bucket and water sit for at least 15 minutes to allow any

After painting anything that has been masked, be gentle when removing the masking tape. Give the surface some time to dry, then pull the tape back on itself. This will provide a crisp edge, which is what you want.

minerals in the water to settle to the bottom.

Keep the sandpaper wet, apply light pressure, and move the sanding block in a circular motion. When finished wet sanding a panel, repeat the process with 1500- to 2000-grit wet-or-dry sandpaper. Repeat with increasingly finer grits until you achieve the desired finish.

Buffing

Like wet sanding, check first with the paint supplier to verify that the paint system being used is compatible with buffing and their specific buffing instructions. In the case of

Meguiar's products have always provided great results, are easy to use, and do not break the bank, making them a favorite of mine. Buffing and polishing compounds are typically available where paint is purchased and/or at local auto parts stores.

Buffing pads can be cloth (used at relatively low speed) or foam (used at relatively high speed). Which type to use depends on the buffing or polishing compound being used, so be sure to read the directions with the product chosen.

Finishing off the cargo area are polished stainless-steel strips with stainless-steel fasteners. They are securing 3/4-inch red oak boards that have been sanded, stained, and then coated with clear satin spar urethane.

single-stage urethane, buffing new paint with gritty compound will dull the surface and ruin the finish. On the other hand, base coat/clear coat or tri-stage systems greatly benefit from buffing, resulting in a more brilliant finish with a much deeper shine.

Bed Wood Installation

Bed wood for use in these trucks is bound to bring up considerable opinions, with most of them being valid to some extent. Which type of wood to use and the type of finish to apply are common questions, but the best answers depend on how the truck will be used. It is quite that simple. About the only thing that is definite is that the thickness of bed wood is 3/4 inch thick.

From the factory, these trucks were equipped with pine wood held down with steel strips. The finish applied at the factory is anyone's guess, as no one source seems to have a definitive answer. Some say the wood was painted, while others say that it was coated with various types of oil-based products. But this is not a restoration book, so that probably does not matter.

Most truck builders use some species of hardwood, which typically lasts longer than any species of softwood. Types of wood range from a common plain grain, such as pine (softwood) and oak (hardwood), to exotics such as leopard wood and zebra wood. If using the truck to actually haul stuff, oak is a common choice. While it is a naturally light-colored wood, it can be stained as dark as desired, and it is very durable with the correct coating. Some of the exotic woods are simply too expensive to use in anything other than a show-only truck.

Regardless of who finishes the wood, softwood will be less expensive than hardwood. Several sources offer bed wood that is already cut to the correct dimensions and with the correct grooves, leaving only final finishing prior to installation. The wood of choice can also be purchased from a woodworking supply house to save some initial expense, but each board will need to have grooves cut and to be finished.

Regardless of the wood species chosen, if the wood is going to be subjected to use, abuse, and weather, an oil-based finish will ultimately be more practical, as it will do a better job of repelling water. If the truck is kept in a garage most of the time, stain the wood to achieve the color that you want and then apply several coats of spar varnish that is sanded between coats. This will provide a smooth, shiny finish. Regardless of the type of finish, be sure to coat the ends of the boards extremely well, as that will be the typical access point for moisture that will ultimately lead to failure of the surface finish.

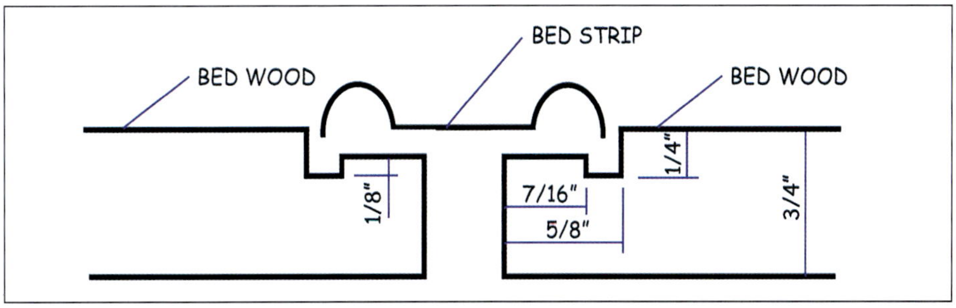

While the width of bed floor material may vary, to use the stock-style bed strips, the grooves must be consistent. The grooves are cut wider than the material of the bed strip to allow for expansion and contraction of the wood between wet and dry seasons. The bolts that secure the bed strips fit between the individual pieces of bed wood.

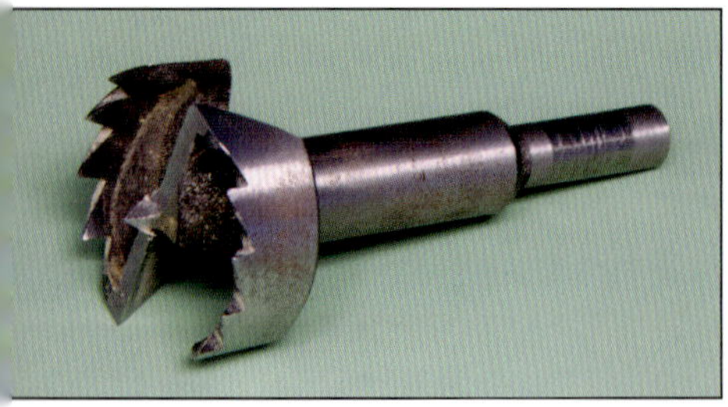

Forstner bits are available in several sizes and are designed to cut a blind hole, providing a flat surface at the bottom of the hole. When drilling the holes for the bed-to-frame mounting bolts, these are required to provide a recess for the offset washers.

Prior to installing the bed wood, the cross sills will need to be installed regardless of the truck being a Stepside or Fleetside. On a Stepside, the cross sills connect to the angle strips at the bottom of the bedsides. On a Fleetside, two cross sills connect to the front and rear of the wheel well, with a third being located just behind the front panel.

Holes in the rear sill and each of the cross sills align and are spaced for the widths of the boards, which are not all the same. If you want to use boards that are different widths than stock, you will be required to drill additional holes in the rear sill and cross sills (or use a different type of hold-down system). Round holes are for bolts that secure the bed strips, while the six square holes are for carriage bolts that secure the bed to the frame.

Prior to staining the wood, the grooves for the bed strips should be cut (with a table saw or a router) and the bed mounting holes drilled. Use a Forstner bit to drill the smooth-bottomed recess for the offset washer.

For the shop truck, I used red oak wood with two coats of Minwax Special Walnut stain. It will then be sealed with three coats of clear semigloss Minwax Indoor/Outdoor Helmsman Spar Urethane. Stainless-steel bed strips will hold it all in place.

If the bolt holes are not drilled before staining, it is not a big deal; however, ensure that all holes are drilled prior to applying a sealer. The stain is merely decorative, while the sealer will protect the wood. Be sure to apply multiple coats, allowing the manufacturers' recommended dry time between coats. Remember to apply sealer to the ends of each board as well.

Bed wood that is cut to length and to the correct profile is available from a variety of sources. Since there are several bed configurations to consider, I refer you to GMC Paul's Truck Parts (gmcpauls.com). The website provides a lot of information about bed wood for GM trucks.

Rather than pay the shipping costs for bed wood on top of the cost of the wood itself, I chose to purchase the wood from a local supplier to cut, drill, and finish myself. This will be more labor intensive, but at least it will be gained experience as well.

While it would be nice to have a truck bed with walnut wood that has been sanded glass smooth and coated with several coats of automotive clear that has been sanded between each coat, that certainly is not practical for any truck that I own. It is not my intention to abuse this truck, but it is a truck and will be a daily driver. It is foreseeable that it will haul hot rod parts to and from swap meets, lumber and landscaping goods for the latest home project, and who knows what else.

For that reason, the wood must be durable and the finish practical. What that translates to is some 3/4-inch red oak boards that will be stained and then coated with spar urethane. With this being an oil-based product, it is suitable to provide protection from sunlight, rain, and temperature changes.

Tailgate Chains

While most everyone can appreciate the vintage styling of these trucks, one of the most common "issues" among builders is what to do with the tailgate chains. In the stock configuration, a length of chain is bolted to the truck bed on each side with a hook on the opposite end that passes through an eyelet on the tailgate to lock it in the upright position or support it in the open position. On a Fleetside bed of this vintage, there is also a short metal bar added to the equation.

This system was quite simple and it worked for the utilitarian purpose of these trucks when they were first built. However, chains, hooks, sheet metal, and paint are rarely a good combination. Today, it is not uncommon for the materials alone for a professional paint job to cost more than the price of one of these trucks new.

Various methods have been used by custom builders of these trucks to replace the chain and hook. A simple way to latch the tailgate in the closed position is to install a hitch pin (found at farm implement stores) or to insert a bolt and secure it with a nut. While these methods secure the tailgate, they do not work for the open position. Various configurations of straps or cables have been used to provide support.

For the shop truck project, a metal strap kit and latch mechanism of unknown manufacturer was purchased from one of the big truck parts suppliers. Hindsight being 20/20, I remind you to initially install these items prior to painting the bed and tailgate. In my case, I was not aware of these products until after the bed had been painted, as I planned to use the stock configuration.

Tailgate Chains to Hinge Conversion

1 *The passenger's side of the tailgate shows the tongue on the outside of the tailgate, which would have a slotted bar placed over it with the hook passing through it to secure the tailgate when closed. The tongue on the inside is for the hook to pass through when supporting the tailgate in the open position.*

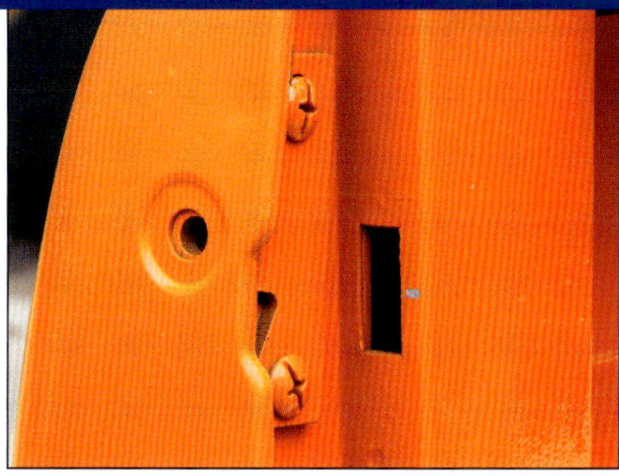

2 *Begin the installation by removing the two screws that secure the brace inside the bed where the stock chain would mount. Retain the two screws, as they will be reused. The kit that I purchased includes two round steel discs to be welded in to fill the remaining hole. Again, install this, then paint.*

3 *While a thought would be to simply install a polished button-head bolt to fill the hole, there is now no longer any threads and you are unable to install a nut on the backside.*

4 *These two pieces will replace the original piece just removed. They will only fit with the original holes in one way, so at least that part is easy. The raised tab is where the upper end of the strap will connect to the truck bed.*

5 *Using the original screws previously removed, secure the new pieces to the bedside.*

6 *To make room for the two pieces of the hinged strap to fold up inside of the tailgate, the edge of the tailgate must be trimmed. A steel template is included with the kit. Clamp the template in place per the kit instructions in order to scribe a line in which to trim. The tailgate is multilevel in this area, so it must be clamped so that it is flat.*

7 *To be more visible when cutting, I placed masking tape along the scribed line. Use a cut-off wheel, jigsaw, pneumatic saw, or plasma arc cutter to make the necessary cuts.*

8 *After trimming the tailgate, use the template in this position to locate the two holes where the opposite end of the hinged strap will connect to the tailgate.*

9 *After locating the holes, use a center punch to provide a divot for the drill bit to start.*

10 *Drill the holes to the correct size for the provided hardware.*

11 *Using the hardware provided, secure the lower end of the hinged strap to the inside of the tailgate.*

12 *Raise the tailgate so that the upper end of the hinged strap can fit over the raised tab previously installed in the truck bed. Raise and lower the tailgate multiple times to check for proper alignment. When everything fits and works as it should, repeat the procedure on the opposite end of the tailgate.*

Tailgate Latch Installation

The hidden latch that I used on the shop truck is installed inside the body of the tailgate. It is spring-loaded and includes a knob that extends through the interior side of the tailgate. Installation is straightforward, as one hole must be drilled to slide the body of the latch into the tailgate, one for a screw to secure it in place, and two to form the ends of a slot for the knob to slide in for each end of the tailgate.

Hidden Tailgate Latch Installation

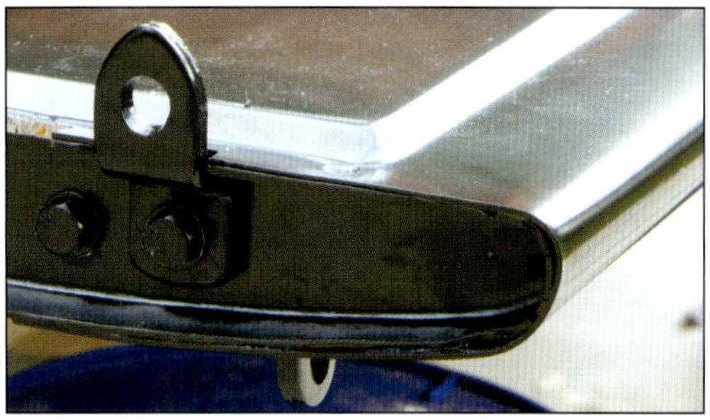

1 *Determine a location in the upper portion of the tailgate for the latch mechanism to be installed. Mark this location with a center punch.*

2 *Drill a 1/4-inch pilot hole, then drill a 5/8-inch hole for the latch mechanism to be installed.*

3 *While the correct location of the mounting hole on the inside of the tailgate is somewhat critical to smooth operation, the instructions provided did not go into much detail on how to determine where it is. The hole must be centered on the latch mechanism and the correct distance from the edge. By installing the housing backward (using the knob to ensure that the mechanism does not disappear forever into the bowels of the tailgate), I was able to visually align the mechanism with masking tape.*

4 *By clamping the mechanism in place on the inside wall of the tailgate with the end flush with the edge of the tailgate, the necessary holes can be determined.*

5 *In total, the centers of three holes are located. The one closest to the center of the tailgate is for the screw that secures the latch mechanism in place. The two holes closest to the edge of the tailgate will form the ends of the slot for the knob that operates the latch to slide.*

6 *Drill the inside hole to be the correct size for the hardware. Slide the mechanism into the end of the tailgate, then thread the screw into the mechanism. After painting and when installing the latch mechanism for the final time, I would believe that a small amount of a thread-locking compound would be prudent.*

7 *After drilling the two other holes, use a small die grinder wheel or whatever is available to remove the material between the two holes to create the slot. For smooth operation, use a file to smooth the inside edges of this slot.*

8 *With the spring-loaded latch in place within the tailgate, close the tailgate. Snap the latch mechanism two or three times to act as a centerpunch, marking the corresponding location for a hole to be drilled in the bedside.*

9 *After drilling the necessary hole, repeat the process for the remaining side. To open or latch the tailgate, slide both latch knobs toward the middle of the tailgate, open or close the tailgate, and then release the latch knob.*

Glass Installation

Installing glass is like most other things; it is easy if you know what you are doing and have enough experience to have picked up some tricks of the trade. However, glass is both expensive and fragile, so making a mistake can take a toll on your budget if you break a piece, such as the windshield or the large back glass. Additionally, if the glass is not sealed properly, it will lead to annoying air and water leaks. For those reasons, there is certainly no disgrace in hiring a professional glass shop to install the glass in your truck.

Windshield and Back Window Glass

If you install the curved glass in the windshield and the back window, begin by laying strips of masking tape around the edge of the window openings to help protect paint from accidental bumps and scrapes. Also consider placing a thick blanket over the hood to protect the paint on it as well.

The windshield and back window glass are installed in much the same way on these trucks. The glass is set inside grooves within a heavy rubber molding, which includes a second groove running around the outer molding perimeter. Fit the molding around the glass and then insert a cord into the outer perimeter groove and pull it taut. Wrap the cord so that both ends meet in the middle of the bottom groove.

Have an assistant (or two) hold the glass and molding unit in place from outside the vehicle, while another person inside the cab pulls the cord. As the cord is pulled away from the rubber it also pulls its edge back, allowing the molding to fit around the sheet metal edges that form the window opening. The inside person pulls one end of the rope, then the other end, easing on the bottom lip first, and then inching up each side and around each top corner, toward the middle of the top groove, at which point the rope pulls free and the last portion of molding pops into place.

Door Glass

Installing the door glass is relatively easy, as it is much smaller than the windshield and is flat glass. Whether using the stock vent win-

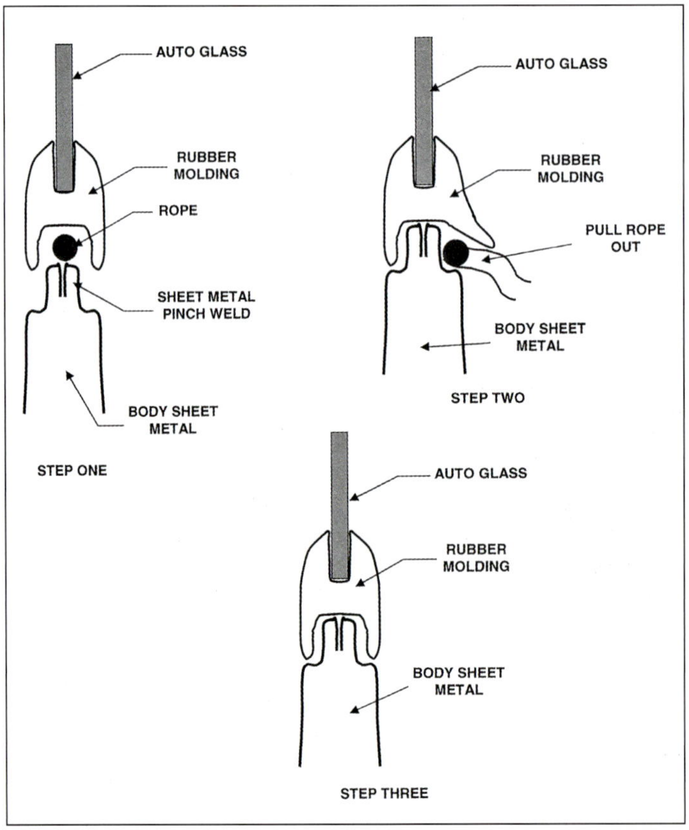

Installation of fixed glass (windshield and rear window) is relatively easy, but there is always the possibility to break the glass during installation. To install the glass, you need the appropriate rubber molding, a length of rope (approximately 3/8-inch diameter and long enough to reach more than all the way around the glass), and some dishwashing liquid and water in a spray bottle. While money can be saved by doing it yourself, if you make a mistake and are forced to purchase more glass, your savings may be lost.

dows or one-piece glass, roll-up or power, the lower edge of the glass is clamped into the window riser mechanism with two to four clamping mechanisms, depending on manufacturer.

The interior door panel needs to be remove to access the window riser. Loosen the clamping mechanisms, slide the glass into them, and tighten the clamping mechanisms slightly. Slowly close the window and check for any binding. If anything binds, stop and determine the cause of the binding. The glass may need to be moved forward or rearward. Run the window through the up/down cycle multiple times, until everything works as it should. Verify that the clamping mechanisms are snug but not so tight that they damage the glass.

Miscellaneous Installations

If you have used a base coat/clear coat paint system that can typically be wet sanded and buffed within a week, you can save some labor time by installing the other parts after the buffing has been completed. However, if you have used a single-stage paint, you may not want to wait 60 to 90 days before installing the remaining parts. For the most part, these exterior parts are easy enough to remove prior to buffing to avoid damaging them and then reinstall when finished.

Bumpers

Whether painted or chrome, recruit an assistance when installing the bumper or bumpers. Installation is easy enough, as they simply bolt on, but a miscue could certainly scratch some paint badly, quickly. Loosely install all the mounting hardware, then step back to verify that the bumper is mounted squarely with the truck, before fully tightening the bolts.

Headlights and Bezels

Install the headlight buckets and secure them to the front fenders with three screws. Plug each headlight into the appropriate electrical plug, position the headlight in place, and secure it by installing the outer retainer.

The headlight buckets fit into the fender one way, due to the shape of the headlight opening in the fender to prevent the headlights from spinning around. If the bucket does not fit flush, rotate it one way or another until it does. Depending on such things as stock versus reproduction fenders and headlight buckets, you may be required to drill the necessary holes.

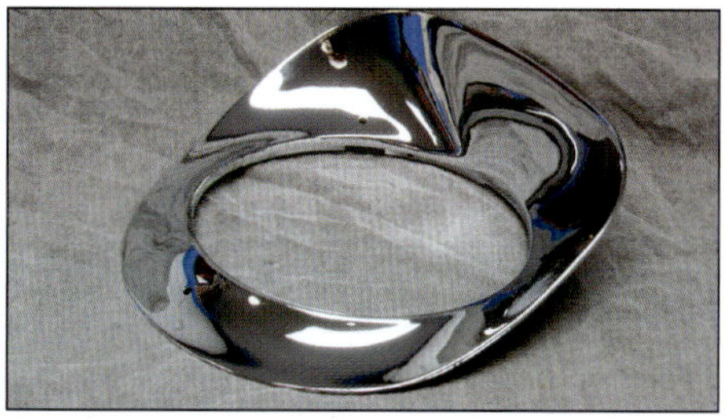

Headlight bezels may be chromed or painted; the choice is yours. From the factory, they were typically painted white, but it is your truck, so you can paint or powder coat them the color of your choice.

While the bezel is necessary to cover the inside opening of the fender, a headlight retainer ring is required to secure the headlight to the truck.

Note that with a four-light system (on the 1958–1959 models), one headlight is for low beam, while the other is for high beam. The light bulbs are specifically high beam or low beam, so be sure that they do not get mixed up. Whether the bezels are painted or polished, now would be a good time to apply some wax or chrome polish as appropriate, to preserve their finish. Install the bezels and secure with three screws.

Exterior Door Handles

Prior to installing the interior door panels, install the exterior door handles. They are secured with two screws. Using a magnetic tip screwdriver helps with this task. A magnet with a telescoping handle or long flexible handle will usually work to retrieve the screws that drop into the bottom of the door.

Exterior Mirrors

For the stock-type exterior mirrors, the one on the driver's side can typically be installed by simply securing it to the door with three screws, as there is a weldnut inside already. You might not have that luxury on the passenger's side, so the interior door panel must be removed to provide access to the inside of the door. After installing the exterior mirrors, be sure to adjust them as necessary to get their full benefit.

Upholstery

Prior to installing the upholstered seats and carpeting, any insulation material that is going to be used should be installed. A quiet and comfortable truck will make your time behind the wheel all that much more pleasant.

Insulation Material

When choosing insulation for the truck, realize that there are two types of insulation to deal with: sound dampening and thermal. While noise caused by vibration from the engine and wind cannot be eliminated, it can be minimized by the addition of sound-dampening insulation. Acoustically dead material, such as Dynamat's Extreme, is a self-adhesive, dense, rubberized asphalt material, weighing 1 or 2 pounds per square foot.

Along with engine noise comes engine heat. With the engine in front of the cab and exhaust below the cab, anything located inside the cab is going to be subjected to engine heat, regardless of the ambient temperature. To minimize this, a thick fibrous material or open-cell foam should be applied to both the firewall and floor at a minimum. It can also be applied to the inside of the roof, doors, and back panel of the cab, if desired.

To minimize the effects of engine noise, wind noise, and engine heat, a layer of Dynamat Extreme was applied to the firewall and floor of the shop truck after the interior was painted. The material has a self-adhesive backing, which makes it quite easy to install, especially to the flat floor of a truck cab.

Begin by cleaning the area to be covered with wax and grease remover. Then, unroll the material until it covers the area to be covered. The material comes in different sizes depending on which specific products are used.

After cutting the material to the approximate size, remove the backing material from the middle of the material and press it into place. Working outward from the middle, peel off more backing and press the insulation material into place. Use a hard roller to push the material into any creases or crevices, such as around the transmission tunnel. Complete the installation by trimming away any excess. Use a utility knife to cut a small X at the location of any seat or seat belt mounting locations.

Insulation Installation

1 ***Sound-deadening material comes in various sizes. The Dynamat Extreme comes in pieces about 2 feet by 3 feet, making them easy to handle. After cutting the material to the required shape and size, the backing can be peeled off, and the material pressed into place. Use a wooden roller to press the material in place.***

2 ***Lay the sound-deadening material in place. Check for any obstacles or any holes for seats or seat belts that need to be opened. Be sure to trim around the cab mounting bolts, as there is always the possibility that the cab may need to be removed sometime in the future.***

3 ***Using a pair of scissors or a utility knife, trim the material as required to fit in the intended area.***

4 *For any required holes, use a utility knife to cut an X in the material. Depending on the thickness of the material, you may need to cut a circle around the outside of the hole, rather than attempting to push the material into the hole.*

5 *After cleaning the surface, peel off the backing from a portion of the material, and press it into place. Peel off more of the backing and press it into place until the entire piece is in position. Then roll the entire surface with a solid roller, especially in any depressed or recessed areas.*

Carpeting

To extend the life and quality of the carpeting, begin by installing carpet padding. Cut the padding slightly oversize and then place it in the floor of the cab so that it is positioned to reach all the way across and front to back. Fold about half of it over and apply spray adhesive to the back of the padding and the floor surface. When the spray adhesive gets tacky, press the padding into place. Now fold the remaining half over, apply spray adhesive as before, and then press it in place after the adhesive gets tacky. Then, trim the padding to size.

Carpeting is installed using the same process as with the carpet padding. Position the carpet centered in the truck. Fold over half and apply spray adhesive to the back of the carpeting and the carpet padding. When the spray adhesive becomes tacky, press it into place. Repeat for the remaining carpet.

Seats

After the carpet or rubber floor mat is installed in your truck, the seating (bench or buckets) can be installed. For a bench seat, get an assistant to help install it and get it positioned. Then, secure the seats to the floor with Grade-8 bolts with washers and lock nuts or mounting plates.

Regardless of the condition of the body, having a project in just one color of primer will typically improve its looks substantially. The shop truck has new doors and back panel, along with a host of other new sheet-metal parts, so most of it is good. However, the lower part of the firewall and the underside require some work. The cab will be removed from the frame for that.

Unlike the cab, the bed is all-new sheet metal. It merely required scuffing of the EDP coating and two coats of epoxy primer for corrosion protection. Two coats of filler primer were then applied and block sanded with 240-grit and then 400-grit sandpaper. After a coat of sealer, three coats of single-stage urethane color was added.

CHAPTER 9

Before the First Drive

By now, we are all looking forward to firing up the engine, rolling the truck out of the garage, and taking that first drive. No doubt about it, this is what we have been working toward. For me, it has been a 15-year adventure in the making. Regardless of the anxiety level, there are some things that need to be checked and attended to before that first drive. Double-check everything to ensure that you and the truck come home safely.

Grasp the belt at about the midway point in the span and pull outward or push inward, depending on accessibility. On most street-driven automotive engines, about 1/2 inch of deflection will get it in the ballpark.

Belts

Verify that all engine belts are tightened to the proper tension. The proper tension depends on the length of the span, but if you have gotten this far building the truck, you probably have a good idea of what looks to be correct.

If the belts are too tight, they will be prone to breakage or damage to bearings of the accessory they are driving. If the belts are too loose, they will simply not be efficient at turning what they are supposed to and will be prone to being thrown off the pulley. Depending on where you are, it could be a long walk back home.

Tire Pressure

Checking the tire pressure is a good habit to get into, regardless of what you are driving or how often you drive. Contemporary tires have stiffer sidewalls than the stock tires for these trucks, so it is not so obvious

Carrying a good air pressure gauge in your truck and checking the air pressure in the tires on a regular basis is a good habit to get into. With all the conveniences, such as tire pressure sensors, in our late-model vehicles, it may be like learning to drive and taking care of a vehicle again.

Regardless of the type of wheels, verify that they are secured with the correct type of lug nut for the wheels and to the proper torque value. Every new wheel that I have purchased had this information in the box, along with other info, such as how often to check for the first so many miles.

when the tires are low on air. Good tires are expensive, but they will typically provide 50,000 to 60,000 miles if properly inflated, balanced, and aligned.

Fasteners

If you have built this truck from the ground up, chances are that most fasteners have been together and apart multiple times during the build. During the final reassembly is the best time to ensure that all fasteners are tightened as required and tightened to specific torqued specs if applicable.

All fasteners should be tight, but double-checking the suspension and steering components is especially prudent. You sure do not want to crash your newly completed truck for any reason, but especially not because a fastener was not tight.

Obviously, the lug nuts must be tight, but they are certainly worth double-checking prior to leaving the garage. They should also be checked after driving approximately 100 miles. Most new wheels will have information included that provides the proper torque specification.

Fluids

Other than windshield washer fluid, most any fluid in your truck is especially important and will rear its ugly head if not at the proper level. Take the time to check all fluids before moving the truck out of the garage under its own power.

Engine Oil

New crate motors and most rebuilt engines require a specific break-in routine that may vary depending upon the engine builder. This break-in routine specified by the engine builder should be followed very closely and may include multiple oil and filter changes in a relatively short time.

If the engine is not a fresh rebuild, it still deserves an oil and filter change. As with any oil change, check the level on the dipstick to verify that the engine oil is refilled to the proper level. Also, verify that it is the proper dipstick for the engine and oil pan. A deep-sump or high-capacity oil pan will require a longer dipstick than stock. Verify that the drain plug is not dripping after oil is added and that the oil fill cap is properly reinstalled.

Transmission Fluid

When using a rebuilt transmission, automatic or manual, it most likely does not have fluid in it when

The two biggest causes of failure to automatic transmissions are excess heat and low fluid. You may need to reach back quite a ways to reach the automatic transmission dipstick, which is something that can be cured somewhat during the construction phase.

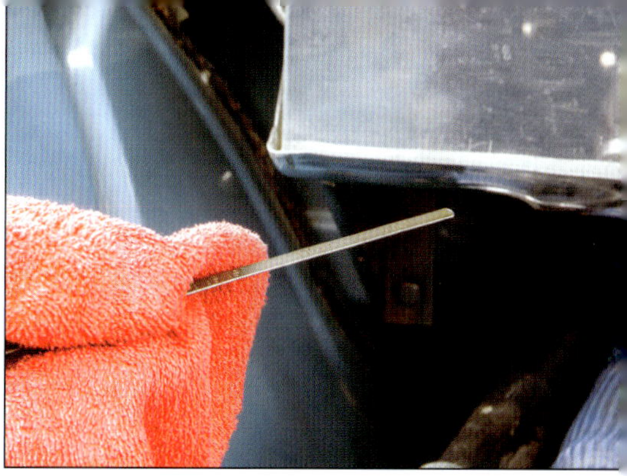

Before firing up that engine for the first time, ensure that it has oil in it, and in the case of a new engine, prime the oil pump. Also, be sure to check the oil level on regular intervals to verify that it is not leaking or burning oil.

When checking the oil level, remember to check the fluid for the power steering pump if the truck is equipped with one.

you take delivery of it. Find out from the rebuilder what transmission fluid they recommend and how much the transmission requires. If you are simply using a transmission from a donor vehicle, a flush and new fluid can breathe new life into an older transmission.

On an automatic transmission, check the fluid level on the dipstick on a regular basis to ensure longevity. Never run the transmission low on fluid.

Rear-End Fluid

Do not forget to fill the rear-end axle housing with an appropriate grade of rear-end fluid. It is often out of sight, out of mind, but without fluid, the gears will quickly let you know that they need some fluid. This has been known to happen to big-name shops, so believe me, it does happen.

Ball Joint Lube

Neither stock nor fully polished independent front suspension components are going to last long if the ball joints are not lubricated. You should also verify that the rubber boots are intact. If the build has taken a long time, the boots may be cracked or torn before there are any miles on the odometer. Lastly, verify that the wheel bearings are packed with grease as well.

Anywhere there is a grease zerk, be sure to hit it with the grease gun. Since it is difficult to see when installed, do not forget to lube the U-joint grease zerk.

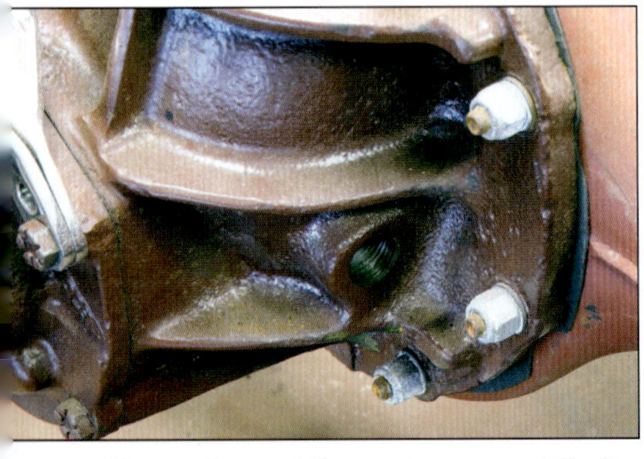

Regardless of the make or model of the rear axle housing, there will be a fill plug on it somewhere. On a 9-inch Ford rear end, the fill hole is located on the driver's side of the third member and is removed with a 3/8-inch ratchet. If you can stick your finger in this hole and reach the fluid, it is full. If not, some needs to be added.

Brake Fluid

Not only should the brake fluid be topped off, the brakes also need to be bled. Begin with the wheel that is farthest away from the master cylinder in terms of brake line. Then, bleed the next farthest, doing the closest one to the master cylinder last. Be sure to refill the master cylinder as necessary during the brake bleeding process.

Check for leaks anywhere in the braking system and resolve any issues prior to driving the truck. After bleeding the brakes or doing any work on the brake system, it is always good to verify that you have a firm brake pedal prior to starting the engine.

Antifreeze/Engine Coolant

In all but extreme locations, a 50/50 mix of antifreeze and water is what you should run as engine coolant in your radiator. Unless you know exactly what the coolant capacity of

Since the chassis was the first thing to be built for this project, those parts are getting old now, despite never having been driven. The rubber bushings for the ball joints need to be replaced, grease zerks installed, and grease added. For some unknown reason, we did not install the jam nuts on the tie-rod ends, and who knows where they are now. They will need to be purchased and installed. Also, it needs cotter pins added to all the castle nuts.

Before firing up the engine for the first time, check the radiator for the proper coolant level. After that, a couple of times a year, check the coolant for the proper mix to verify that it will protect the engine in your climate.

Check the brake fluid level on a regular basis and verify that the cap is on correctly to seal out air. If the master cylinder has been mounted beneath the floor, a remote-fill reservoir mounted somewhere under the hood is a great idea.

your radiator and engine are, mix the antifreeze and water prior to pouring it into the radiator.

Fill the radiator and the overflow tank with the coolant mix until they are both full. Leave the radiator cap off, start the engine, and let it run. Eventually, the coolant level in the radiator will drop, which indicates that any trapped air has been eliminated from the coolant system. Add more coolant into the radiator until it is full again. Replace the cap and shut off the engine.

Check for any leaks in the coolant system. Watch the temperature gauge to ensure that it and the thermostat are working correctly.

A/C Unit

If your truck is equipped with air-conditioning, have the unit charged with R-12 or R-134a by a reputable service technician.

Alignment

Having the truck set to the proper alignment specifications and having all wheel/tire assemblies balanced using a balancer that simulates road force will be the best steps you can take toward achieving the best ride, regardless of your suspension type.

Any reputable alignment shop should be able to align the truck, but you may be required to provide those specifications, as they will most likely not be in their database. I believe that the alignment specifications for these trucks should be the same, regardless of the suspension and/or manufacturer. However, I have not been able to verify that.

If you have a stock suspension, you can verify the alignment specifications with a stock service manual. If you have an aftermarket suspension, the manufacturer should have provided alignment specifications with it. That all said, the alignment specifications from Heidt's for their Superide II kit is as follows:

Caster: 1 degree positive
Camber: 1/4 degree positive
Toe-in: 1/8 +/- 1/16 inch

Headlights, Etc.

Proper aiming of the headlights will certainly make nighttime driving safer and more enjoyable. It does not require specialized equipment or even a lot of time, so do yourself a favor and get the headlights aimed properly.

To do this, approximately 35 to 40 feet of uniformly sloped driving area and a wall are needed. The driving surface does not have to be level if it is consistent. If you have a garage with a straight driveway, you are in luck. Park the truck 2 to 3 feet from the wall or garage door. Turn the low-beam lights on. Using a pencil or some tape, outline the bright spots on the wall.

Back the vehicle straight back to about 25 feet away from the same wall. Again, turn the low-beam headlights on. The top of the low beam shining on the wall should be no higher than the top marks on the wall or lower than the center of the

Squeeze the bulb of the hydrometer, then stick the tube into the radiator to draw a sample of the coolant. An indicator of the hydrometer will show to what temperature the coolant system should be able to handle.

Hoses should be somewhat soft and squishy as shown, but not hard, brittle, or cracked. If they fall into the latter category, they should be replaced. Also check that hose clamps are tight and that hoses are not rubbing on anything.

original area. Adjust as necessary and repeat the aiming procedure until it is dialed in. By aiming the low beams in this manner, the high beams of a two-headlight system will automatically be properly adjusted.

For a four-light headlight system (1958–1959 trucks), aim the high-beam lights to be brightest on the same locations as the original bright spots on the wall at the beginning of the process.

Taillights, Brake Lights, and Turn Signals

Unless there is some glass windows that will reflect, checking the lights will require an assistant. Start the truck, leave it running, and turn the lights on. The headlights and taillights should illuminate. Operate the dimmer switch back and forth. The headlights should change from low beam to high beam and back with no change in the taillights.

Turn the headlights off and step on the brake pedal, all brake lights should illuminate. Turn the headlights on and step on the brake pedal; all brake lights should illuminate. Check the turn signals in both directions with the headlights on and off. The turn signals should work whether the headlights are on or off. When the brake pedal is depressed, the rear turn signals most likely will not flash.

If lighting is sporadic, it is most likely a bad ground. If it is consistent, it is probably a bad connection or a bad bulb.

Horn

Check the horn to ensure that it works when the actuator is pressed and turns off when it is not pressed. While you may never use the horn, it is usually required for state safety inspections.

Wiper Blades

I know that some climates do not require windshield wipers and that some people never drive their trucks in the rain, making windshield wipers unnecessary. However, I believe that all 50 states require windshield wipers to pass safety inspection. Regardless of any legal requirement, having a set of functional windshield wipers is a good thing.

Park the vehicle 2 to 3 feet from a wall or garage door. Measure 25 feet back from the front wheels to where they will need to be for the next step. Note that in all actuality, dusk, dawn, or in the shade would be a much easier situation to do this in, but for the photos, I used the available light.

Turn the low-beam headlights on, and then mark the location of the light beams on the garage door with masking tape. After marking the location of the light beams, back the vehicle 25 feet. The top of the low beam shining on the wall should be no higher than the top marks on the wall or lower than the center of the original area. If the lights are outside of those parameters, adjust them accordingly and retest until they are dialed in.

On Task Force pickups, and on most other vehicles, there are two headlight adjustment screws. Typically, one is located above the top center of the headlight and another to one side. The first allows for adjustment up and down, while the second one provides adjustment left and right.

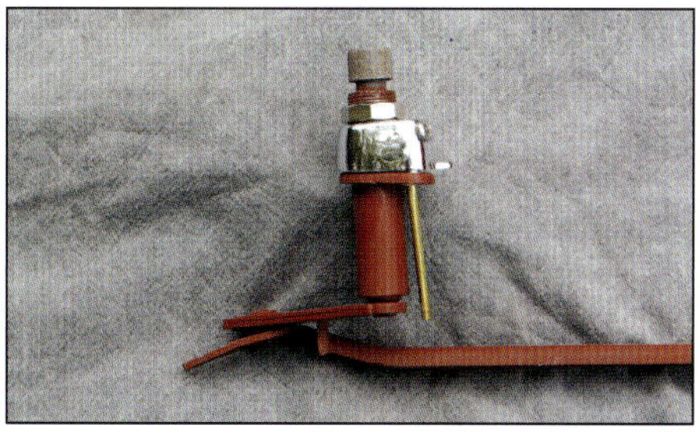

The wiper bezels (shiny part in the photo) were either missing on my truck or had been lost, I'm not sure which. Regardless, they are required for the windshield wipers to function properly. The long brass pin passes through the flange on the wiper transmission to lock it into position.

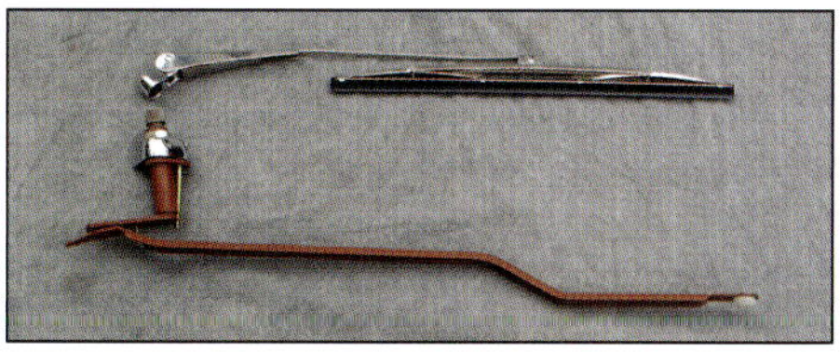

The wiper motor (not shown) attaches to the end of the primed wiper transmission behind the dash (inside the truck) and causes the wiper shaft to rotate in its arc.

The wiper bezel secures the wiper transmission to the outside of the truck's cowl and is secured by a bezel nut.

The wiper arm then slides onto the splined shaft of the wiper transmission.

The First Drive

Now that you have done your pre-trip inspection and everything has checked out, it is now time for the rubber to meet the road. Chances are that this first drive is going to be merely around the block, at least it should be, if that far.

The truck may not be insured at this time, but you would still be liable for any injuries or property damage that may occur. So, if you drive anywhere but on your own property, pick a time when traffic is light and there are not a lot of pedestrians around. There will be plenty of time to show off your truck later, but now is not the time. The purpose of this first drive is to ensure that everything on the truck works as it should.

Do the Brakes Work?

This will be your first real test of the brakes, so test them slowly. Idle the truck out of the garage and then bring it to a safe stop with the brakes. After coming to a complete stop, speed up to about 15 to 20 mph, then apply the brakes to stop the truck. If it is a manual shift, do not forget to apply the clutch also. Increase your speed no more than 10 mph at a time until you feel confident that the truck will stop when necessary from driving speed.

Does It Turn?

The available route for this first drive may restrict some testing, but try to make several turns to the right and several to the left. Does the steering wheel return to the central position? If not, the truck may need an alignment. Does the body sway when turning? If so, a sway bar may need to be installed.

Does It Go Straight?

When driving along a straight, smooth roadway, does the truck drive straight or does it wander? If it wanders, it may be an alignment issue. If an alignment does not fix the issues, inspect the tires carefully.

If no obvious issues are found, have the wheels and tires mounted and balanced using a balancer that simulates applied road force. It may be that the tire should be rotated on the wheel to counteract imbalances in the wheel and the tire.

For all intents and purposes, all wheels are slightly out of balance and all tires are out of balance. If the two are mounted so that the heavy spot on each is in the same location, the out of balance is accentuated. If the heavy spots are located properly, they will counteract each other with less weight being added.

Does It Overheat?

Do not remove the radiator cap if it is steaming. Shut off the engine and let it cool off before doing anything else. When cool enough to check, look for leaks around the water pump, the thermostat housing, the radiator, and the hoses. Verify that the thermostat is installed correctly. Refill the radiator with coolant and let the engine idle and observe for leaks until the problem is solved.

Does Anything Sound Funny or Strange?

Does the drivetrain or suspension make any strange noises? Do the noises increase or decrease upon speeding up or slowing down? Having good answers to these questions will be easier to diagnose the source of the problem.

Are There Any Vibrations?

If the vibration feels like it is coming through the steering wheel, it is probably a wheel alignment related issue. If the vibration feels like it is coming through the seat, chances are that the driveshaft is out of balance.

Does Anything Leak?

After returning home from the first drive, park the truck in a level spot if possible, then let it set for a while. When you move the truck the next time, look for signs of leaks. The color, smell, and location of any liquid will provide a clue as to what is leaking.

Necessary Inspections

Each state has its own rules about the necessary requirements for automotive vehicles, and possibly some that are more strict for custom vehicles. If you are not sure of the requirements in your area, do some research ahead of time to avoid last-minute delays getting the truck on the road.

Safety Suggestions and Recommendations

Safety is of prime importance when it comes to automotive hobbies. Building and driving an old truck is no exception. While experience in building, maintaining, and operating is certainly a bonus, having a second set of eyes inspect the truck after completion is a good idea.

The National Street Rod Association (NSRA) provides its members with a free safety inspection any time they want. This inspection is not mandatory, nor does it replace or supersede any state-required inspections. Its purpose is to advise the owner of any safety items that may have been overlooked. Recommendations of the NSRA are shown in the table "NSRA Safety Recommendations."

Insurance

There are lots of companies to purchase automobile insurance from, so do some comparison shopping. Some are favorable to custom and classic automobiles while others are not. Luckily, I have never needed to file a claim on any of my hobby vehicles. However, they have all been covered through the same insurance company that handles my daily driver vehicles, without any issues or exorbitant prices.

Title and License Requirements

Title and licensing requirements vary from state to state, so check with your state's agencies ahead of time. Presumably, the title was trans-

Most states require at least one outside rearview mirror. If you drive in traffic a lot, one on the passenger's side is a good idea too. While I had planned to go with the small peep mirrors for a real hot rod look, the reality is that I could not see out of them. These original-style mirrors look great and have enough adjustment to do their job.

While it may not mean anything to anyone else, securing the license plate to the shop truck with this license plate frame has been a long time coming. The "Keep on Truckin'" plate frame was on my 1957 GMC, way back when I was a junior in high school. Yes, I am smiling.

NSRA Safety Recommendations	
Required Equipment	
Horn	Electric only
Speed indicator	Speedometer or calibrated tachometer at 65 mph
Rearview mirror	One inside or outside on driver's side of vehicle
Glass	Must be safety plate, Lexan, or tempered glass
Lighting	High-beam; low-beam; tail; brake; license
Windshield wiper	Electric or vacuum operated
Automatic transmission lockout	Neutral and/or park start only
Tires	3/32 tread acceptable. Must meet D.O.T. specifications
Steering	No excessive "play" (2-inch radius maximum) or binding; system must be safely mounted
Throttle linkage	Must not travel past center
Fuel system	Check vent on the trunk and interior-mounted tanks; no clear, plastic lines allowed; no leaks
Exhaust system	No leaks; must pass rear edge of front door and exit exhaust away from vehicle
Self-aligning rod end bearings	Check for fractures, insert sloppiness, or binding
Shock absorbers	One per wheel, no leaks, 2-inch travel in each direction
Brakes	Four-wheel brakes; no leaks; check brake pedal travel; no copper tubing; check length of flexible lines
Scrub line	No steering, suspension, or chassis components should be below this line
Recommended Equipment (may be reason for failure)	
Windshield	Should be AS-1
Shift pattern	Shift pattern should be visible except on 3-speed standard column shift
Fuel lines	Should be safely mounted and routed
Parking brake	Should be activated independent of vehicle's hydraulic system
Self-aligning rod end bearings	Ball should have 1/8-inch spacer on each side of the ball if there is any misalignment. Rod ends should not have more than 10-degree misalignment. Rod ends and four bar-parallel radius rod system rubber bushed ends should have a safety washer at least the same outside diameter as the housing or larger.
Brake lines	Should be safely mounted and routed
Chassis fasteners	Self-locking nuts, lock-washers, safety wire, or cotter pins
For Your Safety	
Safety equipment	Fire extinguisher in driver/passenger compartment, seat belts, a third brake light, and a dual master cylinder

ferred into your name soon after you purchased the truck. Doing that in a timely manner is always a good first step in avoiding issues with the DMV. You are pretty much at their mercy.

Typically, when the title has the seller's signature, you will not have much trouble. However, in some states, if the vehicle and title are from a different state, you may be forced to apply for a new title that simply adds to the cost.

Provided that the truck has passed any state-required safety and/or emissions inspections and the taxes are paid, you should not have any trouble getting it licensed. Some states offer historic, year of manufacturer (YOM), or special-interest plates for hobby vehicles. These typically come with additional expense, and often are contingent upon certain restrictions. Again, check with local agencies ahead of time for specifics.

Keep It Clean

While today's paint products are far superior to those of the past, an

Your favorite auto parts store will have a wide variety of car care products. A clean bucket, clean water, some car-wash liquid, and a good sponge will work wonders for keeping your truck clean and looking its best. You just have to use 'em.

occasional wash and wax is still required to keep the truck looking its best. Keeping a good coat of high-quality wax on all painted surfaces will make the truck easier to keep clean.

A slippery surface helps prevent dirt and road debris from sticking to the surface. Whether driving the truck often or seldom, road rash is bound to happen sooner or later. If these chips or nicks in the paint are left untouched, any exposed metal will quickly begin to oxidize.

Washing and Waxing

Catalyzed paints can be washed safely after a couple of days if mild automotive soap products are used. Uncatalyzed paints should be allowed to cure for at least a week prior to being washed. Most any car wash soap should be safe for washing your newly painted truck. However, always read the label for any warnings prior to using any product on painted surfaces.

The best way to prevent minute scratches or other blemishes on paint is to wash the truck in sections. Wash the dirtiest parts first, such as the rocker panels, fender well lips, and lower front- and rear-end locations, using a soft cotton wash mitt.

Rinse out the mitt and the wash soap bucket and then mix up a new batch of wash soap to clean the vehicle sides. If their condition was relatively clean to start with, continue with that bucket of sudsy water to wash the hood and roof. This process rids the wash mitt and bucket of dirt and other scratch hazards, such as sand and road grit.

How Long Before Waxing?

Although you may desire to get a fresh coat of wax on the freshly painted truck as soon as possible, practice some restraint. As you might imagine, wax forms a protective seal on top of the painted surface, which prevents solvents in the paint from evaporating. Long story short, when those paint solvents are trapped beneath the wax, they will eventually form blisters in the new paint finish.

As a rule of thumb, wait at least 90 to 120 days before waxing a freshly painted vehicle. In locations where the weather is warm and humidity is low, 90 days should be long enough for the solvents to completely evaporate. In locations with cooler temperatures or more humidity, more time is required before applying wax.

Drive and Enjoy

Now that the truck is finished, enjoy it every chance you get, as life is short. In chapter 1, we discussed determining the purpose for the truck as it related to your wants and needs. If you did a good job of determining what you really wanted, you should be successful. However, if you were not honest with yourself or had expectations that could not realistically be met, you may have missed the mark. I hope that is not the case.

After waiting for the paint to fully cure, park the truck in the shade and apply a good coat of automotive wax. Keeping a good coat of wax on the truck will make it easier to keep clean. While you do not want to apply too much wax, if water no longer beads up on the surface, it is time for another wax job.